ADVICE

for an

imperfect

SINGLE

WORLD

I0104271

ADVICE

for an

imperfect

SINGLE
WORLD

Wisdom and Wit
from Friends & Lovers'
Queen of Hearts

PAT GAUDETTE
Founder, Friends & Lovers the Relationships Guide
www.FriendsandLovers.com

Home & Leisure Publishing, Inc.

Advice for an Imperfect Single World:
Wisdom and Wit from Friends & Lovers' Queen of Hearts

Published by Home & Leisure Publishing, Inc.
P. O. Box 968
Lecanto, FL 34460-0968
USA

Copyright © 2004 Pat Gaudette.
All rights reserved. No part of this book may be used or reproduced in any manner whatsoever without written permission, except in the case of brief quotations embodied in critical articles or reviews.

Published 2004

Printed in the United States of America.

ISBN 0-9761210-0-X

*Perfect love is rare indeed - for to be a lover will require
that you continually have the subtlety of the very wise,
the flexibility of the child, the sensitivity of the artist,
the understanding of the philosopher, the acceptance of
the saint, the tolerance of the scholar and the fortitude
of the certain.*
-- Leo Buscaglia

Contents

Since 1996, people have been pouring out their relationship woes via email to a person known simply as "Queenie," the feisty, no-nonsense online advice columnist for *Friends & Lovers the Relationships Guide* (www.FriendsandLovers.com). ***Advice for an Imperfect Single World*** is compiled from Queenie's columns dealing with problems facing singles and is one of a series.

The emails included in this book focus on single relationships. Letters have been edited as needed for clarity, to correct errors in grammar, and to delete or change names, places, dates, locations, and/or other identifying information in order to preserve the anonymity of the writers and those with whom they are involved. Any similarity to persons living or dead is purely coincidental.

Queenie's comments both online and in this book are provided as entertainment only and are not meant to substitute for relationships counseling or other professional and/or medical services or treatments.

Pat Gaudette
Founder, Friends & Lovers the Relationships Guide

The Dating Game

The Dating Game

*"I am looking for my Mr. Right, but I worry I am not
attractive to men. What can I do?"*

Wouldn't it be wonderful if there truly were real rules for dating? How simple it would make this most difficult of games! Not only is the game of love complex, with a muddled set of make-up-as-you-go rules, the game can be downright disastrous when the players aren't on the same page, or even in the same stadium.

Having lived much longer than most of the people who write for my opinion, experience gives me that rare gift of extraordinarily clear backward vision. I've made many of the same mistakes as the people who write to me, and if I haven't made them, I probably have at least one friend who did and learned a lesson the difficult way.

If there's one thing that vast experience has taught me, it is that most people want to talk about their problems, they want to share with anyone who will stand still long enough for them to pour out the whole wretched mess, but no matter what amount of good advice they are given, they will most likely stay on the same course they have already started.

Why? Because each one of us believes that "we" are somewhat smarter than the person whose opinion we have just solicited, that "we" are in a unique situation that only "we" can fully understand, and that despite the experience shared by those who may be much older and wiser, there is no better teacher nor better education than that which is learned the hard way – through personal experience.

Let the games begin!

♥

Dear Queen of Hearts, I met a gentleman this past weekend while taking my mother out for her birthday. We were at a concert in a local night club. When I first saw this man I had to look twice. He was absolutely gorgeous. The funny thing is I usually am not attracted to the "pretty" boys, if you know what I mean. If they are not a Stone Cold Steve Austin look alike (bald headed and muscle bound) I usually do not give them a glance. Anyway, to make a long story short, I was swept off my feet. We danced the night away. When we danced he stared into my soul and said everything without saying a word. I was in total awe by the end of the night. I felt like a true Cinderella. I am still smiling. He asked me how he could get in touch with me and I gave him my home number and cell number. He told me he would be out of town for the rest of the weekend. I did not ask him for his number.

It is now 4 days later and I have not heard a thing. I want so bad to hear from him. It's driving me crazy. My last words to him were "I feel as though I'll wake up tomorrow and tonight would have only been a dream" He kissed me on the forehead and said "This is only the beginning". I have been sick at my stomach since that evening (the good sick).

I am in my thirties and I feel as though I am back in high school. Part of me wants to call information and retrieve his phone number and call him. The adult or stubborn side of me says no... let him call... obviously if he was sincere he will. And what if I don't like what I find by calling him. But the other side of me thinks...what if he lost my number. I do not want to let something as good as the other night slip thru my fingers, nor do I want to be a fool. Please help me! Would it be so wrong to call 411? — Kelley

Kelley, most men like the thrill of the hunt. They stalk their prey, they take their best shot, and, if they hit a bull's eye they move on to the next target. This "gorgeous" man knows he made a bull's eye that night. Even though he was going out of town, if he was as swept away as you were, don't you think he would have found time to make a call "just to chat" and to set up a date when he got back?

Of course, I could be wrong and he might have lost your number. So, there are a couple things you could do.

1) Call 411, track him down and ask him for a date. Risky and you really might get your feelings hurt, or it could be the start of a great love story. Who knows?

2) Go back to the club where you met and maybe you'll run into him again and perhaps the sparks will still fly. Being the suspicious person I am, I always wonder if there's a significant other waiting at home for her smooth-talking man to return. — Queenie

♥

Queenie, I have been having a relationship with a great guy. He's charming funny, and I don't know if he's shy or what. He will not initiate sexual relations, I believe he wants to, but I don't want to be classified as a tramp, by starting the experience. Help! — Joy

Joy, I would suggest you let him take the lead. If he should misinterpret your experience you'll never be able to reverse his impression of you. — Queenie

♥

Hello Queenie, I met a girl and asked her for a date. She agreed and we had a great time dancing, playing darts, etc. That night she told me it was about a year since she parted with her ex-boyfriend with whom she lived for two years. She was not sure if she still loved him or not.

I asked her for another date in a week. She agreed willingly. It was even better this time. We kissed in the backseat of the cab all the way to her place and if it was not for her father staying in her place that night, we could have had sex too. I could see she was happy and that she shed, at least temporarily, the burden of the year-old break-up from her shoulders.

A few weeks later when I asked her for another date she looked at me as if it was the first time we met, trying to tell me that she would not go out with me

again because as she could not afford those entertainments (bowling, night clubs, etc.) I offered her and always paid for myself, she could not accept my invitations anymore. This conversation repeated several times and she never really sounded as if she meant what she was saying.

I understood this was a pretext. I was trying to find out the real reason. She said that she would not tell me not to offend me. But I know she had a great time with me, no one can fake this look and what for?! The question I have is should I try to date her again or I will just annoy her? — Marvin

Marvin, if you had such a good time, why did you wait "a few weeks later" to ask her for another date? Perhaps I have missed something, or perhaps you were a bit too brief in stating what happened, but if you went out on two dates, got close to having sex the second date, and then didn't call her for several weeks, perhaps she thought you weren't interested.

If she turns down your next invitation for a date, and doesn't want to offer any reasons, perhaps it's best that you consider this relationship ended. Next time, don't wait so long to call for the next date. – Queenie

♥

Queenie, I have been attracted to a guy that I met about three years ago. He gave me no indication that he was attracted to me. Nonetheless, I called him up and invited him out periodically. Our dates were ok but I was always the initiator. There was never any intimacy on these dates at all. Nor, did he seem really interested in me for a friendship or otherwise.

I gave up for a while. A couple of months later, I called him and invited him out. He said he had to work late but to my surprise invited me over after work. One thing led to the next, and we ended up spending a very intimate night together. I think that both of us really enjoyed it.

From that point on, he was much more responsive to my calls and, he called me periodically. We still didn't talk very often though (like once ever two or three weeks). I never felt that he wanted a relationship, but it seemed like our intimacy moved him to be friendlier towards me. Interestingly, my strong desire to be involved with him waned, although I had and still do have feelings for him. I began to call him less and less.

After about three months he called me and invited me to dinner. I declined because I felt that I had "gotten him out of my system." He then called me three weeks later and asked if I wanted to meet after work. I was busy. This kept up a couple of more times, but I always declined. Last week he invited me to go with him to a happy hour and I went. We had a great time. When we got to the car, he kissed me lightly on the lips. I was surprised. He then called me that night after he got home and said he had a great time and wanted to get together soon.

All of this to say, I still have feelings for him. And because of the fun time we had the other night, I've been thinking about him a lot. But I don't know what his most recent behavior means. I mean, he always said that he "had a great time" when we went out in the past. Does it mean anything different this time. I definitely felt "energy" between us though when we parted which I had never felt before. Should I pursue this or leave it alone? — Donna

Donna, you're the one who has been avoiding him because you said you weren't interested. And then you wonder what his cool approach means? Was he supposed to try to get you back in bed for another round? He may really like you and want to establish a relationship based on more than just good sex. Or perhaps he thinks you need to be challenged by a man who doesn't try to jump you on the first date. It's up to you as to whether you keep this going. What could a couple more dates hurt? That certainly wouldn't spell a lifetime commitment. – Queenie

♥

Hi Queenie, I'm having a problem with my ex boyfriend who happened to court me thru phone calls and dating. But I just found out this afternoon and have seen him personally with a girl — they are watching movies. It really hurts to learn the truth that he is fishing at two seas. I don't know what to do, should I tell him that I saw him dating with another girl and get rid of him, but what if I still love that guy and how will I know if his feelings for me are real. I'm already 25 years old and old enough to face the reality. What should I do? Please help me? — Monique

Monique, how committed is this relationship supposed to be? Have the two of you agreed that you won't date others, or are you just assuming that since he is dating you, he won't date anyone else? If he has said you're the only one then decide whether you want to have a confrontation about this. If there is no agreement, he can date whoever he wishes, and so can you. Life is far too short to be upset when you don't know the rules. – Queenie

♥

Dear Queenie, I am a Muslim and my girl is a Hindu, but we love each other a lot. Now she has gone to another city to study. The problem is that there are lots of guys out there who are after her. I like that and seem very proud that my girl is wanted and all that, but she doesn't tell them that she is carrying on with me. I know all her friends. They have hints but she doesn't want to confirm it. She likes when attention is bestowed on her. I don't like this cause I feel my girl is taking people for a ride and maybe me too... I am really confused. Please help. I have told her to tell all but she is adamant. — Dascha

Dascha, when people love each other, they do the best they can to not cause the other person undue stress. You have told her how you feel. If she does not wish to change her ways then you must either accept it or consider that perhaps she doesn't care as strongly for you as you do for her. You cannot make someone do anything they don't want to do. You have control only over yourself. – Queenie

♥

Hi Queenie, I am in a relationship presently going on for about 4 months now. He and I met at a night club, against both of our better judgment on the exchanging of numbers. Normally I never give a real number to a man I meet under those circumstances, but for this particular instance, I felt compelled to. Needless to say we talked and had a lot in common; actually it was surprising how much. He came over on several occasions and before 2 months were over, we were intimate with one another. I have never been so in tune nor had my sexual needs seen to as they have been with him. He is like my equal and wants to do all the things I want to do and vice versa.

But there is a downside. I am not an unattractive woman. On the contrary from what I hear from my male co-workers I am a prime catch. He and I were having a conversation and he said something to the nature of I know men bow down to you but I am different and it's the challenge you are attracted to in me!

I just sat there for a second looking at him as if he were the largest idiot I had ever seen. I told him that no, men don't lick the ground I walk on, but I do get compliments on a regular basis, as I was sure he did being handsome as well. Anyway, since that statement/discussion it seems like he is trying to make me chase after him.

He has a busy career, which I understand, whereas I am a fulltime student, fulltime employee and full time mother, so the time I have is limited as well. Before, there seemed to be a need for one to see the other. Now there seems to be my need only. I care for him a lot, but not enough to compromise my pride and run after him .... what should I do...should I tell him all of this? Or just get out of the relationship? — Leila

Leila, if you don't want to chase, don't. No doubt there are other men who'll take you on your terms. Perhaps, since the two of you became intimate fairly soon, the challenge is gone for him. Perhaps you need to turn the tables, stop chasing, and stop "desperately seeking" this man. If it is as good for him as it is for you, he should be knocking on your door fairly soon. If not, well, I'm sure you aren't without your share of dates. – Queenie

♥

Dear Queen, I am looking for my Mr. Right, but I worry I am not attractive to men. What can I do? — Yvonne

Yvonne, if you worry about not being attractive enough, you won't be attractive enough. Have confidence the right man for you will find you to be the most attractive woman he has ever met. Knowing that, you can go through the days with a smile, and that will make you very attractive to everyone you meet.

When you show interest in others, that makes you attractive. When you are pleasant to be around, that makes you attractive. Worrying does not make you attractive. – Queenie

♥

Dear Queen of Hearts, I am 27 and until 3 years ago was very happy with my relationships and women in general. After experiencing 3 very painful endings to short, intense, but loving relationships, I just can't build up the courage to ask anyone new out for a date. I guess I feel scared to get involved. But I really want to. I have had 3 dates in the past two years and I'm not happy. Can you help? — Donnie

Donnie, no one can give you courage but that's what you need if you wish to find true love. It may take many more times of getting hurt before you find the right person. If you don't make the effort, you'll never find her. You're not happy. You can do something about it. Maybe you'll have more painful endings, and maybe not. You won't know unless you try. – Queenie

♥

Hi Queen! I have a sort of dilemma. Well, I just got over a relationship with someone that I have had for two years. I thought that I would never be able to get over him or that I would ever be interested in someone else. But now there is one guy that I really would like to know better. We are both in college, but I am older than he is by about four years. So I don't know if we would really have anything in common or are on the same level. Guys are usually less mature than women. We go to different schools and I only see him at parties. We always hug and talk briefly, but he is really cute and I would like to get to know him better. He's really quiet and shy so I don't know how to approach him with telling him that I would like to get to know him more. I get nervous and shy whenever I am around him. Do you have any advice how I am to go about approaching him? — Rachel

Rachel, keep it light and friendly. Don't approach him as though you want to have his baby. Light conversation about careers, school events, social events, and current movies should enable you to get to know him better and for both of you to relax. Perhaps he already has a girlfriend or maybe he thinks you're not interested in him. You could always invite him to go for a pizza, or to see a movie, perhaps with a few other friends. – Queenie

♥

Dear Queen of Hearts, I met this girl (me 25, her 20). She thought that I was cute and interesting and could not wait until we went out. I acted like I was interested but not pushy. She wanted to go out as soon as possible, so we did. I took her to a nice restaurant. She was thrilled. Took her home and was a perfect gentleman. A little hug and I was on my way. She called my car phone to say that she had a wonderful time.

We saw each other 2 days later. A movie and a late night snack and once again, home and a perfect gentleman.

But we had a misunderstanding, nothing major. No calls for 3 days from either one of us and I brought her flowers to her office, (because she said that she never had gotten flowers there.) She was floored! She said she did not think that she was going to see me again. She said so I will hear from you later? And I called and we made a date for that Friday. So Friday came and she cancelled because she said that she had told her roommate earlier in the week that they would go out. I understood.

She had had a bad week so I told her to give me an hour of her time on Saturday. She did and I surprised her with a professional massage. She was excited about it. After which we were both refreshed and I took her home. She had to baby sit that night. And then our first kiss! Let me tell you. The breath was knocked out of her. She literally could not talk. It was one of those real grab her face and kiss softly type kisses. I though I had made a great impression. She called that night from baby sitting but I was not home.

Sunday came. And then she called on Monday. I was out of town but called her back on Wednesday and tried to make plans for Friday. I called again on Thursday and she had class so she had to go and said she would call me when she got home. It was late so she did not call. Friday, no call. Saturday I stopped by, she opened the door, I grabbed her and kissed her. She was a little reluctant, but then again she was in her robe and no makeup is what she said. I left and called her on the phone and laughed and ask did I make a complete fool of myself. She said that it was cute and said she would call on Saturday. It is Monday and no call. Now, I know what that means. I am not obsessive. Did I not make a move quick enough? Was I intimidating? What do you think? — Gary

Gary, she called to talk Saturday night but you weren't home. So she probably assumed you were out with someone else. You don't say what happened on Sunday. She called again on Monday but you weren't home again. What could she possibly think? You didn't call on Tuesday, but you did finally call on Wednesday. Thursday the two of you didn't connect.

You didn't call her on Friday so she probably assumed you were out with someone else. So you just drop by unannounced on Saturday (probably to see if she's with someone) and you catch her looking the way a lot of girls look when they don't expect to have someone just pop in, and she was embarrassed. Intimidating? Who knows? Quick moves? Yep, with that grab and kiss but it could have worked.

The two of you are not getting off to the best start. I would suggest that if you really want her to think that she's special, and that you're not trying to fit her into an already heavily booked schedule that you send her a few flowers, or a nice little teddy bear with a note of apology, and ask her if she'd be willing to meet a friend of yours, "a really nice, considerate guy."

If she says yes, then set a date and time and you show up and introduce yourself as "a really nice, considerate guy" who'd like to get to know her better. Woo her the old fashioned way, slowly, considerately, and you taking the lead. Believe it or not, even though these are modern times, girls still like guys who take charge. Good luck. – Queenie

♥

Dear Queenie, I met this girl. How do I know she already has a boyfriend? Does wearing a ring (not sure of size yet-looked small) on a necklace mean she has a boyfriend? Or what about wearing rings on certain fingers? Thanks! — Mickey

Mickey, rings on necklaces and fingers are a great starting point for conversation. Point to the necklace and say "Does that ring have special significance?" Perhaps she will say that her favorite aunt gave it to her years ago and it's too small for her to wear on her hand any more. It's the same thing with rings on fingers. Point to the ring in question and ask "Did your boyfriend give you that ring?" If she wants to get to know you better, she'll give you a response that will keep the conversation going. Good luck. – Queenie

♥

Hi Queenie, I recently met this girl who I feel very strongly attracted to. Let me just describe her: she's very independent, strong minded, confident, a bit talkative and in general, a nice young lady, whereas I'm a person who is more like a listener which is just opposite to her. Our background is completely different. It's like she's been to everywhere and met all sorts of people whereas I was like, locked in one place. My life doesn't have much variety.
We've been together for the last couple of weeks. By "together" I mean just going places together. Nothing like lovers. It's a strange thing. Although we are not officially lovers but we seem to complement each other quite well. It's like we were meant for each other, well, there's one thing that worries me.
I am not sure and don't really know how if I can take care of her because of our difference in background. She is always the one who comes up in my mind whenever I needed someone. I've never feel this way before and since I've always been a loner, I don't know how to handle this situation. What should I do? Please help! — Henry

Henry, if the two of you enjoy each other's company, then there's no way this relationship shouldn't work just fine. Opposites can be great together, each providing the other with another perspective. Of course, you've only known each other a few weeks and that's not long enough to make any judgments regarding long term relationship potential. – Queenie

♥

Dear Queenie, an x that I haven't talked to in about 5 months just called. We have both grown up lot and still feel the bond that was always there. We have gone out a couple times and talk a lot. I am happier then I have been in a long time. But some are nervous. We both have responsibility now and hang out with more mature people. I have not gone with anyone since him. Neither has he. We both feel that we were meant to be together. But we are taking it slow. Guess I just want to know if you think that... I don't know what I want. I guess advice is all. What do you think? — Sarah

Sarah, you have the rest of your lives to be together. Take it slow and enjoy each day as though it is the last one you will share together. – Queenie

♥

Hi Queenie, I have been asked to go on a blind date and was told that everybody does not know anything about each other? What should I do? I do not know what I should do in a blind date. — Ben

Ben, blind dates can be horrible or they can be a lot of fun. Just remember that your date is just as worried as you are, even if she may have been on blind dates before. Take it slowly, have fun, be interested in her ideas and talk about yours, too. I know several people who met some pretty great people on blind dates. Just be yourself. – Queenie

♥

Dear Queen of Hearts, I would be considered a nice guy, too nice for any girl to date, so I've been told by them. How do I overcome this or more importantly, how can I date a girl without her telling me this? — Lyle

Lyle, no girl is going to not date a guy because he's too nice, unless she just isn't interested in him to begin with. You haven't given enough information to know how you act on your dates, but if you're too "needy," too "dependent," or too "fast" too quick, these are things that will make girls run the other way. – Queenie

♥

Queenie, there is this guy that I have been going with for 5 months and he has told me that he loves me but lately he been so distant but when I try to talk to him all he says is he does love me and its just that he does have a lot of problems. Well now I am so confused what should I do. — Kelly

Kelly, it sounds as though he needs his "space." So perhaps you should just leave him alone, go on with your life, and let him know that you respect his need for distance. If he understands that you aren't sitting by the phone waiting for his call, perhaps he will become less distant. – Queenie

♥

Queenie, I've been involved with the love of my life for two years. The problem is we haven't ever been a real "couple" so to speak. It always happens that we see each other through our mutual friends, then we go out, have a wonderful

time that usually ends up in the bedroom, then we won't see each other for a few months. We've never even exchanged phone numbers! This past weekend it has happened again, only this time I feel its time to get something started for a change. See, we're both very shy and insecure, but we can never admit that to each other. What is the best way for me to finally open up to him? — Tanya

Tanya, the two of you are too shy to exchange phone numbers but not too shy to be intimate? What's wrong with this picture? If the two of you are ending up in bed, somewhere between hello and goodbye the shyness disappears. If he considered you the love of his life, not only would he have your phone number, he'd be asking for your hand. Better rethink this relationship because it doesn't sound like it's on a solid foundation. — Queenie

♥

Dear Queen of Hearts, I am a college student and I happened to meet this girl who is attending the same course as me. We started a relationship and everything seems to run smoothly. However lately, I have sent 2 e-mails to her but did not receive any reply. In her last letter to me she stated that she seldom checks her mail. Even when I wrote an e-mail to her earlier stating that I was keen to form a study group with her but she did not reply my letter.

She is the top student in my class as well. If she is not interested in me she will not care to even reply her last mail to me or even wave her hand as well as smile to me when we meet each other in college. So can you please tell me what is really happening to me? — Ken

Ken, you may like her and want to be her boyfriend, but it would seem that she is not interested in getting any more seriously involved than just being a casual friend of yours. Don't pressure her for more. We think you should seek out girls who show an interest in you. If she was really interested, she would be replying to your e-mail. Good luck. — Queenie

♥

Hello Queenie, I believe in telling it as it is, for example, the other evening after a wonderful dinner, my companion asked me if I would like to go for a nightcap, and I said "no, because I'm an early bird, early to bed and early to rise". He said that I should have answered "well it's getting late, I would love to go and have a last drink with you but I'll have to leave in an hour". He said that the way I answered, another man would never dare to invite me again because he would think that I'm just not interested. I can see his point because many times I wish "he" would invite me out again, but "he" never did!

Spontaneity means that I'm a responsive person. If I receive a mail, I answer immediately. If I'm invited to a party or anything, I say yes immediately if I know that I'll be free.

I am pretty popular and I am invited to a lot of gatherings but of course there are times that I'm alone but I never pretend that I have other engagements.

When I'm with my friends, I'm all theirs.... It seems with a potential boyfriend, one has to feint busy even when one's not.

There.... I hope he is interested in me as you say he could be, because I like him too. Women are like men, if they like someone they like to be touched :) I'm trying very hard to be mysterious.... Thank you and if you have more advice to give me, gee I'm all open!! — Blondie

Blondie, you sound as though you have yourself very well figured out and you're happy as you are which is as it should be. Of course, sometimes others who are less sure of themselves require that we play the games they know and best understand. Good luck with this man, hopefully the two of you are playing the same game with the same set of rules and the same goal in mind. — Queenie

♥

Hi Queenie, is there a course where courtship is taught here on the web? I mean how does one play hard to get? I need a quick answer so this chance (maybe the last?) would not be "chased" away by my spontaneity and honesty. I met him through one of the dating sites and he said he only chose to write to me based on my description. We have been corresponding almost daily for the past 3 months by e-mail, talking about very common everyday happenings. We've talked maybe 2 or 3 times on the phone. Then he came to visit me for 4 days. We visited museums, flea markets.

He was attentive but not affectionate. In fact during all four days and evenings, he never once touched me. The most I got were two pecks on the mouth, a goodnight kiss and a farewell kiss. I had felt very comfortable with him and I think he enjoyed his stay here (he was in a hotel).

He has invited me to visit him. Since he returned home, he seemed to be more playful and talkative in his writing, and has called me twice in 2 days. I think that he could be interested in me and I do not mind taking things slowly. Only how can I be sure that this time, his interest would not dwindle by my spontaneity. How does one play hard to get anyway and do you think he is interested in me? — Cheri

Cheri, he sounds interested in you if he has continued the contact and has invited you to visit him. A first meeting such as you describe is going to be most uncomfortable for many people. There are so many issues that must be resolved, misconceptions that must be overcome. And perhaps he is shy as you.

Did you expect this man to try to seduce you on your first meeting? If he is the gentleman that you hope him to be, that would have been entirely inappropriate. And, if you are the lady that you appear, he would not have tried for fear of losing favor with you.

He has gotten more comfortable since meeting you and possibly his actions will be a bit more aggressive when you visit him. If you want to play hard to get, does that mean that you "get physical" too quick into a relationship? Or that you become committed too quickly? Or that you believe after one date you and your gentleman are in a serious relationship?

For this relationship to work well, you should be yourself, not someone you think he wants you to be or someone you think you should be. If he is to like someone, it should be the real you. If you operate on this premise, you shouldn't have to "play hard to get," you will relax and enjoy yourself and he will enjoy your spontaneity. Good luck. – Queenie

♥

Dear Queenie, a few weeks ago I was approached by someone and we talked and he asked for my phone number. Two weeks went by without a phone call. Then last Tuesday night he called. He said that he had been out of town for the last two weeks on business. He works from 3:00 p.m. to 3:00 a.m., so he always calls me from work which makes it kind of difficult to talk. Anyway, he continued to call me each night thereafter and we were supposed to go out last Friday night. Well, he called that afternoon at 5:30 and said that he had to work late and had to cancel. (He was going to call later on that night, but he said he went home and went to bed instead.)

I work a part time job on the weekends so he asked for that number because he wanted to see about getting together on Saturday night. Saturday went by-no phone call. Sunday went by- no phone call. Needless to say, I thought the guy was dead or something. I call him on Monday night and he says that he was "monkeyed" into something and couldn't get out of it. (He's in the reserves and they had a drill.)

He said he was sorry and that he was an a—hole and that he should have called. I played it off because he doesn't owe me anything (except respect) since we are not even seeing each other. I did comment that it seemed that he could have found 5 minutes just to let me know something. He apologized profusely. He called me later Monday night and he asked for my work phone number. Of course, I haven't heard a word from him.

I'm already frustrated with this situation. He seems so interested in me when we talk, but then he does just the opposite later on. I'm confused and frustrated. At this point, I'm willing to say that I hope he never calls again. What do you think? — Giselle

Giselle, I think he might be married. — Queenie

♥

Dear Queen of Hearts, I think I'm doomed to be alone all my life. Is it so wrong to be right, is it so wrong to be strong, and I am right and strong most of the time, which seem to chase any man who always started to be attracted to me. I have been told by men and women that I'm beautiful, intelligent and sensual. They fall in love with me without my encouragement and just as soon out of love with me so easily.

For the second time in my 40 years life, I was in love again and was loved back. It only lasted 2 months. I had really thought that he was the one, we talked

24

so easily and many times I didn't even have to finish my sentence, he could guess how I felt. Then why did he fall out of love with me? I don't want to be right, but was I right to break off with him because I felt he was falling out of love with me, because he has been depressive (he told me several times that he didn't want to live anymore), because he kept asking me "what are you doing with a loser"? I think he felt out of love with me because I have such a jealous and capricious nature, but I only asked if he also sent poems to other women.... If despite all this, I still miss him, I miss all the intimate conversations we had. I still love him, isn't love supposed to be blind?

I would give up everything today if I can find that person who would love me unconditionally and completely... I have a good heart and I'm adored by my friends, my employees, but not "the one". They still love me despite my idiosyncrasies and eccentricities.... They adore me because I'm so giving, true, spontaneous....... from the advice I've seen you have given, I have to play hard to get if I want to "catch" him.....??? Should I hide my real character? For my work and position, I do put up a very strict and stern appearance, but inside I'm passionate and kind. How do you think I won the devotion of my friends and employees.. ? I'm tired....... I'm so tired.... or I'm not really fit to play this game of "love". — Rhonda

Rhonda, playing hard to get means not giving too much too soon, not always waiting for his call, not adjusting your life to his schedule or his demands. Many people like the challenge of the chase and if they succeed too quickly in the hunt, they become bored and move on to the next more challenging relationship.

When you enter a relationship, it may serve you best to slow down in your emotional involvement until some time has passed, until you and he have explored a significant portion of your interests, likes and dislikes so you have a broad picture of the person he is and he of you.

Hide your true self? Absolutely not! If you want to find someone to love the real you, they must meet the real you. Not everyone will be attracted to someone who is so strong, sensible and worldly. You are intimidating to some men. And just like you, many men hide their "little child" feelings very well. And some weaker men will be drawn to you because of your strength.

You say your last lover fell out of love with you, yet you broke up with him. Did you do this to protect yourself from being dumped? Since you broke up with him, and you still love him, why don't you call and see if he'd like to get together over a cup of coffee? No one ever said falling in love was easy or forever. Unfortunately, it's the only game in town. – Queenie

♥

Dear Queenie, I seem to be having this problem with my girlfriend. I always want to do something with her on the weekends and she does too but for some strange reason something always seems to come up and we have to cancel.

We have only gone out twice and we've been dating for a month and a half. She always feels really bad when she can't go. Do you think that something's up with her or do I just have bad timing? Is there any way I can convince her to go out? —
Jeff

Jeff, two dates in a month and a half is not exactly a relationship. It would seem there is more going on than just bad timing. If people really want to see each other, they find a way. I'd suggest you look for another girlfriend. – Queenie

♥

Hi Queenie, I've joined an expensive introductions service for meeting singles. I'm a professional male that makes a decent living and I thought I could use a service like this being I have a tendency to have a busy schedule and don't normally have or make the time to meet other singles. I met someone I was really starting to like through the service. I went on two dates with her and she always seemed interested in getting together again. The day of the third date she called and cancelled because she said she had to work all weekend rather than just some of the weekend like she thought. I asked about the following weekend and she said she was going to be busy then as well because her office now hired two new people and she's doing the work of three people which is why she seems to be having trouble getting much free time. This isn't the first time she's cancelled.
I've been very patient with her tight schedule and we have managed to strain out some time together. I just don't know how to help her, or what to do except keep holding on and hope for some changes. I'm beginning to doubt her level of commitment to dating in general which is odd being she's made the same monetary investment as I have in the same service. What to do. — Ron

Ron, when two people have the same strong feelings, they always find a way to get together, no matter how busy their schedules. Cancelled dates and planning to be busy weeks in advance could mean she either doesn't want this relationship to continue or she may have another one that's developing at the same time that has her more interested. After all, if she's in the dating service, too, she's getting other referrals.

Two dates is not enough time to try to build a permanent relationship. Having said that, let's just say there are always exceptions but this doesn't seem to be one. Ask your service for more ladies to date. This one is a bit too busy. – Queenie

♥

Dear Queenie, I got a "sales" call from a dating service today which aroused my curiosity. From what I understand through their website, radio ads, and sales person, they seem too good to be true.
Could you please inform me as to what I can expect if I were to try them out from a consumer point of view? Are there any reasonable complaints from former clients that I need to know about?

I know I can't buy love because love is priceless, but since they claim to be a Fortune 500 franchise, I can't help but be a little suspicious as to how much they will charge me (they appear kind of pricey) to meet that person who is perfect for me. In other words, if I give them a reasonable amount of effort, will I get a decent return on my investment in terms of time and money? Thank you very much. — Fran

Fran, there are many ways to meet people and dating services have been successful for many people. You'll have to do your own investigative work on this one. If you look at your last sentence, you already have the key to a successful search ... a reasonable amount of effort. In other words, no matter what a service does to lead you in the right direction, it will be up to you to make the best of the connection they suggest. – Queenie

♥

Dear Queen of Hearts, this guy, who liked me before a month ago at first really, really liked me but he was really shy. I then decided to call him and I went out with him but only with a group of friends, not alone with him. He wouldn't call me or anything and just recently, him and a group of friends and I spent the night at his house and I had a great time with him.
We didn't actually fool around but we got really close as in cuddling and I really fell for him. Now he tells his best friend that he only wants to be friends with me. I wanted to hear it from him but he can't be open with me. Plus, I am always the one who calls him. He thought I was a great person but he said he didn't know what he wanted and he was afraid that if we got into a relationship, we wouldn't be friends anymore. Now I can't get over him and it's making me depressed. What should I do? — Wanda

Wanda, if you keep pursuing him he's going to continue to run from you. And, your pursuit is not very attractive to him or to others. If he was interested in starting something with you, he would. Right now, he's not interested. Don't wait by the phone expecting him to change his mind. He has the right to decide who he wants to go out with; you can't force him into wanting you as a girlfriend. "Fooling around" is just that — it isn't a relationship commitment. You can get over him if you choose to. Or, if it makes you feel better, you can be depressed and miss out on a lot of fun. He's not the only guy in the world that would be right for you. – Queenie

♥

Dear Queenie, I have searched and searched for an answer for my following question but have not found it. I have dated several girls now and only two or three have gone out with me the second time. My only thought is that maybe I'm doing something terribly wrong on the first date.
What is right on the first date? I have tried kissing on the first date, I have tried NOT kissing on the first date, I've had one girl to kiss me on the cheek

before, I've kissed a girl on the cheek before (and this one is currently working on a second date now) and many other things. I always open doors.

I have tried holding hands and I've tried NOT holding hands. I have no idea what a girl is looking for on the first date. What is it that they want to do? And for the record, I'm a 21 year old male. — Steve

Steve, everyone is looking for someone to talk to, laugh with, and who shares their interests. In other words, everyone wants a friend. (Okay, maybe someone out there doesn't want a friend but they wouldn't be visiting this site too many times because we believe friends are the start of great lifelong relationships.) In other words, date to have fun, to enjoy the things you like best. If you like football, then date girls who like football. If you like computers (of course you do!) date girls who also like computers. This way you have things to talk enthusiastically about. Things to make each of you want to see the other person again because you enjoy being together.

If you meet someone for the first time and you like their looks but you have absolutely no common interests, it's going to be very difficult to maintain an interest level for very long.

As far as should you kiss on the first date? Well, a polite kiss at the door is nice. You're going to have to evaluate each date as it happens to decide if a kiss is appropriate or not. It's the same thing with holding hands. – Queenie

♥

Dear Queenie, I have a serious, bad dating situation on my hands. Due to a health problem I don't participate much in sports, hiking, etc., plus I've never liked these things but I do it in order to cater to others in hopes that maybe someone will take interest in my hobbies. No such luck.

When I am at singles meetings, there are very few women, and a lot of men. I'm not only competing with the guys, but the women seem to talk to everyone else. I can't get more than 5 minutes of conversation with her, and even that is filled with one-word responses.

Women get intimidated when I come up to them to talk, as if I'm hitting on them or something, when nothing could be further from my mind! I just want to make some women friends. I can talk to guys, but women seem to be much harder to talk to. The problem is, I can't get a woman to open up, and I frequent singles groups for as long as 3 months, with no progress.

I don't make lewd comments, I shower, I have good hygiene, and I'm not rude, abusive, or temperamental. I just introduce myself and it goes downhill from there. When I do get a chance to talk to a woman, someone else always interrupts, cuts me off, and no matter how hard I reassert myself, they've got the conversation with her. I wind up sitting on the sidelines, and I don't get cut any slack.

I've been to night clubs, bars, singles bars, coffee shops, supermarkets, etc., etc., and the problem I run into there, is that women don't want to be talked

to. I just introduce myself with my best smile, I try to speak about something relevant in the area, but nothing I do or say, gets them to open up. I get dirty looks from women when I talk to them in supermarkets. Like I'm some sort of serial killer hunting my next prey or something. What is this about meeting in these places? I sure as heck can't even make friends with a woman, and I've been at it for over a year. (Oh and also add to that Laundromats, beach parties, and other things I can't even list here — been there, done that couldn't get a shirt there either.) Finding clubs that interest me are hard: I've checked magazines, the Web, you name it. And as you know, if you're in one of those "geeky" hobbies, you don't try to date outside your interest — not if you don't want to totally disgust a woman who's not into that stuff.

Contrast to when I'm online — I get more email and chat room messages from women than I can keep up with!! One woman would leave her boyfriend for me if she were in my town. I can come home from a horrible night trying to socialize, and get online, and it's a totally opposite ball game. But as you might have figured out, I want a relationship in real life.

I find it ironic that even violent jailbird men have a better time with women than, you guessed it, a polite, appreciative, commitment-oriented nice guy, in a world where "women are looking for commitment and can't find it." Have you ever seen this before? Is there anything I can do about it? To be honest, this is depressing and frightening — I don't know any male who has ever had this many problems, in every situation, with women. I'm a man of thoughts, then action! I'm open to any suggestions or resources I might need to look into. — Claude

Claude, of course I've seen this problem before! If there weren't a lot of people having problems meeting other people, there would be no need for advice columns, or the personals columns or the singles/dating services. You're not alone so don't whine!

You should never pretend interest in something just to meet people with the hope they will also enjoy those things you really like. You already recognize that the things you like are what you think of as "geeky" (although we don't happen to agree) so if you meet people in the glamour sports and then start talking computers, you're setting yourself up for a turnoff. Stick with the clubs and interest groups in which you have the most enthusiasm.

You're probably hitting on the most popular babes at the clubs which could explain why they're already surrounded by guys vying for their attention. Do you ever give any thought to the women who are standing by themselves just absolutely dying to have someone ask them to dance or engage them in conversation? The ones who probably also love computers and all the "geeky" stuff? And, certainly, since you consider some of those other activities boring, that will come through when you're talking.

Big cities might be less friendly places than small towns when it comes to just going up to complete strangers in public places such as the supermarket, library, etc., and starting a conversation. Unless you have a specific reason for talking with someone (and trying to meet new friends is suspect in these surroundings) you'll probably meet with cynicism.

You're trying too hard and that desperation is going to come through loud and clear when you meet someone. Yes, there are so many women who do want to meet commitment-minded guys, but they don't want to meet someone who's desperate for a relationship. Mellow out. Calm down.

Stop with the bad attitude about your situation. (Yes, it is a bad attitude, it comes through loud and clear — or else it's a major case of whining, you take your pick, but it's not something that's going to get you dates.)

The Internet romances are another issue. Plenty of shy people can develop super personalities when they don't have to be face-to-face with someone. They can fantasize about the other person, making them who they want, not the person they actually are. Who knows? Some of the ladies you're conversing with on the Internet may be exactly the ones you ignore in real life because they just don't appeal to you.

My recommendations? Lighten up when you're out in the real world. Evaluate the types of women you're having bad luck with (don't say all of them because no doubt that's not the case). Stay in the clubs and interest groups that best suit you (there are women in those groups too but you probably think they're too "geeky" to meet).

If you want women "friends" then don't discount the workplace. Some of those friends will have girlfriends, sisters, aunts, nieces, etc. they might think would be perfect for you to meet. There are women who can't stand to let a single man remain single — find one! Same thing with the guys you know.

Become a better listener. Learn to listen, ask questions of others to draw them out and then really listen with enthusiasm to what they have to say. You might not get to talk for the rest of the evening, but (believe it or not) the other person will think you're incredibly fascinating! If you don't have a clue as to what is the problem, why not carry a small micro recorder along with you and record some of your encounters (without the knowledge of the other persons, of course) and play them back later. Analyze and correct. – Queenie

Workplace Romance

Workplace Romance

"How does one go out with co-workers without risking committing sexual harassment, especially if one is in a supervisory position and the other rank and file?"

It would be an extraordinary job that required workers to spend eight hours drooling over the babe at the next desk or mooning over the guy in the office across the hall.

Employers hire with an expectation that employees will enhance the financial bottom line using skills to produce whatever it is that the business sells or provides or dispenses. Unfortunately, it doesn't take much for hormones to get the best of close work encounters and, given the sharing and caring that goes on regardless of workplace rules, love (and lust) takes root and flourishes in the work environment.

Meeting a potential mate in a work environment may or may not be less hazardous than hanging out at singles bars. At a singles bar it is assumed everyone is looking for Mr. or Ms. Right (or Right Now) and the inference, by each person's presence, is that they are single and available.

People who work together already have some common interests even if most are initially job related and the close proximity of working together gives men and women a starting point for developing more intimate relationships, particularly if there is a physical or emotional attraction between them.

There are many reasons why work friendships should not go beyond the office including the fact workplace rules will often forbid employees from dating. Unfortunately, lust clouds all rational thinking and many work relationships turn intimate so quickly that the traditional "dating" phase is bypassed completely and the couple proceeds directly to "major relationship".

A couple in "love" can be a joy to behold, unless they work in the same office and their relationship interferes with the work environment. In the best of cases, each is able to contain his or her feelings until the work day is over and the relationship does not have a negative impact on either person's career. In the worst of cases, men and women who are already in committed relationships with others, especially those who are married, may find the lure of an office romance too strong to ignore despite the hazards and potential disaster if their spouse or loved one learns of the relationship.

Regardless of how or where they get started, relationships do end and working around a lover who has moved on to someone else makes a horrible working environment for the one who has been dumped. No matter how secretive the work couple may have been about their relationship when it was all lovey-dovey, when the relationship goes down the toilet, it is probable that there will be a lot of unpleasant exchanges, not to mention a major amount of grist for the office gossip mill.

Looking for love at the office? Keep on reading. Maybe you'll change your mind. Or, at the very least, you'll proceed with a little more caution.

♥

Dear Queenie, I would like to develop a relationship with my manager. We share a healthy work relationship and are both considered to be very good at our work. However we are from 2 different cultures as in religion and social cultures.

I would like to find if he has any interest without arousing any doubts. I am in for a department transfer as a promotion and will not report to him. Thanks. — Olive

Olive, since you asked, I certainly wouldn't suggest you try to develop anything while you still work for this man. However, when you are transferred elsewhere and if your company doesn't prohibit employees dating, you can give him a call and invite him out for lunch "to catch up on how things have gone since I left." If he's interested in you, he might just take this as the opportunity to ask you for a "real" date. – Queenie

♥

Queenie, six months ago, I hired an old friend. I nursed her back to health physically and mentally, now she is seeing someone else but wants to remain status quo. Should I keep trying or get over it and let her go? I'm really sick over this. — Dave

Dave, did you do all these things so that she would be grateful and love you in repayment for your kindness? That's not how it works as you're finding out. Let her go. – Queenie

♥

Dear Queenie, I've liked the same guy for three years, but I haven't gotten the guts to ask him out. I know he's single because I work with him and I'm a good friend of his. The weird thing is that I have no problem asking any other guy out on a date, but when it comes to him i get major butterflies.

I want to know if it's because he's "the one" or if it's just how I am towards him. And also what should I do to get him? And how do I get rid of the butterflies? Thanks for your help... I need it! — Nickie

Nickie, it's a little early to start thinking he's "the one" — there's a lot of time that needs to be spent developing a relationship before that would even be an issue. Since the two of you work together maybe it's not such a good idea to date.

What if it doesn't work out? Are you willing to risk the friendship and your work environment to see if the two of you should have a relationship?

If you've thought it through and have the courage to ask him out, then do it. As far as butterflies, we all get them occasionally but they probably won't stop a relationship that's meant to be. Good luck. – Queenie

♥

Dear Queen of Hearts, how does one go out with co-workers without risking committing sexual harassment, especially if one is in a supervisory position and the other rank and file? Or is it best to play safe and not try anything at all? — Theodore

Theodore, Question #1: One doesn't. Question #2: Yes. – Queenie

♥

Queenie, there's a couple of women at work who always give me big smiles and a hello when I say hi to them. I noticed one of them looking at me while I was standing up in my cube, so I smiled back. They are both very attractive.

The other day coming in from lunch, one of them was coming out as a friend and I were walking in. We were about twenty feet from each other. I glanced at her and then glanced away (don't want to leer); she looked at me, but about thirty seconds later, I noticed she was still looking at me.

I'm kind of shy, but do you think this indicates she likes me? Also, what's the next step? We work on the same floor but on different ends of the building. How do I manage to bump into her and get to know her, without "stalking" around her area? I see her occasionally and say "how are you doing?" and she usually says "good, how are you?".

I'm not really good at this kind of stuff, so any advice can only help. Thanks in advance. — Tim

Tim, it sounds as though you have an admirer! Now the difficult question: is it wise to think about dating a co-worker? After all, if things don't work out, you'll still see each other every day and it can get very painful.

Also, does your company have a rule against co-workers dating? Some thoughts along these lines are appropriate before you make your next move.

Okay, perhaps you're ready to chance dating a co-worker and your company doesn't object. Next time you have the occasion to meet perhaps you can keep the conversation going by something like this:

You: How are you doing?

She: Good, how are you?

You: I'm doing well, but I'd be doing better if you'd agree to meet me for a cup of coffee after work. (Or lunch, or dinner, or a movie, etc.)

She (Option One): I thought you'd never ask! (You're on your own, just take it slow and treat her like the lady she is.)

She (Option Two): I'm afraid I really can't. (Don't take a 'no' personally. If you don't ask, you won't get a 'yes' either.)

You (Option Two Response): Want a rain check? You know where I work should you want to redeem it. (Then smile and keep on with whatever you were doing.)

You won't know unless you ask. – Queenie

♥

Dear Queen of Hearts, I work with this guy and every day after work we would go down to the beach and talk while looking at the stars. Of course we would flirt with each other so i had a friend confront him to see if he liked me or not and he said just as friends because he was trying to hook up with another girl that already has a boyfriend. At first I was just like whatever because he really wasn't my type, but now I'm feeling hurt. What should I do??? — Becky

Becky, was there ever any discussion between the two of you about being boyfriend and girlfriend? Have you ever dated? Did he tell you he loved you? What gave you the idea that there was anything more than friendship between the two of you? Or do you believe that men and women cannot be friends, they must only be lovers?

Why, if you and he talk all the time, did you have to get someone else to ask him if he liked you? And how do you know that what the friend relayed back to you is exactly what he said in reply to the question? After all, everyone interprets things differently. You certainly do or you wouldn't be having a different impression of the relationship between the two of you than what he has.

Flirting is harmless. If you and he were making mad love and telling each other how much you loved each other while doing it, then you'd have a reason to be mad. What should you do? Keep him as a friend, if you can, and look for someone else as a lover. That way, if you and your lover have problems, you'll have a nice guy friend to confide in under the stars. – Queenie

♥

Dear Queenie, I'm 26 years old and have never really had a boyfriend. I have tried asking guys out before, but no one has ever accepted my offers. Recently, I have taken notice of a new guy at work. I have tried to flirt with him, but I don't even know if he has noticed me. A co-worker said she thought he liked me because of the way he smiles when he says hello, but I haven't seen it.

I asked him out to a movie with a group from work, but the others decided not to go. I thought there would be at least two other people and told him I would understand if he decided not to go. He said something about the possibility that his parents would be visiting that night; after that, he said he might make it, he would have to check and see.

He even asked me which theater the movie was playing at, but he didn't show. In fact nobody showed, so I just went home.

How do I find out if he likes me? I'm getting mixed signals. I think he looks at me at work, but maybe he's just trying to find out if I'm watching him.

please give me some advice on how to know for sure. I'm thinking about just asking him out without the group, but if he does like me, I don't want to scare him. What should I do? — Joan

Joan, perhaps you're being a little too aggressive for him? Some guys want to be the one to make the moves. You gave him the opening about the movie and he didn't take it. If it were me, I'd stop trying to get together with him, and see if he makes any moves on his own.

He may be one of those people who believe office romance isn't a good thing since it can really get messy when an office romance ends. It's just a thought. – Queenie

♥

Hi Queenie, I started a relationship with a coworker several months ago. We recognized that it was unwise to do so publicly in the workplace so we decided to make the relationship secret after our first date (i.e. always dated outside work hours, or met for lunch during work hours in secret). Three weeks after our first date, she started having weekly lunches with another male coworker, always in public and platonic in nature.

I objected to this guy at first but she said she loved me, that the other guy was strictly friendship. This has gone on for 5 months, me dating her seriously in secret, she lunching weekly with other man.

Since I am leaving the company soon, I asked her last week to go public with our relationship. She refused on grounds that she wants to avoid questioning from coworkers about our relationship. Moreover, she says she wants to keep us secret from her coworkers indefinitely. I find her position disrespectful to the relationship and me. I think she's being a little selfish. Am I too sensitive and suspicious? — Jason

Jason, I think you're probably being a little suspicious. Do you have reason? Admittedly, my suspicious mind thinks maybe the other man doesn't know about you, and that perhaps she doesn't want him to know the depth of the relationship the two of you share. What do you think? On the other hand, you probably want the other man to know that she is "yours." Am I right?

It's hard to tell exactly what games are being played here, but any time a lover is distressed over the relationship, there is a problem. If the two of you are in love, wouldn't you think she'd want to shout it to the world the same as you do? — Queenie

♥

Dear Queenie, my problem is sort of different. I already know what to do, I just can't do it. I was dumped by a girl I am seriously in love with, because I crowded her out. I understand that I did do this, but I am just taken back by the fact that she has completely ignored me since the breakup. She has told me numerous times that she was in love with me, and that she had never met anyone who was this good to her and her daughter.

I understand why she has broken things off with me, but I do not understand why she acts like she absolutely hates me. Two weeks ago, everything was fine and now "just the sound of my voice makes her sick". Now, I know that I should be going out with my friends and finding someone else, but everyone I meet I just compare to her, because in my eyes this girl is perfect. I cannot get her out of my head, no matter what I do.

I am trying to forget about her but I really can't. It doesn't help matters that she works where I do, so I see her quite often. Just seeing her makes my heart flutter but I feel lower than dirt when she won't even say hello. What can I do to get myself to let go of her, and to realize that there will never be a chance for me and her? Please help me. — Stan

Stan, if you know what to do but can't do it, why should you do it if I suggest the same thing? She is doing what she must to get over a broken heart. She loved you. It didn't work. She's in pain the same as you are. She's doing what she must in order to get over it. That means ignoring you so she won't remember how she used to feel when she was near you. She doesn't hate you, she's just trying to put the love she used to have for you in its proper place — in the history books.

Perhaps, once she's had a chance to sort things out, and once you've let go, the two of you can be friends. Perhaps not. Working together is going to make this relationship so much harder to conclude. If working elsewhere is out of the question, try your best to treat her the same as any other coworker, without letting your emotions rule. Good luck. – Queenie

♥

Dear Queenie, lately I've been slightly interested in a young man who just happens to be my TA in one of my classes. We are both the same age, we are both graduate students, and we both have expressed a mutual attraction for one another through flirting, joking, and a few short conversations after class.

Friday I needed help with a project for another class and I asked him if he would help me, since it was in his field of expertise. He agreed to help, but once I met him, we got sidetracked. Neither one of us were able to concentrate on the project—we were both talking and flirting outrageously with one another! We tried to finish it up that night, but still we kept talking, getting to know one another. After connecting in so many ways at dinner, we ended up at his apartment and he kissed me. I was totally unprepared for it.

One thing led to another, and soon I was feeling a little pressured to have sex, so I told him that it was going too fast, that I'd like to get to know him better. "I totally respect that," he said, and said how his physical relationships in the past had lacked meaning and longevity, that there was no substance and they died out. We kissed and made out for hours, culminating in a very sensual backrub for him. He gazed at me with a dreamy-eyed expression and said, "You really know how to take good care of me." He walked me down to my car, holding my hand, telling me *that he had a great time, but also that I should keep quiet about this for now, because he could get into trouble. The last look he gave me before I left was a deep, dreamy look of longing that seemed to say he didn't want me to go.*

Monday morning was awkward, to say the least. Today I had to get something from him after class and we flirted and joked. But he acted as if nothing happened. Is he scared that someone will find out what happened, or would he be scared that he experienced some pretty powerful emotions Friday night and maybe isn't ready to deal with him? Finals are next week and I may not have him as a TA next term.

What should I do? Should I continue to wait and see if he will pursue me when it's safe, or should I forget about it and move on? I hope time will tell. Thanks again for your help! — Cheryl

Cheryl, it sounds like the two of you get an "A+" in "Foreplay" for this evening. Don't expect, though, that he interpreted the evening in the same way you did. Guys like getting physical and don't necessarily build long term romance from having sex. Women have a tendency to believe that sex and love go together.

I certainly wouldn't suggest putting your life on hold waiting for him to make a move. Sneaking or keeping quiet about dating someone sets the wrong tone for what should be a very open and happy relationship. Perhaps he already has a girlfriend? You might be better off with a TA to whom you weren't so physically attracted. PS: Bravo for saying "no" on the first date (even if you did get a little carried away.) – Queenie

♥

Dear Queenie, I am currently involved with my boss, who is 20 years my senior. I know very taboo, right? But we have been casually dating now for 5 months and the other night I mentioned to him that it was common knowledge at work that we are involved. He seemed to be quite disturbed at this, although it was he who told many of his male employees, so I felt why should I hide or deny it. I must tell you that we DO NOT flirt at work and it is business as usual.

The reason I am asking for advice is that he commented that if it became public knowledge things would end. It has been public knowledge for weeks now and I am wondering how I could know this and he didn't... if he should brake things off (which I am hoping won't occur, as I am content in our relationship) how should I handle the situation? — Tamara

Tamara, you're in a very bad spot. You probably like the guy and when it's over, you either have to find another place to work or learn how to handle a broken heart while you still work for him. This is one of the main reasons you shouldn't date your boss.

Since you're "casually dating" why don't you, nicely and politely, let him know that you think it best for you, him and the business, that the two of you don't date any more. In other words, save face, get out while you still can without causing problems in your working relationship. It, and you, can't be too important to him, if he will end the relationship if it becomes public knowledge.

Incidentally, is he married? – Queenie

♥

Hi Queenie, I become friends with this girl at work we would talk a lot and help each other with our problems. I fell in love with her. She doesn't want any relationships in her life right now so I didn't tell her this because I was afraid to loose our friendship. It became too hard to be around her all the time. So I ignored her for a whole day thinking that maybe I wouldn't feel as sad if I had nothing to do with her. This made things worse. Now she is ignoring me and I miss the friendship.

I'm confused and afraid that if I apologize I will have to tell her I love her because I don't want to lie to her and then will be so uncomfortable at work I might have to quit. Help me PLEASE!!! — David

David, you don't love her, you like her a lot. You have a physical attraction to her. There's a difference. Love happens between two people, and right now, only one of you is steamed up.

If you don't have the maturity to apologize and tell her that you care a little more for her than you should under the circumstances but that you'd like to remain her friend, then we suppose you should quit your job. Otherwise, neither one of you will be comfortable at work. Good luck. – Queenie

♥

Queenie, I went out with a man ten years older than me who I work with. I felt everything was going great, though both of us were hassled because of the age difference. Then, one night, he rings and tells me that it's over. I got no explanation just that everything was against us, even though he loved me. We went out for less than two months, but I do love him as well. We are friends now, but I still find myself thinking we'll get back together.

Recently, he has started seeing another girl at our work. I find myself being bitchy to this girl, yet I deny to everyone that I care about him no longer. I even deny it to him. But there is another guy who I like and we went out last night. I just kept thinking it was my ex.

I like this guy, but I don't want to end up hurting him when I still care about the other guy. I don't know what to do. Every time I see the ex, I get upset, yet I don't think I could just never see him again. Also, I'm not sure whether I am just interested in the other guy to spite him. I am so confused, I care about them both. What do I do? — Delores

Delores, you don't have a choice as far as whether or not you date the first guy. He's gone. Your best effort would be to forget about him, stop thinking about what might have been, and get on with your life. Don't be bitchy to his new girlfriend. It may be just a month or two before she's feeling the same way you do and watching him dating someone else from work.

Dating someone you work with can be hazardous to a relationship. It also makes it much more difficult to forget about the person when they're where you can see them every day and watch what they're doing. If you find yourself obsessing about him perhaps you should look for another job.

Going out with this other guy doesn't mean you have to be madly in love with him. Have fun, relax, enjoy yourself. Who knows? You may find that he's a much better boyfriend than this other guy could ever be. You'll never know until you give him a chance. A couple dates does not make you committed. – Queenie

♥

Hi Queenie, I find myself extremely attracted to an employee of mine. She has shown some signs of interest in me, but all members of management were required to sign a paper saying we would not have relationships with employees. I think about her all of the time. What should I do if I cannot just forget about her? — Bennie

Bennie, this is not a major problem. Simply quit your job and ask her out. You're obviously not getting any work done with her around, and you're not management material anymore since you're a breath away from breaking some very important company rules that can impact not only you but the entire corporation. If you were in the military, you would be advancing toward court martial. – Queenie

♥

Dear Queenie, I had a very good male friend at work. We spent a lot of time together and after a while, I got the definite feeling of chemistry growing between us. I'm a 36 female and I don't believe that I'm prone to jumping to conclusions. Anyway, one day when I really felt the chemistry, I finally asked him what was going on between us. I was floored when he said "nothing." He also said that he felt "set up" the last time we went out with friends (something he'd suggested!).

The real problem is, however, that I more or less told him that I didn't think we could continue to be friends. I do believe that he was "playing on both teams" or at least striving to be deliberately confusing. I wrote him a note telling him that I was confused by his behavior and that while I wouldn't insist that he was coming on to me, I was choosing to keep my distance.

Since then he's been acting very "uncool" i.e., he's been acting very superior, as if he's managed to pull one over on me. He also seems amused by my decision to keep my distance. I believe my decision was a good one. There have been other indications that he "plays games."

How do I handle his "amused" and superior attitude? His salacious smiles really bring out the worst in me — I feel he's really managed to make a fool out of

me. I'm being cool, but this only seems to make him more amused. I stay out of his way and he makes a point of arranging his schedule so we'll "accidentally — on purpose" run into each other? (I've changed my schedule to avoid him). Any advice (besides get over it?) Part of me is tempted to confront him in a nice way in order to diffuse things. Smart Idea? — Anna

Anna, no one can "make" a fool of us. We make fools of ourselves. It's time you take control of this situation, and you can. If you simply ignore him he won't have a game player with which to play. All of the things he does require a reaction from you in order to be effective. Ignore him.

Since he's a co-worker you shouldn't do anything that would upset your working relationship. You must be the adult. Confrontation probably is not a good idea. A simple smile whenever you run into him, regardless of his attitude, will confuse him. Right now, he knows how to push your "hot" buttons. Get over it. – Queenie

♥

Dear Queenie, you have helped me out a lot in the past and now I am back again. This guy and I have decided to start dating, we have known each other for 2 years and we work together. The other night he told me that there was a woman that we both work with and that he has been friends with for a long time. She is married with kids. She wanted him to have an affair with her. He said no (thank God). He did say he told her that he had feelings for her, but it was wrong. They are no longer friends.

When he told me this it really hurt!! The next day I told him that it hurt me in a way. I also asked him if I was pushing him in to a relationship with me that maybe he didn't really want. He said that he really has feelings for me and that thing with the co-worker was over, but what he told me after words scared me and I didn't know what to say, he said that he feels like he is not good enough for me and that he sees himself as a loser. I told him that it wasn't true and that he was a good person, etc. He said that he has wanted to kiss me a thousand times, but he feels uncomfortable. What should I do, and what should I say to him? Thank you so very much, Gabriella

Gabriella, I'm not certain what he was trying to accomplish by telling you about your co-worker unless he expected she might say something to you and he wanted his version to be heard first. That disclosure certainly can't make the work atmosphere too pleasant for you.

One thing I have learned is that when someone says they're a loser, they generally are. You see, the stage is set so that when he is caught doing something wrong, he can easily say "see, I told you I was no good." Then you have no one but yourself to blame because you didn't listen when he warned you.

He probably isn't good enough for you but you're going to make your own decisions. Just be cautious and careful. (It's not such a great idea dating a co-worker.) Good luck. – Queenie

♥

Queenie, there is this guy at work that I really like. I am very shy. He always says hello to me and gives me a sexy smile. We are always busy and we work in different departments. He talked to me two weeks ago. We talked about the merchandize that I sell. We talked for 4 minutes but I enjoyed so much. I like his voice, his smile. I like him so much.

The problem is that I have not seen him n two weeks because our schedules changed. I have been thinking about him. I want to get to know him. I don't know how to approach him. — Sandy

Sandy, are you making a smile more than just a smile? Being a shy person, perhaps you are making his conversation and his being nice into something more than it may be. What do you know about him? Is he married? Does he already have a girlfriend? Is he also too shy to make a first move?

Answers to all of these questions would make the problem of how to approach him a little easier. Obviously, if he's married or already committed, you need to redirect your interest. If he's available (not married, etc.), and your company does not have a policy against employees dating, then you can always make the first move. That means shoving shyness aside and calling him and inviting him out for a quick lunch or a cup of coffee or something light and non-threatening so that you can get to know each other better.

You'd hate to miss a chance to meet someone because you were too shy to make a move. Especially if years later that same person was to say to you, "I really liked you but you were always so stuck up." Sometimes people don't know you're shy, they believe you're not talking to them because you're "stuck up." — Queenie

♥

Hi Queenie, while I am moving to another department for the next few months I will still be talking work with person. Also when I move to the other department, our desks will be only 2 minutes away from each other though we may not really have reason to cross desks. But we will be working at very close distance. I asked him if he was back with his e-girlfriend and he informed me he was on a casual date a couple of times with another female. When I asked if he believes in marrying within the community as is common in his culture he said in the past he has had a girl friend that was not from his culture. I recently had my appraisal and he, his manager and my new manager all gave excellent reviews.

He knows that I am paying attention to his religion, trying to understand and appreciate the same. All this story but what would be a logical and practical approach. Yes, we are allowed to date and marry with someone at work. — Kayla

Kayla, once you are no longer supervised by him, you might then offer to buy his lunch and "catch up" since you're no longer working in the same department. He'll recognize this as a maneuver to get to know him better and if he's interested, he'll take you up on your offer. If he says yes, then keep the "date" casual and non-serious. Ask him about himself and let him talk about those things that interest him. Hopefully, he'll want to know the same about you. If he says no, don't take it as personal rejection, as he might have a very good reason for not being able to do something at that particular time and date. Tell him that you'll give him a "rain check" for another time. That allows him to call you in the future should he want to get together.

Please remember, work relationships can be wonderful but if they end they can create very real problems for both persons involved. He may be unwilling to get involved with a co-worker for just this reason. – Queenie

♥

Queenie, I just met an attractive, single woman (secretary to a high profile person) from my office and want to ask her out for a date. Trouble is that because of her work demands, most of her time, she doesn't have much free time to herself even in the weekends but I fully understand her high work commitment and dedication to her boss. My question is should I continue to ask her out. To my knowledge, she's not going out with anyone at the moment. Besides her, I am also seeing other women. — Chris

Chris, if you've already asked her out and she has turned you down, you should back off. Regardless of whether or not she is dating someone, she is under no obligation to date everyone who asks her out. It sounds as though the lady is trying to keep her personal life separate from her career. Respect her wishes. — Queenie

♥

Hi Queen of Hearts, there is this guy at work to whom I am attracted to. Until he invited me to his party, we never really talked to each other unless it was related to work. Now we talk all the time. As a matter of fact, the party was the first time that we have ever seen each other in regular clothes (we wear uniforms to work). Last week he invited me to a Halloween party. I unfortunately was not able to go. When I told him this, he seemed somewhat disappointed to my surprise. However, when concerning if it would have been a date, I am clueless.

That is not the problem though the problem is that I do not know how to approach it. I don't want to seem too aggressive. I basically want to know of a way that I can catch his attention and let him know I am interested. If you can help I'd greatly appreciate it. – Alexia

Alexia, the next time you talk to him say "Hey, I really hated missing the Halloween party. Any other parties I can pencil into my schedule now so I don't miss the next one?" This will let him know it wasn't a personal rejection of him, just that you honestly couldn't go to the party. It also shows you're interested. – Queenie

♥

Dear Queen, there is this certain young lady I have developed very strong feelings for, she is aware of me, in fact we know each other quite well, as we have chatted on more than one occasion. I would definitely like to pursue this relationship, in fact, I have been thinking of asking her out to lunch one of these days, but have run into a roadblock or two. 1) I haven't garnered enough nerve to actually ask her if she would like to have lunch, 2) The fact that I'm a bit short on cash with 4 days to go until payday.

In one of the gutsiest moves on my part, I bought her a half dozen roses from a nearby florist and left them at the entrance of our workplace. It turns out she didn't pick them up until 2 days ago (I overheard her talking with some other female workers about how someone left her a half dozen roses but she was saying that she never heard her being paged, and that "they couldn't get a description of the guy who delivered them").

As I mentioned, this is a relationship I would like to pursue further. We did exchange smiles yesterday morning. Whether or not that gave her a hint, I suppose I'll never know. I would like to reveal to her that I was the one who left her the roses, but I fear the rejection and disappointment factor.

Part of me, though, wants to take the anonymous route and simply leave an anonymous note in her locker letting her know my feelings for her and that I am not one of the most obvious suspects, but the person she would least expect to do something like I did. Can you give me a bit of advice on how to handle this? — Claude

Claude, anonymous actions are draining your available cash and not giving you even the slightest chance with this lady. For a romantic encounter we would suggest that you buy one rose from the florist and deliver it to her yourself with a comment such as "This is the way my other roses should have looked, sorry I was too shy to hand them to you myself."

Then invite her out for lunch or a movie or something else simple and inexpensive. If she is interested, she will be flattered. If she isn't interested in dating you, it's better you know now. – Queenie

♥

Hi Queenie, recently I met a guy at work and we were getting along great and having some fun at work and at lunches, until some nosy coworkers caused trouble. He is now off on a 3 week vacation. Before he left there was an uncomfortable feeling between us. I was left to deal with this all myself and it hasn't been easy. I did get a postcard from him. I am feeling very uncomfortable about seeing him again when he returns.

I know Cancer and Scorpios are a very compatible together. I really like him and I think he has some feelings towards me. We have only known each other for a little over 2 months. I'm not sure as how to act towards him when I do see him. Act like I don't care and show him I've missed him.

I do want him in my life. I'm just not sure as what to do now. HELP — Sandra

Sandra, there's not enough information to give you any suggestions at this point. You're finding out why it isn't a good idea to date co-workers, even if you are compatible. Is this man currently involved with someone? Did he go on vacation by himself?

What is the rest of the story? If he is involved, you need to back away until he is unattached, and then the two of you should cool it during working hours and around co-workers.

As far as the astro signs, there are millions of people sharing each of the 12 signs so..... there are plenty of people you're compatible with including or excluding this man. – Queenie

♥

Dear Queenie, a new male friend and I were becoming close until a few coworkers messed that up by sticking their nose where it didn't belong. He went on vacation for 3 weeks and I didn't talk to him until he'd been back for a week. I'm not sure of how to handle talking to him now, the situation seems weird and a bit uncomfortable.

I know he likes being around me as I do him. How should I handle this situation to get us back on the terms we were before all the mess started? I'm Cancer and he's Scorpio. I know of all the signs we are the most compatible. HELP!!! — Sandra

Sandra, you're still not giving enough information so I have to make a couple assumptions and see if either one could provide a possible answer. First, is this man married or otherwise involved with someone, is he your boss, or is he considerably older than you? Any one of these could be reason he might not keep the relationship continuing.

If he is not any of the above, could it be that he has just decided the relationship could be getting a bit more serious than he wanted it to get and he is backing away?

If the two of you are single, unattached adults, there shouldn't be a reason for anything to be messed up, but there is a key element you are not telling us about this relationship. It takes more than compatible signs to make a good relationship. – Queenie

♥

Dear Queen of Hearts, my new male friend and I were getting along great, until a few coworkers said something to our supervisor and we were called for our behavior, there was nothing wrong except we were laughing and maybe they didn't like it or they were jealous.

Anyway, he went on vacation for 3 weeks, during this time, not one person from work would talk to me nor go to lunch with me, (I really could care less).

I did hear from him by postcards while he was gone. He's back and the situation is strange. I'm not sure how to act around him or really want to say. We have talked a couple of times since he's been back.

How can I make this situation more comfortable for the both of us? I really like him, he makes me feel good about myself and makes me laugh and this has been a long time since I did either. Please help us. — Sandra

Sandra, this seems to be a correspondence course that has started and as I see it, there are several issues involved. First, getting involved with a coworker is not a good idea. You've learned one of the reasons why not. The office or workplace is not your personal space, it is your employer's, which means you should be working to perform the job for which you were hired and being paid, not using the time to establish a personal relationship.

Second, if this man wants to continue this relationship, on non-company time, he knows how. He apparently doesn't feel a need to expand it into something more. Your continual attention is probably making him very uncomfortable. It also could be having a bad effect on his job security.

Third, your bad attitude about your coworkers needs to be corrected. No matter what pain someone has caused you in the past, it is no reason to be angry at the people you work with now. You cannot possibly be doing the best you can in this job considering how much time and energy you're spending on disliking "them" and trying to establish a relationship with "him." If you need this job, our best advice is to put your full attention to doing what you are being paid to do, and do it to the best of your ability. If you cannot, then get a job elsewhere.

I'm going to drop out of the role of counselor for you because I'm not qualified. All I can do is offer an opinion, which I have done. This will be the last response to your questions on this issue. It's up to you now. Good luck. – Queenie

♥

Queenie, I'm head over heels with a co-worker. I was instantly attracted to her the first time I saw her, and wouldn't mind getting to know her better. When we talk or work, she would lightly brush against me (I don't know if it's by accident or on purpose), but continue on talking after that as if nothing had happened. I've been working with her for 3 years.

Then, 2 years ago during a Christmas party we sat together in the same table, and engaged in light conversation. Then, during the late hours of the party, she put her right leg over my left hip (under the table), while we were surrounded by other co-workers and friends. (We weren't caught, thank God!). I was thinking: If I put my hand on her hip, I might not look at her straight in the eye the next day. You see, I'm a nice guy; meaning that I don't sleep around or do things like that. So, I did nothing until the end of the party (including talk). She didn't take away her leg, though. On the way home, we were talking about the party, but it's as if nothing had happened!!

The main thing that I was thinking was: "Is she a slut or is just making the first move?" Months later, I assumed the latter was true, so I asked her out to a movie and months later, a concert. She was enthusiastic on going to both, but

she said that she was busy to go to the movie. Also, she phoned me up 4 hours before the concert, saying that she was sick.

I'm now thinking that she's just trying to avoid me, and still be nice - but she would still brush against me at work even today, and she would look at me in the eyes while we talk. We even had hour long conversations over the phone! I think that it was just lust that I had in the beginning, but now, I think about her in a more 'romantic' sort of way. I really like her a lot, but I couldn't express my feelings about her. My observations about her would be that she wasn't flirting with me, and she's basically a nice girl.

My question(s) would be: 1. What's going on? She's giving me mixed signals here! Does she feel the same way about me, or not, or just confused? 2. If the answer to the above question is 'just confused', or 'she feels the same way', how can I make the first move? What should I do? What should I say? Can you give concrete examples on the above advice? — Randy

Randy, if this lady is dating someone else she's playing with you and you need to walk away from her. If she is not dating anyone, she still seems to be playing with you.

(1) If she felt the same way about you that you do about her, the two of you would be dating and enjoying each other's company in a romantic sort of way. She might be confused or she may be just teasing to see what effect she can have on you.

You don't provide an option (3) but my advice would be to find someone else to date. – Queenie

♥

Queenie, there is this man I met on the job. We work at the same organization, however, not in the same building so we are not constantly bumping into each other. I would love to get to know him better, but he is moving so slow. He invited me to Thanksgiving Dinner, but didn't ask for my telephone number until three months later?

What is the problem? How can I get a relationship going with this guy? — Stacee

Stacee, perhaps this man is involved in one of those on-again off-again relationships with someone he can't get out of his system. So, when he thinks it is off-again, he contacts you. And then it picks up again. If that's the case, you better walk away from this one for a while.

The other possibility is that this man is very shy and needs some encouragement from you. You can speed up the dating process or at least test whether he is interested in dating you by casually mentioning that you have a couple tickets to a concert or a sports event or something else very non-intimate in nature and see if he'd like to join you. If he says "yes" then go out and buy the tickets! If he says "no," and says he'll take a rain check, give him a couple weeks to return the lets-get-together suggestion.

Or, if you think he is still too shy, ask him if he would like to join you for some other innocent activity (hopefully by now you have engaged

48

in enough conversation to know what his hobbies and interests are so you can tailor your suggestion accordingly).

If he continues to turn you down — and he might not turn down even the first invitation — then you might want to turn your attention elsewhere. No sense getting your ego deflated with repeated turndowns.

What does the "info hotline" say about this guy's personal life? There is always someone in an organization who knows everything about everyone, whether it's true or not. You don't have to seek out this person but this is one way to find out some of what you want to know. And, knowing there is always office gossip, should you and he start dating, you need to keep it as private around the organization as possible. Good luck! – Queenie

And Baby Makes Three

And Baby Makes Three

*"My girl friend is having twins but I don't know if I love her
enough to spend the rest of my life with her, she is cool and all
but I just don't know if I'm ready to be a father since I am
starting my career."*

If you're looking for a reason for love being so crazy-making at times, blame good ol' Mother Nature. We're all hard-wired with the need to reproduce in order to keep the earth populated and it's that need that can push us into love relationships that don't make much sense. These matings may not make sense to us but they apparently make good sense in the overall scheme of things when considering the prime need to perpetuate our species above all else.

It doesn't take brains to make a baby. All it takes is a fertile female, a willing and able male, lust, and little or no thought about birth control in order to set the stage to make a baby regardless of whether the couple is ready, willing, or able to make a family.

Most relationships begin because of the physical attraction each feels for the other. If the lust is strong enough it is quite often mistaken for love. Unfortunately, lust doesn't last and if love hasn't developed by the time the lust leaves a relationship, there's not much left to hold the relationship together.

The birth of a child might inspire some couples to rethink their feelings for each other but the responsibilities of caring for a child can blow a relationship apart just as easily.

Dating takes on a whole different perspective for single parents because some potential partners aren't ready to step into an instant family situation. Many potential marriage partners won't make it past the "and I have a child" stage of dating. Some people can't deal with the very heavy baggage children bring into a relationship, the necessary time spent with the ex, the shared history that can't be undone, and the contacts with the ex that will continue through the years.

How do you date when you have dependent children? As a single parent your first responsibility is toward your child or children. Should you date and keep your kids a secret until the relationship gets serious?

How soon should you introduce your children to someone you're dating? Should you have someone over "for the night" when you have children? How do you introduce your date to your child?

And, what about the child's other biological parent? Are the two of you on good terms or was the creative process the highlight of your relationship?

Dating is tough enough when there's just two, add in a child and things can get scary.

♥

Dear Queenie, my boyfriend and I have been seeing each other for almost 2 months. I want a child, but feel it might be too soon. Is it? — Anna

Anna, aren't you getting things out of order? Has he asked you to marry him? Is he ready for a lifetime commitment with you? Yes, it is much too soon. — Queenie

♥

Dear Queen of Hearts, my girl friend is having twins but I don't know if I love her enough to spend the rest of my life with her, she is cool and all but I just don't know if I'm ready to be a father since I am starting my career. — Charles

Charles, aren't you about 9 months late in deciding that you might not love her enough? You don't know if you're ready to be a father? What about her? She might not feel that she's ready to be a mother, but she's accepting the responsibility, not once but twice! It's time to grow up so your kids will have someone they can be proud to look up to. — Queenie

♥

Dear Queenie, a few weeks ago my girlfriend broke up with me. I was puzzled by the thought because I couldn't realize why she would break up with me, when she used to tell me that she loved me and all and say that we were soul mates. So finally after a week of being broken up I demanded the truth, and the truth I got, in specific detail which I wasn't too keen about. It happens that the reason we broke up was because for the past 6 months while she has been away on scholarship she was having an affair with another guy. All the time she was talking to me and telling me how much she loved me.

Now she is 2 months pregnant, he dumped her ass when he found out she was pregnant. She went on and on about how she loved him and all the wonderful things they did together, while I sat there and gagged.

Now she is back home and can't go through an abortion and she is asking me if I will go back with her and take care of her and the baby, what do I do? Is she a major loser? Psychopath?

She has even asked me to be the guardian of the child, but problem is I love her but this is the third time she has cheated on me. Gosh if only I knew how this soap opera ended. — Matt

Matt, people treat us the way we allow ourselves to be treated. She knows she can get away with just about anything and you'll still be there. Some people would be outta there after being cheated on once. She does it three times and you're seriously considering taking care of her *and* her baby? You do know that the other guy is legally responsible for *his* child don't you? So maybe you're a nice guy. In this case, a nice guy (you) is finishing last. —Queenie

♥

Dear Queenie, I am a college student with a 29 yr old fiancée. We've been together for four years and engaged for one. My fiancée says he will not marry me unless I get pregnant first. I've always wanted children but I'm not ready yet. He says he will not wait any longer than 2-3 more years.

What am I to do? I love him a lot and I want to have his baby. In my eyes he is not financially set and neither am I. My parents want me to finish school first before I do anything. I know he will be a great daddy seeing how he reacts with children. I also would like to know if you think it would be the right move to move in with him while I am still in school before we get married. Please help me!
— Cookie

Cookie, your fiancé is a few sandwiches short of a picnic in his thinking. I'd suggest you give his ring back and tell him you have a life to lead. You need a good education (particularly if you marry this loon) and it sounds as though he wants to stop your personal growth as quickly as he can. Move in with him? Absolutely not! Dump him and get your degree. It doesn't matter how great a daddy he might be, he doesn't sound like he's much in the way of husband material.—Queenie

♥

Dear Queenie, I was with a guy for a few months in an off and on kind of way but there was really no commitment and I became pregnant and I decided to keep it thinking that we will end up together some how because I love him a lot but I don't think he feels the same wat about me. During my pregnancy he started going with his ex girlfriend again this really hurt me and made me jealous but the one thing I don't understand is he still calls me at night to have sex and I do being stupid because I just want to be with him.

I just want to know what I should do with these mixed feelings and emotions I've already tried to talk to him about it and it didn't work what should I do? — Christie

Christie, do you understand that sex isn't the same as love? Do you understand that a guy will be glad to call if he can get sex without commitment? I don't know if you're mature enough to stop having sex with him. I definitely hope you are using protection so that you don't have another child by him. As far as love, I don't see it.

What should you do? If it were me I'd drop him fast and forever and try to make the best life possible for my child. What will you do? Depends on how desperate you are to make this loser fall in love with you. Sorry to be so harsh, but somebody has to grow up around here. — Queenie

♥

Dear Queenie, my boyfriend and I have been dating for over a year and a half now. When I found out I was pregnant and because of the suddenness and uncertainty of the situation, I decided to have an abortion. He was very supportive through the ordeal, even went with me.

We have discussed marriage and children many times and we both know that we want to be together for the rest of our lives. We are very happy together and spend all of our free time together. He still lives with his parents. He comes from a very close-knit family who are very religious but his father is very much in control. Now, in spite of my perfect pill-taking record since the abortion, I am pregnant once more. I was shocked to find out and so was he. However, my attitudes have changed. I don't want to go through another abortion, not just because it would tear me up emotionally but also because of possible physical risks that could plague me for the rest of my life. I feel as though my boyfriend and are capable of making this work.

He says he will be there for me no matter what I decide to do but I'm detecting an uncertainty and above all, fear perhaps of what his father might say or do. I don't want him to marry me just because of the baby, but I wish I were more certain of his feelings about it. I want to be able to ease his mind and discuss how we could actually make this work but I'm afraid he would feel pushed into something he is not ready for. If he decides not to take an active role, not only would I be astoundingly hurt, I would feel all alone with my responsibility. Please respond and give me some advice. I need an opinion!! — Krystal

Krystal, marriage under the best of terms is a gamble. So is parenthood. It has to be your decision regarding your unborn child as you are the one who will have ultimate responsibility for the next 18 or so years for his or her livelihood. Marriage doesn't change the responsibility that comes with being a parent although, if you have a supportive spouse, it can make parenting a little less of a challenge.

Your boyfriend's image of family life has been instilled in him by what he has learned as he has grown up. He may not have inherited his father's qualities or he may have not yet have had a chance to exercise them while living under his father's control. This is another one of those things you learn once you marry someone. Whether or not your boyfriend wants to assume responsibility for a child it's a little late for him to say "I'm not ready". It's also a little late to start worrying about his father's response.

Tell your boyfriend immediately that you plan to have this child. Then start planning your life as a parent. Hopefully he will be grown-up enough to accept the responsibility of fatherhood.—Queenie

♥

Dear Queen of Hearts, he cheated on me once we just got back together and had a son he seems to be so sincere I need to know in my mind that it will not ever happen again. — Deb

Deb, no one has those kinds of guarantees. You simply have to trust that he has learned what is most important to him. — Queenie

♥

Dear Queenie, I have been dating the same person since February of this year. He and I seem to have a lot in common, as far as goals for the future and our overall aspect of life itself. We have an extremely competent sex life and our appetites are very close to one another's. But, it seems both of is have a fear of commitment. I have been on birth control since he and I decided to become sexual and neither of us care for condoms. I went to the doctors last week, for spotting and since my cycle is extremely regular, I was concerned. Guess what I found out...you got it...pregnant.

My friend is out of town on business all week and I am going on a vacation before he gets back so another week will go past before I can tell him. My fear is that he will think: 1.) I did it on purpose, 2.) he will not want it, 3.) he will not be there for me and 4.) that he will ask whether its his or not.

I don't really believe in people getting married because of children, these days. But I am not a firm believer of abortion either. I care for him a lot, but I don't know for a fact if he is THE person for me. Nor I him. But a child is a connection that will be there for the rest of our lives.

A child is a commitment of parenthood on both ends, and lastly a child is a part of me and him. So, what do I do? How do I handle this? — Georgia

Georgia, too bad you can't take a "do over" on this but it's too late for that. It's unfortunate but very few people think past the passion to the possibility that their few moments of passionate sex might turn into a lifetime commitment. It's time for you to turn into a responsible adult. Fast! Whether you're ready or not to give up your freedom, you've got a new life starting within you that is going to need to be your first priority for the next 18 or so years.

You need a plan for yourself and for the baby. Do you have a good job? Can you support yourself? You need to be able to survive as a single parent — you need to know that you can do this as so many other women have done and are doing this — so that if your boyfriend turns and runs, you will realize that you will survive.

If your boyfriend doesn't believe it is his and doesn't want to take the responsibility (financial support, at the very least), there are simple blood tests that will confirm the father's identity. It might not be a good way to start the parenting part of your relationship but some guys get so freaked when they think about kids that they do and say things they later wish they hadn't. Good luck. — Queenie

♥

Dear Queenie, I've wanted to have a baby since I was 20, now I'm 36 and the clock is really ticking. What do you think about single mother's doing it on their own?

Would you consider a sperm bank? What do you tell the child when he starts looking for his father? That you really didn't know the guy he was just a number??

Looking for answers to this dilemma. — Leslie

Leslie, being a kid is difficult enough without not knowing who your father is or knowing that your father came from a sperm bank.

Being a single parent is very difficult and I'd suggest that you do a search on the Internet using the phrase "single parenting" to see what information shows up. If you have enough financial resources to provide adequately for his or her first 18 years, that will help. Figure about $100,000 as the absolute bare minimum, excluding college expenses, unless inflation gets much more out of hand.

Ask yourself exactly why you want to have a baby. Just being a parent isn't good enough. Neither is wanting to reproduce yourself. If you believe it is the only way you can get someone to totally love you, this is also not a good reason. You can always consider being a foster parent or adopting a needy child. Once you make the commitment there is absolutely no turning back. Good luck. — Queenie

Fatal Flaws

Fatal Flaws

"Every time we're in an argument she always says cruel and nasty things about me."

Some relationships should never happen. They are flawed from the start. These relationships begin, intensify, and then slowly begin unraveling. That should be the end of it but when one person wants out and the other person thinks they have found their one-and-only, the stage is set for the agonies of love gone wrong but not yet laid to rest.

It is too bad that couples in these fatally flawed relationships don't have the clarity of vision about the future that outsiders looking in have. If they did, they'd get out at the first signs of trouble or they'd recognize the flaws and avoid getting involved to begin with.

♥

Hi Queenie, I am 43 and finally found the woman I would like to marry. We have many shared interests and are very compatible. However, she seems to be either insecure or paranoid, always thinking there is some dark motive to events conspiring against her. She also doesn't take advice well at all. Often if I suggest a better way to do something, she'll take it as an indication that she's totally wrong, or I'm just trying to prove I know more than her.

I don't know if it's a lack of trust or what, but I get annoyed when she thinks these things about me and others. Is there anything I can say that will convince her maybe there isn't a "Machiavellian plot" (her words) in everything that goes on? I have tried but then she'll either stick to her paranoid opinion or say I'm defending the other person. I really love her a lot but this bothers me. — Gillis

Gillis, how can I delicately put this? Maybe there isn't a delicate way of saying I think the lady may be just a tad bit too paranoid to be normal. Perhaps counseling could be suggested? I doubt that without proper help she will get better with time; and I suspect this problem will get to a point that it will become intolerable. It's your life and I hope you'll think of your options before making a decision that is painful for you and for her. — Queenie

♥

Dear Queenie, my girlfriend is going through a lot of stress. I'm always there to listen to her and to help her, but she rejects me. We have a communication problem, she doesn't tell me much, never the less respects me. When I ask her about her problem or ask where she went during the day she responds with: "What's it to you" or "why do you care" or "it's none of your business". So what should I do? I also suspect she's up to something in terms of that she's seeing another guy. I don't know what to do. I'm really upset and I haven't called her for days. I miss her very much and I want the best for her. I need help. — Stan

Stan, this does not sound like a loving relationship. As a matter of fact, it doesn't sound like a relationship at all. Has there ever been a good relationship between the two of you? If you think there's another guy, and if she's treating you this way, I would suggest that you consider getting yourself another girlfriend. I just don't see any other way. — Queenie

♥

Dear Queen of Hearts, I am engaged to a lady from Mexico. I write, e-mail and call often, but she rarely communicates with me and hardly ever writes. When we do communicate she is very sweet and tells me how much she loves me. When I love someone I have to have frequent communication, but she is different. I am afraid that she doesn't love as I love her. Why does she not have the desire to communicate with me more often? — Walt

Walt, I don't know why she isn't on the same communication level as you but if the two of you are engaged and you have these problems, the marriage doesn't seem destined for success. Why don't you take a couple steps back, rethink the engagement and get yourselves more in tune to each other before making such a giant commitment. – Queenie

♥

Hi Queenie, my lover has a gastrointestinal issue, and we have been together for three years. I recently just moved in with her, we both wanted to make sure we could live together before marrying. I never realized it would be this bad. She now tells me that the reason why I never knew about it was that she would actually go through pain holding it in when we were together. And now that we live together she discussed with me that it is to uncomfortable to constantly hide it. And to me this is extremely unfair to her, but then again I find it offensive.

In the middle of the night in her sleep I am kept awake with her problem and she doesn't know I hear her. I find myself feeling selfish, but feeling disgusted with her and also with myself. What am I to do????? Please help! Thank You, Stephen

Stephen, if you love her, get her to a doctor. This is a physical problem that may have a very simple cure. Of course, if you're looking for a reason to break off the relationship, this is as good as any. — Queenie

♥

Hello Queenie: This problem started several months ago and is still affecting me. My g/f of 8 years went on a short ski trip with her family. She had my permission to go as I couldn't take time off from work on such short notice. When she returned she acted distant to me till she finally admitted someone on the trip was interested in her and she couldn't see or talk to me as I have an "unfair advantage" because we both live in the same state and he lives elsewhere.

I went from seeing her almost every day before the trip to nothing after the trip. I had to go to therapy to help deal with this and I finished my therapy but

I still have thoughts that maybe I did something wrong here and some days I feel guilty. Maybe if I just didn't allow her to go everything would be OK. I have recurring thoughts like this. Is this going to scar me for the rest of my Life? Any tips? — Eddie

Eddie, if she had to get your permission to go on a trip with her family (or needs your permission to go anywhere, for that matter) I am amazed this relationship has lasted this long. If she is older than 21, she shouldn't need anyone's permission to do anything! It sounds as though she doesn't want to be controlled any more. Perhaps you need to talk to your therapist regarding this relationship a few more times. Good luck. – Queenie

♥

Dear Queenie, about 3 weeks ago, my boyfriend of almost 4 years broke up with me. Over the previous 18 months I had been basically punishing him verbally through insults and constant reminders of a brief affair he had. I had a very hard time dealing with this so I dealt with it by arguing with him constantly. Underneath I still loved him deeply but I was very hurt by what he had done.

Now he has a new girlfriend. However he says he isn't sitting well with his decision and would like to be back with me but he has too much anger. He calls me every day and I have cried and pleaded with him to give me another chance. I see things totally differently and I understand now that everyone is entitled to make a mistake.

There are 4 children that are hurting in this as well (his 2 from a previous relationship, my 1 from a previous relationship, and we have a child together.) I tried to ask him to give our family a chance and he says not right now....yet when I have a male friend over, he has a fit and tells me that I don't love him and I haven't changed. He then asked me to show him that I had changed by leaving my male friends alone and showing him through my behavior, however he won't spend any time with me to see that I have changed.

I don't know what to do. I'm tired of crying and pleading my case to him, but if there's a chance that my baby could have both his parents together... shouldn't I do whatever's necessary to allow that to happen? — Myra

Myra, I'm a bit confused. He broke up with you after you spent 18 months verbally abusing him after he had an affair. Now he has a girlfriend, you want him back but he wants you to 'prove' yourself.

Perhaps the best thing to do is just get on with your life. He's probably making you pay for making him so miserable. Who knows when he'll think you've learned your lesson. By that time you may not like him any more and if he does come back you'll probably hold his current girlfriend over his head until he leaves again.

Perhaps if you just get on with your life, and let him get on with his, sometime in the future the two of you *might* realize you belong together and at that point you both might be mature enough to enter into a more forgiving, less abusive relationship. Your children would benefit from a more mature approach to relationships. Good luck. – Queenie

♥

Dear Queenie, I'm so angry my boyfriend of five years just came over the other night and we had great sex, then he has gone off again, and I think that I am more angry at myself for falling for it again, he says he doesn't want a commitment then when we break up he is always back I don't know how to let go but he is driving me insane with his mixed messages and he wont even acknowledge the fact that I feel hurt and used when he does this, how do I let go, without him I am very lonely and its really hard for me to meet new people. — Naomi

Naomi, what reason does he have to treat you well? You'll give him 'great sex' no matter how he treats you so he does what he wants. The sooner you get over him, the sooner you'll start feeling better about yourself. You have to like yourself before others will have a reason to like you. — Queenie

♥

Dear Queen of Hearts, I have been with this man for 10 years. We have not had sex for a year and a half. He said it wasn't me, but that he had no sex-drive. Well he seems to have a sex-drive when he thinks I am asleep or when I leave the house!

The relationship has been steadily declining for awhile, and at this point it's like living with my brother, but I don't know how to end it! He's a good man but we obviously just don't do it for each other anymore. He has had some terrible luck over the past few months, and I feel guilty about wanting to split up, when he's down on his luck but I am miserable!!

Any suggestions on how to break it off, and get my guts up to do it? — Cherry

Cherry, if having sex with him is the only reason you're still together, then I doubt you could leave soon enough. If, however, you love him, then wouldn't you rather understand his situation and be an understanding partner?

I suspect his terrible luck has driven his confidence into the dumpster and perhaps he just doesn't have enough confidence to believe he could please you. If he were to try and fail, it would only be that much worse. Pressuring him for physical intimacy can only add more stress.

He knows you're upset, he knows he's not making you happy in this very important area of your relationship. So take the pressure off. There are other ways you can get the physical relief you need by yourself. Perhaps with a new, caring, no pressure attitude, he'll relax and respond. For that matter, show him what you do — it might inspire him. Good luck. – Queenie

♥

Queenie, what is the proper and most effective way of dealing with a boyfriend who constantly interrupts you? What can I do about helping him to correct this behavior; and how can I keep myself from getting upset about this situation?

Some Background: We love each other very much, and have been going out for 3 years. He goes through phases when he starts interrupting me all the time to just some of the time. In its worse phase, I can't stand to even talk to him, because I end up yelling at him to let me say something... Please help. — Nora

Nora, while there are certainly people who would say you need to do something about his behavior, our thought is that you need to do something about your own. We're not being unkind, we're being practical. If you truly love him, and this is the only major fault he has, would it be worth dumping him because he does this? If so, dump him. If not, learn to accept this as his particular 'uniqueness' and look past it.

Perhaps he needs special reassurance of his importance in your life at these times, and this is the only way he knows to make you 'see' him. Perhaps, too, at these times you're paying less attention to him and more attention to someone or something else. Why not just stop talking the next time he does this, and listen to him. If he stops, ask him to continue. If he says, 'no you were talking' then say to him 'yes, but you wanted to talk also and I will wait until you are through.' Do you have the patience to do this?

There's only one person you can change in your life. That's you. You can't change him, but he will react differently depending upon what you do. Good luck. – Queenie

♥

Dear Queenie, I hurt my boyfriend of three years after we started having problems, I cheated on him. He said he no longer can trusts me and does not want to get back together. This I completely understand. He started seeing someone else which I can also understand.

I left him alone so I could get over him and this is where my confusion begins. He became really angry when I stopped returning his calls because he was calling for no reason. He said he realizes I have not changed and he was thinking about getting back together until I started playing this game. It is not a game, I love him and want to work things out if possible, but now he is giving me mixed signals and this hurts worse. What should I do? — Donna

Donna, it sounds as though he is playing his own games. Perhaps he wants to make you 'pay' for hurting him and this is the best he can do. We suggest you refuse to play the game. Perhaps if you leave him alone and let him get this anger and his other relationships out of his system, there might be some hope for the two of you. If you want him back, that is. My guess is there are still problems that will make the two of you a 'less than perfect' match. Think about it. – Queenie

♥

Dear Queenie, one of my friends has asked me for my advice and I am trying to help her, but I would also like your input. She has been engaged for almost a year and she has been with this guy for almost two years.

The problem is another man has turned her head and she is very attracted to him and may want more than a sexual relationship with him. This man is not only her supervisor at work, but he also has a girlfriend and has admitted to my friend he is and has cheated on his girlfriend with different people. He would do anything to get my friend in bed.

She takes up for him, saying they are good friends and they can finish each other's sentences and they think about each other all the time. She realizes he is the opposite of what she wants for a husband and a father, but that challenge and sexual attraction is confusing her.

If she gave up her current relationship, she would lose a stable, secure, healthy relationship. Her fiancé gives her everything and their sex life is still going strong, so what's her problem? I don't get it. Please help!! — Jennifer

Jennifer, lust is part of the problem. Unfortunately, it will probably cause her to lose the great guy she's engaged to, her job, and her self-respect. A small price to pay to sleep with a loser, wouldn't you say?

It's that 'emotionally and physically abusive' relationship that says a lot about her needs and why she'd do something like this. She probably needs some counseling to find out why she needs so much pain in her life. – Queenie

♥

Dear Queen of Hearts, my boyfriend of 4 months has low self esteem. It's rather exhausting at times to believe more in him than he does in himself and to endure the victim act. I don't want to drop him because he is very sweet and I'm starting to care about him.

We're both in our mid twenties. I want to talk to him, suggest he see a therapist. I've told him I am unable to make him happy or I would do so. I think he dates so he can "fix" himself but of course that never works. He instead might consider making himself happy and letting that energy carry over to the relationship.

What can I do? Or should I end it and tell him to call me once he finds himself? I really hate to do that. Sometimes though he is so glum and won't smile for hours. How can I still date him without "rescuing" him or attempting to do so (I tend to try and rescue guys...) He's a wonderful person, just like me. — Lydia

Lydia, you could be setting yourself up for heartbreak. Once he's "fixed" he may no longer need you. I have seen it happen lots of times. I think you should be more concerned about your personal happiness and assure him that you think he's great, you care for him, but you're not qualified to be his "shrink" and you're going to get on with your life and if he'd like to come along, it's up to him.

You might call it "tough love" but if he really cares for you, he'll rise up to meet you, not keep pulling you down to his unhappy level. Good luck. – Queenie

♥

Dear Queenie, I've been seeing this guy for about a month. Up until last weekend everything was fine. We had an argument. I apologized and everything was fine or so I thought. You see, his ex-girlfriend was a major pain. She argued about something continuously and she drank and became violent. He put up with her for longer than he should have because she said she would kill herself if they broke up. I'm NOTHING like her, but because we had a little dispute, he's decided that he's backing off. He says that it's not only about the dispute we had, but the problems he's been experiencing financially with his business.

A part of me feels like it's my fault, and then part of me says that's stupid. I could understand it if I was a constant nagger and bickered about every little thing he did, but I don't. I'm only human and I don't feel that I should zip my lip if there's something bothering me. Am I wrong?

You have always given good advice, even if it does hurt sometimes. Thanks.
— Lydia

Lydia, for you, the "fire" lasted about 30 minutes. For him, it may have brought back a rush of bad memories of his ex. You have no control over his memories, and it isn't your fault that something you might say might trigger a negative response. Unfortunately, when you date someone, you cannot erase all the negatives of prior relationships that can come flooding back on you.

The fact that he has financial problems is significant at this point. Men worry much more than women about their financial status since it is how they measure themselves and their success, and how they consider themselves measured by the world at large. With this stress in his life, it may be easier for him to have no relationships to have to worry about.

As far as whether you're wrong about being yourself, no, you're not wrong. As an adult you realize that you can do or be anything you want to do or be. The second part of that is the knowledge that whatever you choose to do or be has consequences that you also much be prepared to accept.

If you choose to not control your anger then you must accept fully the consequences of that action. In this case, it caused a negative response in a man you'd like to know better. If you had chosen to hold back, would you still be facing his decision to back off on the relationship? It's difficult to say.

I appreciate the comments about the good advice, and I don't try to hurt anyone although sometimes a blunt, straight-on response can do that at first. Good luck. – Queenie

♥

Dear Queenie, when does dishonesty become too much, is the question I guess... I have been together with a wonderful woman for 8 months now. On the whole, our relationship has been great. We are alike professionally, socially, emotionally, and spiritually.

There has been one chronic problem. She tells me white (and some not so white) lies about her relationship with her ex and even about smoking dope. The bottom line is that she lies when it is the easy way out, or when she wants to do what she wants to do, and not be questioned about it. She says that she learned this as a defense mechanism growing up.

When do lies become too many? I know that she loves me, and would never cheat on me or lie about loving me, yet some friends tell me that "small lies become big lies." We talked many times about this, and she kept saying she would try not to do it anymore. Finally I made it clear that I couldn't remain in the relationship if she lied to me. It got better for a while, much better, but yesterday she told a "half-lie." Once again saying she really wasn't trying to hide anything from me.

Her lying has made me suspicious to the point where I don't know when she is or isn't telling the truth, and I get suspicious. The one yesterday was that she told me that her friend (the long ago ex) may or may not sleep over on her couch, then it happened anyway and I found out that that was the plan all along and she knew it.

I broke up with her today. Did I do the right thing? Do you think she can change? Do you think I ended this at a time when she was on the verge of totally embracing honesty? Please answer soon, because we ended things today, and I can still salvage if you think I am overreacting. My friends tell me to get out, but they may just be telling me what they think I want to hear. What do you think? Thanks. — Daniel

Daniel, trust is critical to the success of a relationship. Can you trust her? It would seem you can't since she lies to you. A lie is a lie. Where do you draw the line? She has lied about meeting her ex. You want to trust her but you find it difficult. Most people would.

Her lies are not insignificant. Smoking dope when it is in violation of your profession is a morality issue. Lying about her ex, and involving him in the lying, is also a morality issue. Listen to your instincts and try not to be blinded by need.

She won't get better at least that's my personal opinion. Your friends may be right. As an adult, she doesn't have to use old defense mechanisms to protect herself. She knows that what she is doing is going to cause trouble (as it would in any relationship), so she pulls out an "I can't help it" defense. Yes she can.

Make up with her if you wish, but I don't think you're overreacting. As a matter of fact, most guys I know wouldn't have hung in this long. Good luck. – Queenie

♥

Hi Queenie, I am a very jealous person!!!! My girlfriend has many guy friends, who would like to be more than just friends. She sees nothing wrong with being their friend. It just really hurts me, for her to be with a guy who has more feelings for her than she has for them. It's really been hard on our relationship, and I do love her! So how can I save this! Somebody help, it's driving me crazy!!!!
— Stony

Stony, there is absolutely nothing wrong with your girlfriend being friends with other men as long as she isn't flirting and leading them to believe that she's interested in more than friendship. Perhaps some of the men would like to be her boyfriend, but she chooses YOU!! Doesn't that make you feel special over them? It should.

Are you so suspicious that you believe she will do something behind your back with one of these guys? Do you trust her? If so, STOP torturing yourself with what might happen. If you don't trust her, then get out of the relationship and find a girlfriend who you can trust.

It is unrealistic to expect any female to only have one male friend just as it is unrealistic to expect any male to have only one female friend.

There is a phrase: "Without love, there is no jealousy; without jealousy, there is no love." In other words, when you deeply love someone you will be jealous of the time and attention they spend with others because you want all of their attention directed your way. When jealousy begins to harm a relationship, then it is being done to excess. – Queenie

♥

Dear Queen of Hearts, first blind date ever and we hit it off. We fell in love in a matter of weeks. We talked of marriage and a lifetime together. She moved away for school and we saw each other weekends; she then moved to a school 1.5 hours away and continued weekends. The next year she moved into my place and commuted. We got engaged and were happier than either had been. I was hesitant about the engagement because she had been engaged and lived with a guy before; she convinced me that this was different. The last year of our relationship had not gone as smoothly as the first 8 months. Some of this was my fault... didn't spend as much time with her as I should have... too much time with my friends.

This last summer we were getting along very poorly so we went to a marriage counselor and started to talk the issues out. She decided she needed some space and got her own apartment closer to school but didn't tell me she had done this until we were talking. When she moved she left her engagement ring because she didn't feel comfortable or right wearing it.

I was crushed at this point, but we continued with the counselor and things really started to turn around; I thought things were going great, but the last three weeks have been not good. She says that she is deeply in love with me and has never felt so close to anyone, but that she has never been attracted to me physically.

The situation is tearing me apart...we both agree that this is the hardest that both of us have ever worked on a relationship. She is saying that the lack of

physical "compatibility" is beginning to make her resent the relationship, and she's not sure if we should continue. I've suggested we go back to the counselor and look for sex therapy...she is willing, but states over and over that how can they fix something that doesn't exist (her lack of attraction)? I don't know what to do in this situation...I've never loved a person so completely, and I truly believe that to be her feelings also... except the lack of "sexual compatibility".

She tells me it's her problem that I'm attractive looking and that technique, etc., in bed is as good if not better than she's had in the past. I have told her that I don't think I could handle being around her if we were "friends only" and knowing that she's seeing others for romance. Please give your best insight. — George

George, since she has agreed to further counseling, I suggest you give it your best shot. Sexual compatibility is very important in a love relationship, but I'm sure I don't have to tell you that.

There isn't a significant age difference however you might be right about her not being experienced enough to commit, particularly if she has been engaged once before. Good luck. – Queenie

♥

Dear Queenie, my girlfriend and I have been dating for 6 months now. I am the first real boyfriend she's had in a long time - she hasn't dated seriously for 2-3 years, and the longest relationship she's had was about 8 months. I've been in a few longer relationships. We started out spending a lot of time together, and got along really good. We stayed over at each other's place quite often, met the family and all that, and everything was really good. We had a great sex life, and I basically have gotten her to "like sex" - according to her friends she never really liked it before but now has bragged to them about how great the sex we have is.

About 3 months into the relationship, she had been planning to go on a holiday with a couple of friends. They backed out and I said that if she wanted, I'd go with her. At first she was a little hesitant (it's a pretty big thing to plan a trip 3 months into the future with someone you've only dated for 3 months) but after we talked she decided it would be okay.

Basically, 2 weeks before the trip we had an argument (the first real one we'd had), but resolved it. Then we went on the trip, and as soon as we left her attitude seemed to change. I don't know if it was the pressure of being with me 2 weeks straight (we obviously stayed in one room), or what it was. Basically, she just seemed to lose interest in things I said. I felt that when I said something it was annoying to her - that I didn't really have anything interesting to say.

At the same time, we seemed to be arguing about so many little things - we seemed to jump on anything the other person said and fire it right back at them. It became a little unfair. Near the end of the trip, we got into a huge fight one night, and went home in a taxi with both of us really upset. Once back, she left the room for about 2 hours. When she came back she was upset and had been crying the whole time.

I pressed her to talk. We talked about a lot of things, and I told her how I was feeling. She basically said that whenever we argue that she feels like it's always *right and wrong - I have to be right and she has to be wrong. I can see that - I like winning. I apologized for that. I then tried to explain how I left, and she didn't really seem to internalize - she was just waiting for the whole conversation to end. We went to sleep, with me still feeling there was lots to be said, but I didn't want to press her too much.*

Again, she said we'd talk about it - we didn't. We got back a week ago, and since then, we've talked on the phone pretty well every day, but I haven't seen her since getting back. When I am talking to her on the phone, her attitude seems to be the same as before we left - we're in a relationship and that's not going to change. She's asked if I want to go skiing with her and her friends in a few weeks. We're going to a friend's wedding in a couple of weeks.

I guess what's bothering me is that I don't really know how she feels and I don't know how to get her to tell me. I seem to get really insecure about it, but I guess that's human nature to assume the worst when you just don't know. It's just little things, like a couple of nights this week she stayed home and didn't go out. Normally, she would invite me over to watch TV or a movie with her. But this week, when we've talked, she says she's staying home and that's it. It feels like she doesn't really want to see me.

How can I get her to talk to me and tell me HONESTLY how she feels, without trying to change the subject, or just saying what she thinks I want to hear?

I've read John Gray's Mars & Venus, and see some valid points - particularly that I seem to always want to fix her problems. But I need some advice on how to get her to open up to me so that I can feel more confident in knowing how she feels. Thanks so much for any advice you can give. — Henry

Henry, you would be most comfortable if you could crawl inside her brain and study all of her thoughts, wouldn't you? You want her to spell out in complete terms what she's thinking, how she's feeling, and when she does, you psychoanalyze and critique, probably offering options for thoughts and actions that would be better for her (in your opinion).

Why is it so important that you have this look into the deepest recesses of her emotions? Why must you know every thought she thinks? Why must you understand every mood that she has? You don't have to know how she feels all the time, in minute detail. Allow her some privacy, some thoughts that are hers alone, some emotional space for herself.

She doesn't want to talk, talk, talk, about feelings and emotions. Some people don't. That's not a failing. Or, if it is, it is just as much of a failing as someone who must constantly talk about them.

You've been dating almost 6 months. You have a need to be close — all the time — and she doesn't have the same need. Who do you think is going to have a problem in this relationship? Both of you, of course. If she spends all of her time with you (to make you happy) she will be unhappy.

If you must spend some time away from her (to make her happy) you will be unhappy. It's a situation of opposite needs trying to compromise enough to make a relationship work. Are you up to it?

And stop discussing your sex life with all your/her friends! There are some things that should be between just the two of you and what you do in the bedroom is one of those things. – Queenie

♥

Dear Queen of Hearts, I'm in a relationship with a girl for almost 3 months now. From the beginning we had arguments at least once a week, and I think it's normal for couples to have arguments in a relationship. But lately, we argue everyday, literally.

For example, her roommate's car broke down once and I gave her roommate a ride back to her dorm. We argued to one in the morning because she said she felt I would give a ride to anyone, and she doesn't feel special. We're talking about her roommate who is also a friend of mine! We also argue because I talk to other girls who are my friends. She talks to guy friends of hers all the time, and when I say something about it she says they were just talking.

That's not the worst part of it. Every time we're in an argument she always says cruel and nasty things about me. And afterwards she always says that she didn't mean it. I have tried calling the relationship off a few times because I didn't want to be emotionally hurt anymore, but she won't let me. Sometimes she apologizes for what she said and sometimes she gets physical. Last time she jumped on the hood of my car and wouldn't let me leave.

Also, whenever she's stressed out or angry about something she would release it out on me. She expects me to take her out all the time. She expects me to be with her all the time. I can't leave her to go home without her getting mad. If I don't see her for one day she says that I only come over to her place when it's convenient for me. I drive 45 minutes to see her everyday but sometimes I get tied up doing other things I just can't make it. These aren't dates we're talking about either, just me being there.

With all the cruel things she said about me, I can't/don't feel the same about her like when we first got together. She was not like this when we first met, and I'm afraid this is the real her I'm seeing now. I've told her I wanted to end it but she wants a reason, and every time I give her one, she says it's not good enough. I really need help on this one. I don't know what to do anymore. Am I wrong in trying to end this? Should I try to keep this going? Help. — Joel

Joel, you have been dating this girl for only 3 months and she is trying to completely dominate you. This is not a good relationship and I doubt it's going to get any better. You don't have to give her a "good" reason for splitting up. If you don't want to stay in this abusive relationship just tell her goodbye. That is all you need to say. And you can tell her that by phone if there's a potential for physical harm from her if you talk to her in person. Then stay away. – Queenie

♥

Dear Queen of Hearts, I met her four years ago in an office where we both worked. She and I hit it off instantly and became very close friends. Although I

was attracted to her, I never made a pass at her because I thought she was for the most part happy with her boyfriend. Then I quit my job and after a couple of weeks she called up and invited me over for a beer. I soon learned she was very unhappy with her current boyfriend and that she was very attracted to me. One thing led to another and we have been nearly inseparable ever since.

In an effort to be brief, I have been seeing her for the past several months and things have been pretty rocky. She finally broke up with her other boyfriend. And we spent two fantastic weeks together.

The last night we had together she was acting weird and I couldn't get her to talk about it. I've told her how I feel about her. Now, (for the third time) she says we were only meant to be friends and nothing more. She has not gone back to her old boyfriend and she's not seeing anyone else.

My better judgment tells me to just leave it alone and never see her again. She wants to have dinner, go to the movies and just be friends. But history repeats itself and I know we will end up making love and here we go again. I'm crazy in love with her but I can't take the abuse.

We made holiday plans etc... etc.. What side of the fence is she standing on?? What gives?? — Bobby

Bobby, she is not on the same side of the fence you're on. Now maybe you can have some insight into what her other boyfriend was feeling, particularly when you and she were making it together and she and he were still involved.

You were too caught up in your own feelings to see the bigger picture, but perhaps now you can step back and see this woman for the bad news she is. You don't need "friends" like this.

Whatever her problems are, whatever motivates her to destroy relationships, if you have a need to be a part of her little game, accept that you'll keep getting hurt. Your "better judgement" is right on! – Queenie

♥

Hi Queenie, my boyfriend (now ex-boyfriend) and I were fighting a lot due to the fact that I was under a lot of stress because my mother died suddenly. Because we were fighting we broke up. I want him back now that I feel I have my life in order but he seems to be playing games.

I asked him if we could get together and talk and he said yes, but he said that he is really busy working all the time and does not know when he will be able to get together.

I feel that this is just an excuse. We used to work together and he quit the job and I feel like it was because of me, so he didn't have to be around me. I really miss him and I still love him a lot. I don't know whether I should just forget about him or whether I should wait and see what he decides.

He said that I really hurt him when I broke up with him. But he doesn't understand what I was going through with my mother dying all of the sudden. It was a real shock and I have to take care of my little brother and it's just a lot of work I was not ready to deal with. Please help me. — Danielle

73

Danielle, the death of a family member or someone we deeply love can put a tremendous strain on relationships. How we deal with our grief and grieving impact on those around us, particularly those who have no concept of the depths to which our grief can take us.

If your boyfriend had been more caring and mature, he would have had more tolerance for the situation. He would have backed away and let you go through the process of grieving, offering support and solace when you asked it of him, and being someone you turn to for comfort.

Instead, your boyfriend is punishing you for the pain you caused him. He doesn't have any understanding of the stresses and pain in your life, nor does he care. He selfishly believes that the world revolves around him and him alone.

You don't need him in your life. Don't wait for him, don't beg him to come back, don't degrade yourself. With the situation you are in as a result of your mother's death and the added responsibility of your little brother, you need a man in your life not this immature boy. Relax. If you will relax, you will probably find that there is someone close by who is falling in love with you even now. Open your eyes. – Queenie

♥

Queenie, I am a 35, professional white female. I recently started dating again after a few years of . . . abstinence (to tell you the truth, I was going through a lot of shit and I couldn't deal with dating).

Here is the problem. I made a casual date with an acquaintance from school. I invited him to a picnic/cookout. We met at the party, had a great time and agreed to see each other again. Yesterday, I was supposed to meet him at this park where he said he'd be playing basketball with his friends. We would go do something from there.

The M— —f— — didn't show up.

I am furious. This person seemed to be interested in me. He was polite and we had a good time at the picnic. Not to mention, he approached me originally with the idea that we should go do something together. What I'm trying to say is that he acted like he liked me.

Then he didn't show up, didn't call. I was so humiliated. I just want to give up on this whole dating thing. Why didn't I see this coming? I am very angry. What am I supposed to do (that's legal). If he comes up with a good excuse, what then? — Rosy

Rosy, get a grip!! You are humiliated, angry and all bent out of a shape because he didn't show up after your first casual date. Perhaps something happened to him that prevented him from playing basketball with his friends. Maybe he was in a car wreck. Perhaps he got ill. Any number of emergencies could have occurred. Did it matter enough to you to call and find out if he was okay? Dating has changed in the past few years with women taking more of an active role. If you're concerned about whether or not he'll show up, you might want to call to confirm the date.

You are still angry from your prior experience(s). You are still dredging up a lot of emotional s—t and you may not yet be ready for dating. Dating is not easy. Sometimes you'll meet someone, everything will click and you think you've found the perfect soul mate. That's your view of the meeting. His view may be entirely different. You think "we could make beautiful music together." He thinks "nice, but no bells." He thinks that saying "I'll call you" or "let's do this again" are a required part of the first date conversation.

You believe that when he says "I'll call you," he will, or "let's do this again," he means "I like you enough to get to know you much better." You start planning your life around these few statements and then are angry when he doesn't become a part of the program.

To date successfully you must be able to not take the other person's casual approach to dating as a personal insult or affront. You may not have any other dating interests in your life at this time, but men you meet may be interested in meeting or dating others. Until you become committed, every man you meet is merely a casual acquaintance who may or may not become something more.

Chill out. Dump that anger. If you care about this guy, call him and gently, casually, cheerfully, with a modicum of concern, ask about yesterday. Do not shout, demand, cajole, whine, or threaten him. If he has a good excuse, what then?

Are you ready to be a good companion? Not with your current bad attitude. Can you be a good companion? Sure ... but it takes work to become the interesting, optimistic, cheerful, understanding, empathetic type of person he and most men would like to meet.

You don't need to be Mary Poppins. Just be yourself ... without an attitude. And good luck. — Queenie

Virginity

Virginity

"I'm a virgin. She is not. She is 29 years old and I guess it's
not a surprise that she isn't a virgin."

Millions of women grew up in the "you don't do 'it' until your wedding night" decade, the "if you 'do' him, you marry him" generation. Whether or not a young woman's first sex partner was a suitable life partner, she was obligated to "make right" her decision to give up her most precious asset by marrying him – if he was willing – which guaranteed a plethora of divorces decades later. Holding onto her virginity was a full-time job for a girl coming into full bloom.

For boys with raging hormones the virginity issue was only a problem if they were virgins when their peers weren't – the sooner they "did it" the sooner they joined the ranks of "real men". The logic was flawed because if maintaining virginity until the wedding night was a requirement for "good girls" just how was a boy expected get his manly experience? What made it acceptable for boys to "prime the pump" prior to marriage when that same sexual experience could brand his good girl partner "easy" and a "slut"?

Interestingly, in the majority of emails I've received about the virginity issue, it seems to be a more important requirement to young men who wrote wailing about the lack of virginal young women or their partner's non-virgin status than it seems to be for today's young women. Or, perhaps, young women are subscribing to Wendy Keller's "born-again virgin" movement (*The Cult of the Born-Again Virgin*, Health Communications Inc.) and reclaiming their virginity when it suits their needs.

❤

Hi Queenie, I know this is a long letter, but I would appreciate it very much if you would help. I do believe this is somewhat unique (reversed role situation?) I know you have heard similar stories, but I've searched everywhere on the internet and have found no postings related to it.

I am a 23 year old virgin male. It is by choice and not for any other reason (like I can't get any). I just graduated from college and basically didn't date (again, believe it or not, by choice). I am a much focused person and have strong feelings about my education. Besides, I was so busy that I didn't have the time that women need and that I would like to give them.

Now, I'm not trying to be self-deceived, I'm not a ladies' man...I'm a shy 'nice guy'. I realize that I am the type of guy that women want to marry, not date (for many women anyway). I hear (quite often) that I am such a sweet guy and that some women is going to be lucky to find me (men, women, friends and family say this).

Weeks after my graduation I met someone. I was the pursuer. She was very friendly and was easy to talk to. So, after knowing her for about one month, I asked her out. We had a great time...and we have ever since. I'm ready now, after my years at college, to get serious. We hit it off like I can't even explain. We are the exact same person...almost. Like I said before, I'm a virgin. She is not. She is 29 years old and I guess it's not a surprise that she isn't a virgin.

We have discussed this difference and she says that she is fine with it. I think that's why we hit it off so quickly and so well. She knows that there will be no pressure. We have moved very quickly and feel very strongly for each other. I just want to be different, but I can't help thinking of the other guys she has been with. If 'we' work out, will I be compared? Does she have any diseases? Will it be special to her? Am I different than the others? I have asked her those questions and she has given answers that are satisfactory. All of her relationships have been long-term monogamous ones.

To tell you the truth, it eats away at me to think that she was with someone else (more than one). It actually makes me physically ill. I have always wanted to share that most intimate experience with another like myself. To learn together is a dream of mine. In fact, it was virtually at the top of 'the list'. I think about it all the time. I think that a 'perfect' mate for me is not realistic. Temptation, for most, is just too great. If I had found a virgin, she would most likely be way to hung up and be a bore (there are other things couples can do...). I've always wanted to find someone like me that wants to have a little fun, but won't go over the ultimate line. Along with a perfect personality, I just don't think that person exists, if she does, it would be almost impossible to find her. I also don't want to lose what I have because it is absolutely perfect except for that one thing.

Now I know I'm not very experienced, but I'm talking about any kind of relationship/friendship. She has fallen for me extremely hard. I'm not trying to kid myself, I have fallen for her too. I also observe how she treats others and her actions are sweet and genuine. She tells me that one of the reasons she loves me so much is because of the way I treat others.

Not to sound like I have an ego or anything, but I know that I am everything (so far) that she has ever wanted. She has told me that she has always settled before. She has actually asked me if 'I was perfect'... 'Is there anything wrong with you?' Her friends have asked me if 'I have a brother'.

Please don't tell me that I need to talk to her about this... I have. I believe what she says, but that's not the issue. I understand that things could change... and probably will to some degree. We could have a longer 'honeymoon stage' than usual.

Don't tell me it's just something I need to choose for myself... that's obvious. Or that I need to date more and get that experience to compare. I don't want to lose her. I really doubt that I'll find someone as compatible. I am a very intelligent person and I know how things should go. I want an opinion and/or experienced thoughts.

I also know that she is kind of 'my first serious' and that it might (might?) play a role in my feelings... there are plenty of other fish in the sea... blah blah blah. I don't know exactly what I'm looking for in an answer, but please, just ramble. I would like to hear lots of insight. I would prefer not to get any open ended comments or return questions. "Everything she has done everything that has happened to her and all her experiences have resulted in exactly who and what she now is."

80

That's the problem! I realize these experiences are what have caused her to appreciate me so much. She has had a sexual past.

It's hard for someone who does not hold virginity (sex) in such a high regard to understand my feelings. What can I do to get over it? I'm not sure that I ever will. Was this person sent to me as some sort of test? Don't I deserve everything I want in a companion? She is everything, except for her sexual past.

It may sound insensitive, but to me, if I share my life with someone who has had a sexual past... it's left-overs! After all those jerks use her for that (and most do use women for that), I get the left-overs. I don't want that. 90% of men are dogs! Of what is remaining, 9% are undateable for whatever reason. Which leaves 1% (maybe) to go around.

I feel sorry for women. I think that if I was a woman I would either forget about companionship with men or look toward woman to fill that need. Women are so much more caring. The reason this is bothering me so much is because she is everything I have ever wanted... except her sexual past. Is it so wrong of me to want exactly what she has (we have)...plus the other?

What is my problem (hang-up)? Not that I want to leave her...I don't plan on it. If our chemistry continues and she remains the person I know now, we'll be together for a long time. (I know 7 months isn't really that long to think like this). Can you put my mind at ease? Can you tell me what you think? Will it last? Or am I just too hung-up to not forget about it and have it affect the future? It has not been a problem at all between us...yet?

Should I just 'Get over it, you stupid ass! You have a great catch!'? Am I crazy to even think there is a problem with this virtually perfect person... or am I settling, as she has before? I know I'm new to this, but I know how people should treat each other and this is exactly how it should be. I care for her deeply, as she does for me. But why does this bother me so much? Is it worth the risk to move on? Sincerely, Chad

Chad, you are so completely obsessed about your virginity and her lack of the same that I can't help but feel this relationship is probably doomed unless you get some counseling to put the whole thing into proper perspective.

She has done nothing wrong! Yet, you believe she is dirty for having done a perfectly natural act at a time that she thought it was appropriate. This is erroneous thinking on your part and it isn't a simple issue but rather one that is very complex and extremely important with regard to any relationship you might ever have.

Would you be settling by being in love with someone who didn't wait for you? No, you wouldn't be settling should she decide to stay with you when she can see past her love and see how much pain you and your obsession can cause her. Shall I continue to repeat it? She has done nothing wrong!! Eight months ago she didn't even know you existed. How could she possibly have 'saved' herself for you? Please get counseling. — Queenie

♥

Dear Queen of Hearts, I'm 18 years old and my problem is that I have never kissed a boy. The first reason is that I'm afraid maybe I will do something wrong and the second reason is that I find is that I find the kiss very disgusting. But the first reason is the most important. Because I can't kiss anyone I am always alone. I never had a relationship. I'm looking forward to your answer. Thank you very much. Angelina

Angelina, don't worry about not having kissed someone yet. With the right person a kiss is never disgusting and it may take years for that right person to come into your life. There are some guys who would consider you to be perfect girlfriend material because of your unkissed status. – Queenie

♥

Dear Queenie, I have a problem and I hope you can help me. I am in love with a girl, but I am not her first man. She lost her virginity at age 14; the relationship carried on then that bloke left her for another girl. She says she has only slept with that one guy.

We discussed our previous relationships in detail and then let it slide. However the fact, that I am not her first worries me, sometimes it hurts me. I think I might be too jealous. What can I do to get rid of these nasty feelings because it is ruining my life? She can see that something is wrong but I cannot tell her. I have never told her and I never will, she might take offense and I won't risk losing her for the world. I love her too much.

Why do magazines always say that a woman first man is the most important? Things like that makes me feel insecure, even if I know in my heart that she loves me. Help if you can please. — Brian

Brian, nothing I can say can possibly help you if you are silly enough to believe everything you read. The first rule in any relationship is not to discuss the past. Forget it. It doesn't exist. It's history. It cannot be changed. Never, never, discuss your sexual history or ask your current girlfriend for details about her past! It doesn't matter.

Now, if you want to lose her over something over which you have absolutely no control, keep getting upset about what happened long ago. Forget it. – Queenie

♥

Dear Queen of Hearts, I recently found out that my girlfriend is not a virgin anymore when she told me that she was. I was devastated by the news. We have had our intimate moments and I can't help but feeling disgusted and sick that someone else had the same moments with her before. What should I do?? Bradley

Bradley, you can either readjust your thinking, or you can just go ahead and dump her and look for someone else and require that they have a virginity test before you get involved with them. If you're this concerned over something that you and she cannot change, and if you can't get it out of your mind, then there's not too much anyone can do to help you. — Queenie

♥

Dear Queen of Hearts, my boyfriend and I met at an event at which we were both entertaining. The night before the banquet, we had a dress rehearsal. He said he thought I had a beautiful smile, and has caught his eyes. He caught my eyes too. At the banquet, we made no attempt to introduce ourselves to each other. We followed each other around, but never had the nerve to say "Hello. My name is..." He finally took the first move and asked me to dance. We talked the rest of the night about everything you can think of. In fact, I even gave him my number (I never give my number to anyone!) I felt I could trust him...

We have only been going out for two months, when I asked him whether or not he was a virgin. He was a little hesitant to answer me (knowing I was a virgin). But, he did tell me the truth. I asked him how many he has slept with, and he told me two. He's had two girlfriends.

I was hurt when he told me. I guess, I expected him to be a virgin like me. I didn't know what to do or what to say to him. I thought, "How could he sleep with those other girls?", "Why do I have to be the 'third' one" "Why can't he be inexperienced like me (thinking the fun of exploring together)?"

I guess I just wanted to be the "first one". I told him, and you know what he said, "you're the first one that I've asked out."

We've now just celebrated our two year anniversary. Why do I still think about his past girlfriends? Why can't I just be happy of how everything is going? Please Help! Thank you, Melanie

Melanie, you were foolish to question his sexual past and you are foolish now to continue to obsess about something that was none of your business. There is always going to be someone who is "the first one" for everyone. How could he know to wait for you? He didn't even know you existed when he had the need for his first sexual experience. And you... if he's not the right one, and you meet someone later who is a virgin, who wishes you had not had a sexual experience, what can you say to him as to why he is not the first?

Keep thinking about the first two girlfriends if you must. It will continue to make the relationship you have with him less than it could be. Why would you want to do that over ghosts of the past? That is history, done and gone, unable to be changed. If you keep worrying about it, perhaps something will happen between the two of you that will spoil what you share. Forget and move on! – Queenie

♥

Dear Queenie, last year, at the age of 23, I fell in love for the first time with the most wonderful woman I've ever known. We worked in the same building

for 2 years but didn't really start talking until about 6 months before we got together. We began talking over our building's E-mail service. I would write my poems, riddles, my thoughts to her and she would do the same to me. She's so incredibly intelligent, kind, spiritual, and beautiful. Oh, I can't begin to put into words what I feel when I look at her.

We've been together now for a year and living together for about 7 months and I'm happy to say that the feelings we had at the very first are still there. For some time now we've talked about marriage and a life together, and although the thought of marriage and children, both, things I've always wanted to have, are immense, when I do think of them, I gladly see her there with me.

This is my first relationship and she was also my first sexual experience. I had chances to have sex before her but, it never felt right. I wanted my first experience to be special, with someone I would want to remember, not just some casual, drunk fling.

My girlfriend will soon turn 30 and needless to say she as had a few relationships in those years and, although her past 3 boyfriends do get to me, its the "wild" time in her life, about six months when she had casual sex with 4 guys, plus some other short "thing" with other guys, that really bothers me.

It just kills me to think of her being intimate with another man, much less one she doesn't care about, and who hasn't done anything to deserve her attentions or her body.

Even though she tells me she doesn't think about them, that her mementos of them are more mementos of her life, that she has never loved like she loves me, that I'm the best boyfriend she's ever had, still, if I hear the name of one of her ex-lovers, or the city where she went on vacation with one of them, whenever I think of her holding, kissing, laughing, snuggling, or, sleeping with some other man, it crushes me.

Recently she's been looking for jobs out west and plans to move there when she finds one. She really wants me to go and I too would like to go with her, but a move like this will mean more than just relocation, it will mean a redefinition of our relationship, a serious commitment, an engagement.

Again, it's not that commitment scares me, I want her, I just wonder if I need other experiences, if, because I don't have other relationships to compare this one with or a "wild" time in my life, I'm not ready.

I do so love her. I don't want this move to destroy something I honestly believe could be my life's gift, my life's love. I just don't want to have regrets down the line, and I don't want to hurt her either.

She has suggested that I stay for a while to have some experiences, to live a little life, but I know that beneath her calm rational attitude the thought of me with someone else would really hurt her and that the time away from her would be terrible for me. I've grown so used to having her with me every morning, every night.

So the questions in my mind aren't about whether or not I want to be with her, they are more about whether I will be okay with her being my only, and her having been with so many in such casual ways. What's your advise on my situation? — Jeff

Jeff, stop obsessing about her past or it will destroy that poetic spirit you treasure. She didn't know you then, her life was different, her life was hers to live as she saw fit, as it remains so now.

If you love her, you will put her past behind you. If you have a need to get even for her past life, that may cost you this wonderful woman.

You must understand, we all believe our choices to be appropriate at the time they are made. None of us are able to return to our past and erase choices that, though appropriate at the time, appear inappropriate in the future.

Due to the age difference between you, perhaps you need to mature some more before you think about commitment to her or anyone else. – Queenie

♥

Dear Queen of Hearts, I can't seem to find that special person. I hold this rare belief that sex is something to be saved for marriage. I'm not sure of the exact origin of this belief, most likely something to do with religious upbringing. No matter what the reason, I am a 22 year old virgin, trying very hard to find a female around my age that is also.

Many friends of mine have decided to give up on introducing me to new women because of my "narrow mindedness". I personally don't think that I am narrow minded, just old fashioned. I have no plans to change my morals in the near future, so people are just going to have to accept me for who I am. The problem is meeting women. Where do you meet women who share these out of date morals? I have tried every thing including church! Just isn't working. Any advice would help. — Douglas

Douglas, if you want to be old fashioned (or narrow minded, perhaps) you will have to accept the consequences. I won't belabor the point, but if people must accept you for who you are, you must accept that your "pool" of possible soul mates is extremely limited. Particularly if church isn't providing you with the dating possibilities that you are seeking.

It was not so many years ago that women were brought up to believe only "bad" girls weren't virgins on their wedding night. That caused a lot of sneaking around and lying as well as creative sex play with everything except penetration. During those same times, young men weren't chastised or taught to wait for their one true love. It was an interesting double standard, to be sure. I, personally, believe today's times are much more honest.

In the aforementioned days, women who truly waited often got married for the wrong reason or to the wrong guy. Some women placed such a high value on virginity and waiting that when it came time to surrender on their wedding night, they were severely disappointed with the act of love. Will you accept any female (within an acceptable age range) as long as she is a virgin, or do you consider other characteristics such as kind nature, pleasing personality, and shared interests to be important?

There are much more important qualities that will last much longer than virginity will. – Queenie

♥

Dear Queenie, I have been dating my girlfriend for almost a year and a half now, and we have a very solid and strong relationship. It has been perfect happiness for both us until lately. She just recently told me that due to her religious commitments, she cannot get "close" anymore. When she says "close", she means anything past kissing on the lips and hugging. Any other gesture or means of expression are automatically "sinful" and inappropriate.

We have never had sex, and have agreed to abstain until marriage. We have held each other passionately, and I have kissed her on other parts of her body. Also, I enjoy rubbing my hand against her body, and have given her many massages. However, all these expressions are now against her set of moral beliefs. She says that she feels guilty for all the times that we have shared our bodies in passion. I am willing to do anything for her, but I just am concerned because I have grown so attached to sharing my body and love with her.

She always says, "if you really love me, you would never need to do anything physical." I agree somewhat with what she says, but I also feel that there needs to be a sense of physical passion. I know that I always feel good whenever she used to share a part of herself with me. She says that she will compromise if I REALLY want her to, but she will continue to feel guilty. I do not want her to feel any guilt, so I have agreed to sacrifice my feelings for her happiness. Yet, I don't feel as happy as before. I will do anything for her, even this ... but I just wish that there could be some sort of compromise where we both could be satisfied. I am so worried because this one issue is just tearing me and my relationship apart. We have enjoyed more than a year of love, and I don't want it to end because of this...
Sincerely, Manny

Manny, your girlfriend has been compromising her feelings for you. She's probably more sad and confused than you are. She knows that the way things are going with the massages and more that sooner or later (and most probably sooner) you will have had complete sex. Up to this point you have had everything except the actual act of penetration. You've probably had better sex than many couples who "go all the way."

If this is against her religious commitments, against her moral code, and she is feeling the guilt, it is not a pleasant experience for her. Why would you want this most intimate of love expressions to be anything less than perfect for her? How you treat her now, how you care for her needs in this very important matter, will tell a lot about your true feelings for her.

Sex between two consenting adults is fine. A key word here is "consenting." It means that both partners are in complete agreement with the activities being performed. Anything else is inappropriate and not the way lovers treat each other.

If you're considering ending the relationship because she is having difficulty adjusting her personal commitments to fit your physical needs, then perhaps the relationship isn't as solid and strong as you think it is — and perhaps you need to take another look at what it means to love someone. You apparently want to have sex. She wants to wait until it's appropriate to make love. There's a world of difference between the two acts. Is she worth waiting for? – Queenie

♥

I am 37 years old, Asian male. I am not the best looking bloke in town nor obsessed with making money. So, it seems in the foreseeable future, my face will not grace the pages of Fortune magazine or be picking up anyone I might date in a Ferrari. Lacking what seems to really matter these days that are expected from a man. Without much to offer in terms of security, I can only realistically anticipate a life of loneliness and in my case eternal celebacy! You see, I am hung up with chastity and true love and predestination.

So much about my down side, I am, on the other hand, not the gloomy type. I am a pretty carefree person. There are probably many "good men" like me out there who are lonely, yet happy, young at heart but insist on extinct ideals when it comes to love & relationships. What will your advice be? Continue as we are as long as we are happy? Or we need to wake up and join the rest of the world? Thank you. — Meesha

Meesha, what type of woman do you seek? An 18-year-old with today's ambitions and ideals, who may still be a virgin? Or a woman closer to your age, with maturity and experience who understands that money is cold and looks fade but a good heart is priceless. A woman who may have already had one or more failed relationships so she would not fit your "chastity" criteria, yet she could be the person best suited to you.

There is nothing wrong with having high ideals. Sometimes, however, strict adherence to what we think "should be" restricts our opportunities for happiness. If you believe having a virginal wife is the most important issue, you eliminate all of the fine good-hearted women who, by experience, know the value of a good man.

Does predestination mean you will wait for destiny to come to you or does it mean your actions will take you on a predetermined path? Would you stand in the middle of a busy highway and proclaim that if you're struck by a car it was destiny? Or would you use your intelligence to move to a safe spot?

Temper your beliefs with reality and you may find that destiny has been waiting for you to make the next move. Do whatever makes you happiest. Your inquiry shows you wish for more than you currently have. — Queenie

♥

Dear Queen of Hearts, sex to me is something that is very sacred and special. I am 19 years old, and have never had sex simply because of the fact that I made a solemn promise to myself that I would never have sex with someone

unless I was in love with him. This is the way I have always been, and I am going to stick by that.

The problem: My boyfriend of 4 months now, who has had a bunch of sexual partners in the past, wants to have sex with me. It isn't that I don't, because sometimes in the heat of passion I feel like I do, but then when I am alone I thank God that I didn't follow through on my thoughts. I told myself that with this boy, I was going to wait until he said he was IN LOVE with me. I feel like I am with him. One night I managed to tell him these feelings of mine, and we began to argue. He said that he cared for me, but as for love... Lynn

Lynn, stick to your personal beliefs. The right man won't try to force you into sex; that isn't something a person who loves you would do. And why have sex with anyone else?

Guys have shorter fuses than women when it comes to the "heat of passion." Their physical need at the moment overpowers their common sense. YOU need to limit the passion so it doesn't get too far out of hand. – Queenie

♥

Dear Queenie, my boyfriend of six months wants to have sex with me. It's totally against my religious beliefs, but I want to make him happy. Is there a way to do that without sleeping with him? — Naomi

Naomi, if he really wants to have sex, regardless of your feelings, then you probably won't make him happy unless you compromise yourself and have sex with him. That is not the right reason to become intimate! Sex is the most emotionally intimate of acts.

You don't have sex with someone just to make them happy. What about what makes you happy? Going against your personal beliefs will only make you unhappy and your feelings are more important than his in this situation.

He has nothing to lose, and you have a great deal to lose. Wait until you meet a guy who values you and respects your religious beliefs over and above his need for a few minutes of physical pleasure no matter the cost to you. When you meet the right person, you won't need to write for advice. Losing your virginity is a one time deal; once you've "done it", you can't undo it. – Queenie

♥

Dear Queenie, please give me advice, I've known this guy since the beginning of the year, and we've become very best friends, since then. Well this past august we decided to experiment sexually and we promised ourselves if we went that step we hope it wouldn't mess up our best friend relationship. Well it didn't. We still talk perfectly fine, so the friendship part is still there.

When we first started experimenting, it felt like a experiment, now it's become completely different. The kisses, caresses and everything else we do has

become so passionate where now I think I'm kind of falling for him. I think he feels the same way too, because he has also changed.

When he asked me if I was falling for him I said no because I didn't want to get rejected as far as he not feeling the same way, when I asked him he also said no, and also says he's with me because I'm safe, and he only likes me for friends and that he hope he's not misleading me. But then other times he tells me I'm really great with the personality and the sex part, (it kind of turns him on), and he misses me a lot when I'm not there.

I don't really know what to think, I mean, we won't do anything unless I want it, not when he wants it, and I'm still a virgin, and want him to be the first. I want to know does he seem like he's falling for me also, because his actions tells a completely different story from what he says when he tells me he just want to be friends. Am I probably being mislead? — Bonnie

Bonnie, actions are a much more reliable gauge of what a person is feeling than words. If he is falling in love with you and if you are falling in love with him, where do you want this love to go? Do you want to get married and raise a family? Or do you just want to have someone available to date during the school year? Can you picture the two of you growing old together after raising a family?

Ask him the same questions. If you two are good friends, they are not outrageous questions to ask, particularly since you are fast approaching an important intimacy decision.

To give up your virginity without being in love with him would be a shame since you'd like to save that wonderful experience for someone you deeply love and not just a great friend. If you and he are only going to be friends and don't plan on being anything more, then you should stop with the sexual experimentation and start dating other people.

The next time he asks if you're falling for him, tell him the truth. Ask for the truth from him, also. That's the start of a good relationship. You can build from there. Don't expect that love will never hurt you, hurt is part of the package. And that means sometimes finding out that someone we love doesn't love us in return. (I suspect that's not the case here.) — Queenie

Sex

Sex

"If sex is no good anymore, and you fantasize about someone else, is the relationship in trouble?"

Can there be anything about which men and women understand less than sex or that, what they think they do understand, couldn't be farther apart?

For him, love equals sex. "If you love me, have sex with me." For her, sex equals love. "We've had sex therefore he loves me."

It is a quick leap for her to mentally and emotionally go from bed to bride even as he is eyeing his next sexual challenge. For him, sex is the prize for which he will use any and all means to get, even the promise of commitment. For her, sex is the means she will use in order to get the prize: commitment. All the while Mother Nature smiles as the human race continues to make more babies and the earth's population continues to grow.

Can a relationship flourish if a couple's sexual needs aren't in sync? If sex is important within a relationship, how long should a couple wait before determining their compatibility? Can "having sex" be just as satisfying as "making love"?

If he follows his urges and has sex when he is presented the opportunity, will he think any less of a potential mate who does the same? How much of their sexual history is it safe for a couple to share with each other?

Does sex on the first date spell doom for a relationship? Does porn equal real intimacy? Is masturbation cheating? Can a relationship based on lust survive?

♥

Hi Queenie, I've been dating the same guy for 3yrs and living w/him for 2yrs. My biggest problem is that he won't have sex w/me. I am not ugly or fat. I consider myself relatively attractive.

We won't have sex unless I initiate it and even then he says he's tired. We've talked about it and argued even more. He does masturbate every day and it drives me crazy! Why is he doing this?

He knows I want to have sex. He says it is not me and that it's him. He even wants to get married and I don't because of this. I would say that in a month, we'll probably have sex twice, but I might be stretching it a little. I am so sexually frustrated. When I come home from work and I'd like to have sex w/him, my drive goes away and I want it elsewhere. He is very selfish and I know I won't be satisfied so I don't even bother. Please help me out and give me some honest advice. — Monica

Monica, you want honest advice? Here it is: forget about marriage with this man. There's too much anger in this relationship for it to succeed. If he isn't willing to see a doctor to make certain he doesn't have a physical problem and then go to a counselor to see if there is an emotional problem,

I don't think there's much hope for the two of you ever having a happy life together. I, personally, think a breakup may be in order. – Queenie

♥

Hi Queenie, my girlfriend is 19 and I am 22 we have been together for about six months and have known each other as friends for about a year and a half. My problem is before she met me she was extremely sexually promiscuous. She's had about 20 sexual partners, several of them one night stands. We had been together about 3 months before we ever became intimate because we both wanted to make it clear that it wasn't about sex.

And, I'm okay about all of her sexual past... Except about six months after I met her she had sex with four male friends of hers at the same time. She says that she was under the influence of things that affected her judgment and they talked her into it.

I try to understand and never bring it up, but, it still bothers me more then I can say. Not only because I'm angry with her because I knew her then and we were really close, at the time talking about getting in a relationship, but, also because I feel disgusted every time I touch her. We still have a fine sex life. And, I make sure that she always feels wanted and that she's satisfied. I just feel really sick and disgusted after. Ideas? — Eric

Eric, I hope you're using protection when you have sex with this woman because you're looking death in the face if you don't. With so many sexual partners she is putting herself and every one of them at risk of any number of sexually transmitted diseases. Never forget that whenever you have sex with her you are having sex with all of her previous and present partners, and their partners, and their partners, and on and on. Somewhere in that vast mix of sexual activity is more than one deadly disease.

She obviously has a problem with saying "no" and she is in desperate need of more help than you can give her in order to understand why she has such little respect for herself. She needs counseling quick. — Queenie

♥

Dear Queen of Hearts, if sex is no good anymore, and you fantasize about someone else, is the relationship in trouble? — Josie

Josie, I'd say the relationship was well on its way to being over. — Queenie

♥

Dear Queenie, I have been seeing a man I really like and care for a lot. We've been dating for 4 months. The first date we went on we had sex, and in these past 4 months I've seen him only for about 5 or 6 times. We have phone conversations everyday. I'm really confused and I don't know what to do because I'm falling head over heals for him. But I don't think he knows how much I care

for him. We haven't talked about our feeling about each other. Please help. —
Sandy

Sandy, you put the sex before the feelings and got this relationship off to a bad start. The only way to salvage this relationship might be to start completely over and this time stay away from sex until you've had a chance to discuss your feelings for each other and make sure you and he have the same view of where this relationship is heading. — Queenie

♥

Dear Queenie, I've always heard when your done having sex, the last thing you should do is try to talk to the guy, they only have 'rest' on their minds at this point. I've been dating this guy for a short time, and we had sex. He went to the bathroom and when he came back I was half asleep counting on him to do the same, but he didn't, he came into bed and started talking about the whole experience, he was actually shocked about some stuff, but he said he enjoyed it very, very very much. I could just muster enough strength to say "mhm". He talked quiet a bit and he actually resembled a boy talking about this surprise his parents gave him, he was sweet yet he seemed a bit scared.. .but I was confused, and still am.

I am not complaining about this, I just want to know if I should throw away that "I want to sleep" conception and take advantage of that "open" state he falls into, or maybe it was just his reaction to our first time together. Thanks —
Mary Ann

Mary Ann, assuming this wasn't a one night stand you should have your answer as to whether his talkative nature was the way he is after sex or his reaction to your first time together.

Let me say this: to suggest that all men are the same after sex is to say that all people are short or fat or old or young. In other words, different men are going to act differently in bed, both before, during and after. Learn to adjust to your current man's actions and you'll be fine. – Queenie

♥

Queenie: I have been living with my boyfriend for over a year now. I don't know what to do about something that has been bothering me and keeps resurfacing even after talking about it with my boyfriend. It is an awkward and uncomfortable thing for me to talk about and that is why I have resulted to getting advice from an anonymous source over the internet.

So here it goes, I find evidence from my boyfriend masturbating. I feel like he does it in the morning when I get out of bed and into the shower. I think that he also does it while I am out of the house. I have found the evidence on his clothing, etc. I have brought it up on several occasions and he claims that I am "Delusion". He said that it is something that he only does if he has gone a long time without being sexually active, which we don't. He told me that he has not done it for a long time.

It really is taking over my sanity and starting to affect our Relationship because I can't get my self to talk to him about it because he has already told me that I am delusion and basically made me feel like I was crazy. I really love him and fear that if I bring it up he will think that I am even crazier. But at the same time I have a hard time acting like nothing is wrong when it is. The anger it drives me just stays stored inside me to the point were I will not act myself and say that nothing is bothering me when he notices that something is. What do I do? Is this a normal way for women to feel or am I really crazy? I need to do something and get this out of my head because it is really affecting my life in a negative way. — Bobbie Sue

Bobbie Sue, what your boyfriend is doing is perfectly natural. Many people who have sex on a regular basis will also pleasure themselves. Note I said "people" — there are women as well as men who enjoy solo sex in addition to sex with a partner. The problem is with your opinion of the act itself. It is normal, natural, it isn't dirty and it's nothing to be ashamed of.

Leave him alone, stop checking his clothing, and stop obsessing about this. It isn't a sign that he's not satisfied with the sex life the two of you have, or that you're not doing enough for him, it only means that he's a very sexual guy who likes sex with you and sometimes without you. His hand is a much better substitute than another woman. — Queenie

♥

Dear Queen of Hearts, how much should someone's sexual history matter in a healthy relationship? I have a very healthy relationship where our fights focused on my past sexual history that took placed in college and my current boyfriend can't seem to deal with my past. what can I do to ease him with the past and focus on the present? — Tori

Tori, in my opinion (which doesn't account for anything if you were to ask your boyfriend), the only time a person's sexual history becomes an issue is if they have been promiscuous and haven't practiced safe sex. Then they bring to a new relationship the potential of diseases from their past relationships.

AIDS is a very real threat and the HIV virus can stay dormant for years. Having said that, I don't believe there's any reason to discuss past sexual history with a current lover. There is no "need to know" other than what I said above. Anything else is potential for problems as you're finding out.

You did what you did before you met him believing that those to whom you were doing what you were doing were people you had feelings for at the time.

Some guys don't want to know that their girlfriends have been sexually active with anyone but them. It's a nice dream but unrealistic in today's world and very unrealistic for the guy who has been getting all he can throughout his dating years. Maybe your guy can't get past it. If not, let him go or you'll spend a lifetime of misery as he continues to treat you as less than the good person you are. — Queenie

♥

Dear Queen of Hearts:
1. What do you do if a boy wants to have sex with you and you don't want to? 2. When will the boy ask you to marry him? 3. When to tell he if really loves you? — Melissa

Melissa, you NEVER have sex when you don't want to. He really loves you if he doesn't pressure you into doing something you don't want to do. And he's more apt to ask you to marry him if you don't have sex with him before you and he are seriously in love. Having sex will not make a guy love you. Sometimes it will even make him like you less than he did before the two of you had sex. — Queenie

♥

Dear Queenie, I don't seem to understand why my boyfriend is so superficial. He told me that if the sex wasn't good he would have moved on to find someone else. He told me its just a normal thing. Also, he then told me that he knew I was a 'good one' and that's why he gave me chance to get better at sex. By the way he told me this after stating that he was falling in love with me. I think this is very superficial, especially considering that he is a psychiatrist. Are all men this superficial? Please help. Thanks — Connie

Connie, I don't know how this particular statement came about. No doubt there was much more to this conversation but this particular issue stuck in your mind because you want to think that you've got more to offer than just being a good lay or a sex object.
Your boyfriend isn't being superficial; he's being honest about what he needs in a woman. Good sex is important to men, much more so than it is to a great number of women. It comes down to whether or not you like this man enough to continue dating him now that he has pronounced you a 'good one'. — Queenie

♥

Dear Queen of Hearts, I have had an allergic reaction called PID, and this has made things very complicated to have children, but very easy to have tubal pregnancies according to the doctors. I have also been molested as a child and I am still working on things, I have a lot of insecurities, I do not know when I should tell a person I date this information.
I usually tell men I date within a month or two, because I feel it is fair and I don't want them to think I am a liar when I tell them, I feel like this is information they may need to know. The reaction I get is usually a back off or I get used because they think they have nothing to worry about.
When is it a proper time to mention this? I am tired of these reactions! — Tara

Tara, personally, I don't think your childhood molestations are anyone's business. If you're in counseling and working things through, you don't need to expose your insecurities to guys who are new in your life. That's the kind of information you would probably want to share with your husband someday but it's a bit too serious for dating discussions.

PID, (pelvic inflammatory disease), is a sexually transmitted disease that can be life-threatening if you are careless with your sexual partners. You must use birth control (condoms) every time you have sex. As far as when to tell a man about your PID — definitely do it before you and he have sex for the first time and I'd suggest that you not have sex until the two of you have dated seriously for a while. — Queenie

♥

Dear Queenie, just one question, in the first week of going out with a guy, and you really like him, how far would you go? — Anastasia

Anastasia, I wouldn't go anywhere if I wanted him to really, really like me. Guys like ladies. They also like a challenge. Ladies who are a challenge are worth waiting for, regardless of how eager a guy seems to be. – Queenie

♥

Dear Queen of Hearts, I'm 20 years old and have dated quite a few women. I've learned that the issue of sex always comes up after dating a while. But when I think seriously about having sex with this girl I'm dating, the thoughts of AIDS, HIV infection, and other STDs and stuff like that automatically jumps into my head. I've been preached abstinence all my life (I just blew it off then), but it seems like if I do sleep with this girl I'm dating that I will get infected by some horrible disease, even if I use protection.

I worry about that every time I get serious with a girl because it seems that the odds of getting disease are really high, compared to hard facts that say the odds are very slim—even slimmer if the girl and I know each other very well. In that case, am I worrying too much?

Am I overestimating the odds of getting disease, even if the girl says she doesn't have it? I believe that's my problem—overestimating the chances of condom failure and getting disease...?? —Frank

Frank, you're smart to be concerned. Somewhere along the line, someone you meet and casually have sex with may have someone in their past, who had someone in their past, who had someone in their past, who had someone in their past, (and on, and on) who had a bad sexual disease.

You should not be totally paranoid about the dangers of disease, but you should care enough about yourself to be in love before you have sex. And then use protection. – Queenie

♥

Dear Queenie, this is unusual, I'm certain, but it is causing a little debate between me and my SO. Whenever we get intimate, I put my two cats in the bedroom, or in the living room, depending on where we decide to do it. She thinks its silly, but I feel embarrassed when Ivan and Gorky watch us. They are like my children. Am I weird? Jason

Jason, if having the cats in the same room inhibits you, we don't think it's silly to move them elsewhere. Nope, I don't think you're weird... although the cats might. – Queenie

♥

Dear Queen of Hearts, I can not seem to find someone who, wants to be with me any other way except sexually (except Lamont, and he wants that too). If I meet someone I like, I don't believe in waiting, and just recently I met someone, and we had a good time together, and I explained to him my fears about my sexuality as far as wanting to wait. I have not heard from him in a couple of days.

I really enjoy sex, but once I engage in sex with someone, that is all the relationship becomes. I see the person for sex. I am lonely and want someone to hold at night. Someone to do things with. Someone to just be with. Recently I found that in someone. All but the sex.

He is older, he buys me things (something I have never really had, not since I broke up a long relationship about 3 years ago) he just wants to spend time with me, he insists on giving me rides home when I am not feeling well, or it is raining. At these times he can lose his job, but he does them anyway.

The problem is he lives with a woman already. I don't try to get in the way of that at all. In fact quite the opposite, I tell him okay you need to go home to her now. Okay isn't she out of work now you should go home. We hug, in the beginning he really tried to get me to kiss him, and was always talking about sex, still does, but not the same way of just trying to get some.

He is always talking about sex. He loves women, and sex. I love women too. I am in no way bi-sexual, have never tried it and only have a mild interest in the idea of it. But he can talk to me about seeing women waking in tight clothing, he'll see them, and oogle the way men do. It does not offend me. We have both said we need to stop seeing each other, I am not trying to take anyone's man, and I am not sure I want him. He is older, and I am attracted to younger men. I am 34. He must be 54 give or take 5 years.

But, what about this situation, and what about my loneliness, and not being able to sustain a relationship. I am not a very social person. I go to work, come home take care of my home and children. Don't have friends, except for a few. One woman, beside my sister. Two really good male friends, including the guy I just mentioned. Confusing I know. Please help if you can. — Tamara

Tamara, I'm afraid I can't be of much assistance. You sound as though you are searching desperately for someone to keep you from being lonely. Unfortunately, your desperation will drive people away instead of to you.

Perhaps if you can learn to wait two or three months before having sex with someone you're dating, you might have better luck getting to know more about them, and they about you. As you have found, when a relationship gets sexual too early, most men move on to the next 'mystery lady.'

Men enjoy sex. They also enjoy being with a woman who enjoys sex. But most 'sex first' relationships don't last. Most men look for more restraint in their ladies for long term relationships.

In other words, most men don't want their "soul mate" to be "easy." Right now, it sounds as though you're very easy, except with Lamont, which is why he hangs around. At least that's what it seems from what you've said. — Queenie

♥

Dear Queenie, I've been going out with my boyfriend who is 17 years old for about 4 months now. We've now been living together for 3 months. I'm 21 years old. Even though my boyfriend is 4 years younger than me, he is very mature for his age and he is truly the first guy who truly cares about me. In the beginning, the sex was excellent. We did it once or twice a week. For the past month and a half, we have not had sex. He told me his sex drive is really down because he has been really stressed lately. My sex drive on the other hand is really high. I don't know what to do. Can you help me? — Pamela

Pamela, you need a lot more help than I can offer. – Queenie

♥

Dear Queen of Hearts, I feel I made a huge mistake in the heat of a passionate night and feel terribly sorry and guilty about it. Basically, I've been dating this great girl on casual terms for about a month and a half. We greatly enjoy each other's company and had mutually agreed that she wouldn't expect a long-term emotional commitment from me while I wouldn't push her too hard on the physical front until she feels ready. However, the other night we were fooling around and one thing led to another, I ended up breaking my previously confirmed word that I would wait until she really wanted to sleep with me.

No, I did not rape her by any account, just that I continuously persisted and was making my moves until she couldn't resist anymore and I ended up going "all the way" forgetting that few minutes prior to that I had told her I would be patient and let her make her own decision as to when the "right time" would be.

I immediately sensed that something was "wrong", feeling that I inadvertently lost her trust and self-respect. I tried to explain to her the following day of my "mistake" that occurred in the heat of passion and told her how sorry I felt but that as a human of male sex, there was not much I could've done in that moment, considering she did not give me a resounding "NO" but said "it's not ok with me but it's up to YOU". While I took full responsibility for not exercising sufficient self-control, what was I supposed to do in that moment of passion for G-

d's sake, considering I am a 21 year old inexperienced guy. I didn't point out to her that it takes two to dance a tango, instead taking full responsibility afraid that it would aggravate her, but that was the case somewhat!

Anyway, we decided to take a break and think about what we want from the relationship if there's still any benefit to it etc., hoping time would heal that "screw-up". I would appreciate any advice on this matter because I am kind of unsure what the best strategy is to get back the great fun we were having. — Paul

Paul, you're pissed off that she isn't as delighted with the sexual aspect of this relationship as you are and you're using the old "hey, I'm a guy and guys can't handle their hormones" routine. Oooops! See what happens when you forget that zippers don't come down by themselves?

The two of you were playing a dumb game. She didn't want the sexual intimacy and that was her right. She, unfortunately, played the game with you and allowed it to go too far. She told it wasn't okay with her.

You remember her words so you weren't in a total stupor. You made a choice to have sex with her despite the fact she wasn't as enthusiastic and ready as you were.

I don't know if it was date rape but if she didn't want to have sex and you (the 21-year old inexperienced guy that you are) couldn't control yourself so you "did it" to her, I suspect some legal authorities might consider it to be.

She knows it will be very difficult to see you again and keep from having sex now that it's been done once. And you know, in your little devious mind and that part of you just full of youthful raging hormones, that if you broke her down once, you can break her down again and again. After all, what's the big deal now that you've done it?

The fact the two of you have broken up tells me a lot about your relationship. Try to treat her like a lady, respect her wishes if you're lucky enough to get another chance, and think with your heart not your crotch the next time you have a lady in your arms.

Incidentally, "making love" is what consenting adults do together, with no regrets. "Having sex" has much fewer requirements and can be done by anyone, with or without a partner, willing or otherwise. – Queenie

♥

Dear Queen of Hearts, I need to know if there is a problem with a person wanting to watch their lover have sex with another man. Please respond! — Matt

Matt, if all of you are consenting adults I don't see that there should be a problem. The key words are "consenting adults," which means *all* people involved are completely comfortable and agreeable to the act, and everyone is of legal age and emotionally mature enough to deal with this type of sexual activity.

If these conditions are met, then you should also be prepared to accept anything that may happen as a result of this sexual encounter, including the possibility that your lover will dump you to be with the other man. Quite frankly, I wouldn't want to risk it. Do you? – Queenie

♥

Dear Queenie, my fiancé just recently revealed a secret to me. Before we dated, he employed the services of a professional masseuse; however a massage was not all he got. I am just shocked that he would even allow something like this to happen! It makes me wonder what other kinds of secrets he has. I find this act disgraceful but he can't understand why I am so upset? Am I blowing this out of proportion or do I have a right to be concerned? — Melanie

Melanie, you find sex disgraceful? I can't help but feel that you and he will have a difficult long term relationship if you continue to feel that way. You're way too upset about something that is perfectly normal.

Paying for sex is done all the time. In some parts of the U.S., and in many of parts of the world, it's a legitimate business. In other places it has to be disguised as another business, such as "massages."

Your feelings would be understandable if he was doing this as a steady practice now that you and he are in a relationship... but with your current attitude about the whole issue, one of you is going to be less than happy in the long term. Good luck. – Queenie

♥

Dear Queenie, I am in a relationship with this girl for awhile now. We are both in love. We don't have sex that often and when we do I have to make the first step. The problem is that I want to make love. It's always a rush "let's get it over with" thing.

I don't know what to think? I have told her about it, but it did not seem to do any good. It's making me a mess. I want to marry this girl but this sits over my head. Do you think I am over reacting? Jon

Jon, no you aren't over reacting. Being sexually compatible is a major part of a successful marriage. If you're having problems now, just being married won't make them any better unless she feels uncomfortable about sex before marriage. Married, she might become more relaxed, making love within the guidelines that are acceptable to her. Have you talked with her to see if this is the problem?

Or... she may be shy about sex and, again, needs to be in a more committed relationship to relax and enjoy. Or... she may have been taught that sex is bad, which it is not, but done with the wrong person, for the wrong reason, or under the wrong circumstances, it is not worth doing. Good luck. — Queenie

♥

Dear Queen of Hearts, I am a 23 yr. old girl, who has a problem. I have a great friend at work and he had been after me for awhile, he wanted to get intimate

with me. But I kept saying NO because of the fact that we work together. Anyways, after a few months of saying NO I finally said yes.

But now I have all these feelings for him. And he tells me that we can not have a relationship because of the fact that we work together he tells me that he really cares for me and he really likes me but there is something that is holding him back. He lets me in and when he realizes it, he quickly pulls away... HELP... What can I do? — Karen

Karen, I will assume that when the next man asks you for sex and keeps after you, that you will respect yourself enough to tell him to get honest or get lost.

Sure he really cares for you and really likes you. And, guess what? You're safer than a one night stand, and cheaper than buying it on the street.

Am I angry? Yes! And you should be too. Show this creep the door and explain how it works. – Queenie

♥

Dear Queenie, I work in a store and one day a customer approached me and asked me if I wanted to go out with him. I am a foreign student and I do not have much experience dating American guys. I though he was being disrespectful and said NO! to him in a mean way. When I told my friends, they told me there was nothing wrong with that. Some months later, I saw the guy again. I smiled at him and apologized for what happened. He invited me to go out again. This time I said yes. We slept together in our first date. He lives in another town so we did not talk to each other during that week.

One day he came back and spent a little time together but he did not talk much. That night we slept together again and he left. I asked him if he wanted to visit me the next day and he said "maybe". He did not.

After two weeks I called him and he did not want to talk much. I asked if he wanted to go out with me and he said I don't know. I asked him "yes or no?" He was quiet for a time and then said no.

I live in a small town and they are not used to foreign people. My friend told me that maybe he was just curious about sleeping with a foreign girl and now he does not want to see me anymore. I learned that I should not sleep with a guy until we are emotionally connected. — Rosie

Rosie, how sad you had to learn this lesson this way! He didn't understand that you don't sleep with every man who dates you, but he didn't know that because he could only base his opinion on his experience with you and the short time it took to get you to have sex.

Consider this as a lesson learned the hard way and don't ever give of yourself until you believe yourself to be in love, truly in love. Then it will be a sweet experience for both of you. – Queenie

♥

Dear Queen of Hearts, this guy and I have been good friends for three weeks now. I've known him for three years. Anyway, we aren't going out and we haven't been with each other yet, but he reckons we are with each other.

Anyway I went to this disco and he and his best friend was there. He decided to go and get drunk, so I talked to his best friend. By the end of the night, I had been with his best friend, and he was really pissed off. I am really scared what everyone is going to think and I still have feelings for this guy, but I also like his best friend. If it was between those two, I would go for the guy I'm suppose to be with. But I don't know how I'm going to tell him and apologize for what I have done. Please help! Depressed! — Amanda

Amanda, how is everyone going to know unless you or he talk about what happened? I trust you aren't going to blab and if he does then he's not a gentleman. If you're saying "been with" for having sex, it is better to "make love" after you're "in love" than have sex without love and regret it.

Apologize if you feel you must but since you're not married or otherwise committed, you may do with yourself what you will with whom you will whenever you wish to do it — assuming you're over the legal age for doing it... and are capable of accepting the consequences for your actions. – Queenie

♥

Dear Queen of Hearts, a little history here: I'm a pretty, sexy, independent female who hasn't been into a long term relationship for 3 years. I was very hurt. I'm also very conservative sexually, and haven't "gotten off" with a man in a long time (but can very easily by myself). A month ago, I acquired a male roommate, a wonderful man, whom I've grown fond of. We also recently became intimate and haven't quit since then (every day). We still tell each other we're free to date other people.

I'd love to have an orgasm with him, but I'm afraid to, as I don't want to fall in love with him (or maybe am afraid I WILL fall in love with him). I find him very sexy, attentive, warm, funny...and we get along fantastically in other ways. I'm a bit confused at how to handle this type of relationship, as I've never before been other than platonic with a male roommate.

Men have either been long term boyfriends or one-night stands. "S" is neither, as we're great friends and now, good lovers. I'm afraid that he might get tired of my not attaining an orgasm, while I'm wondering that if I do, I'll never be able to bear his being with another woman.

I guess my emotions are a bit confused, and perhaps, I'm trying to be a bit more "cool" than I really am. I'm not sure if I'd be hurt if he made love to another woman, yet I'm feeling more sexy than ever and find myself thinking about sexual fantasies like never before. It's almost like he woke up a hidden part of me and I guess I'm a bit miffed because I don't know what to do about it... enjoy it? Don't worry about growing too close? Get other men too? Go ahead and get an orgasm with him? Save it for someone else? — Tamara

Tamara, I have to question your reference to yourselves as "good lovers" considering your "problem." While orgasm in your mind's eye might be the line between love and lust, most suggest that it's the initial decision to make love that determines the direction of the affair other than in the instance of a one night stand.

Engaging in the act of loving and not "going for the gold," it would seem, misses a point if not *the* point. It would be surprising to learn that "S" is as well holding back other than to hold back to prolong what sounds like a spirited romp in the hay.

Of your multiple choices, the most relevant one seems to be "go ahead and get an orgasm with him" and hope that choice isn't the only multiple in the event. Deal with the emotional choices as they come. – Queenie

Dumped!!

Dumped!!

"Anytime I have dumped a woman (which hasn't been very often), I have considered it simple, decent, human courtesy to make sure she left knowing the reasons. She might not have liked the reasons, and she might not have agreed with the reasons, but she left knowing the reasons."

Are you keeping the eternal flame burning in the hope that he or she will return? If phone calls are brief and impersonal or messages not returned, take the hint. Give your ex space. If he or she wants to get back into your life, let them make the first move. At that point you will have the option of responding. Perhaps by that time you will have new interests and won't be interested in renewing the relationship. It could happen.

Saying mean and nasty things about your ex to friends and family is a silly thing to do in addition to being unworthy of you. Should you and he (or she) reconcile at some future date, you'll have discredited yourself badly and you might find that family or friends are less forgiving of your ex than you are.

Keep your worst thoughts to yourself. You never know when a new and interesting person will be nearby.

Getting dumped allows you a chance to take a fresh look at your life. It gives you a chance to get in touch with your feelings. It provides time for introspection.

Getting dumped teaches you about freedom. You may now, for the first time, be making decisions without explaining the reasons to anyone. This is a freedom few people take the time to appreciate.

Is this your first failed relationship or do you have a history of failures? What is different about this one than the last and the one before that? You should be able to draw parallels, see patterns.

Does each relationship have the same blueprint? Are your choices setting you up for heartache? If you can see the patterns, you can learn and make changes so that future relationships stand more of a chance of survival.

Try to avoid those things you did as a couple that will trigger memories. Memories are fine but if a particular place or a special song reminds you of your lost love, now is not the time. There will come a time when you can do "special things" without getting the blues.

Mourn your lost love. Then move on. It will take time, but the pain will get less and less, and one day it will be gone.

Everyone gets dumped sometime.

♥

Dear Queenie, I've just been dumped and rather suddenly. We had been together for two years and thought strongly about getting married. We both wanted to. I love her more than anything and am wondering how I can get her back. Also "should" we get back together? I'm empty without her. I love her with all my heart. — Steve

Steve, why did she end this relationship? If she isn't involved with someone else and you know the problem, fix it. Tell her how you feel. You have me convinced. – Queenie

♥

Dear Queenie, my boyfriend just broke up with me. We have been together for almost three years, and we never fight. I have felt our relationship getting weaker however over the last year or so.

Tuesday we were talking and all of a sudden all of these concerns came up from both of us. I felt like he wasn't giving me the attention I deserved, and he feels that he doesn't want a girlfriend right now. I told him I loved him, but he didn't say it back.

As a matter of fact we have been telling each other I love you for quite some time. I have just been scared to say it recently because I was afraid that he wouldn't say it back.

Anyway, I just want to know if I should bother trying to get him back. I love him so much, and I feel that he is my soul mate, but I don't want to try to force someone to love me that doesn't. Should I try to get him back, or do you think he is just scared of commitment and will eventually come back on his own? — Laura

Laura, it sounds as though the two of you need some time away from each other. Let him go and take the time to date others. If the two of you are meant to be, you'll get back together. — Queenie

♥

Dear Queenie, I have been with my high school sweetheart for six years and things with us were great until I went away to college. During my third year away he started lying to me and he even stopped calling me. I was hurt so I cheated on him resulting in me having a baby. I moved back home and we've been trying to mend our relationship.

The problem is that it's been over a year and he tells me that he loves me and that he wants us to be together but he's not doing anything to prove what he's saying. Should I keep trying or should I just let him go. — Lana

Lana, you got hurt because he was lying to you and stopped calling you so you cheated on him and had a baby as a result. Now the two of you are trying to make a go of it but he isn't "doing anything to prove what he's saying"?

He says he loves you. No doubt you want him to marry you but he's holding off. Maybe he's trying to come to grips with having to support someone else's baby. That might make him a little commitment shy. However, if you can't wait for him to get marriage serious then you probably should let him go and hunt down someone who will marry you. Otherwise who knows what you might do if he hurts you again. — Queenie

♥

Dear Queenie, my best friend and I have known each other for years and after we had only known each other for a few months we started a "friends with benefits" relationship. This has been going on for about 4 1/2 years and I made the mistake of getting attached.

He does things though that makes me think he likes me as well. Such as he will call when he knows I will not be home, doesn't tell me about any girls he knows or works with, and if a guy hits on me he has to let me know a girl hit on him, but only if he knows a guy hit on me.

However, lately he has been very distant and acts as if he doesn't even want to be my friend? I am trying to figure out what is going on and I need some advice that will stick. If you would please help I would appreciate it, I am driving myself stir crazy. Thank you. — Dixie

Dixie, this sleeping arrangement is not the same as a real love relationship. It's a relationship of sexual convenience. I'd suggest that you disentangle yourself from him and stop playing mind games with each other. This isn't love. This is stupid. — Queenie

♥

Dear Queenie, he is asking me to move on with my life. His decision is that i can stay at the house while we sleep in separate rooms. We talk a lot but there is something different about it, he listens to me more earnestly. One reason for this is that his business is encountering a lot of problems. He says he just can't give me the comfort that i need because he can't even give it to himself at a time like this.

The next reason is that I tend to bring up the involvement he had with another woman six months ago to frequently. Which he specifically told me to put behind us. So now he says a relationship is not what he wants with me or anyone. I am willing to change because I did not realize what damage it could have done. This relationship means an awful lot to me not being how it used to be is hurtful. What do I do? I still think deep down inside that it can be nurtured back because I know him better that he knows himself.

Could he just be saying this because of the extreme pressure of life? He says sometimes he doesn't know where he is heading. Or should I just be strong for both of us at this moment? Things are never always terrible it has to get better someway or the other. No one will ever understand how much I care about him or no one will ever care as much as I do. I don't want to be like his exes who ran off but it is hard when that someone shuts you off but not fully and says things to you that is not positive. — Nanci

Nanci, this sounds like a relationship with problems, and they don't particularly sound as though they are caused by you. He told you to put his involvement behind you? That's fine, but you had unresolved feelings of betrayal. Despite his need for you to forget, it doesn't happen overnight (but you knew that already, didn't you?).

If his business stresses are causing him to be confused about life in general, there may be nothing you can do at this point except take care of yourself. Can you stay in the same house with him as a "platonic friend"? I, personally, think this could be extremely painful. What happens if he decides he wants to date someone else? Could you handle it, him dating and perhaps bringing her home?

Life will get better but only after you take control and make some decisions about your personal happiness. – Queenie

♥

Dear Queenie, I have written to your column before, so I guess I'll try it again. Your responses have always been pretty interesting. Once again, I find myself so mad at the entire female race in general, I could spit fire. My girlfriend of about seven months - a woman who I really wanted to build a life with - just ended our relationship. Like every woman born, she says I didn't do anything wrong or anything like that. She tells me that she has been seeing a married co-worker of hers, and that this man makes her feel "a giddy, in-love feeling" that I just couldn't give her. That she would risk destroying a family to get her "giddy little thrill" is absolutely the dumbest, most irresponsible, and most selfish thing I have ever seen anyone do. In one of your recent columns, you said it best when you said that no one has the right to steal someone else's spouse (or something like that).

So, once again, I find myself devastated because of this "Prince Charming/ seeing skyrockets" crap. Once again, I find myself feeling inadequate and substandard because a woman I dated didn't get that "giddy" feeling. I just want to scream at all you mothers out there who continue to put this unrealistic fairy tale into your daughters' heads.

I am a 36-year-old professional man - never married, no great vices, and I would like to at least think not too hideous to look at. I am reserved, kind of analytical, and I don't get terribly emotional over much of anything. At times, I'm afraid that that this may outwardly come across as cold or uninterested. In the times I have been in love, like in this relationship that just ended, I think I would describe the feeling as a warm, quiet, contented feeling. I don't get "giddy" or "see skyrockets" about anything.

This breakup now has got me scared to death that every woman I date will be looking for this unrealistic "giddiness", but I am old enough to know that the skyrockets are frivolous and short-lived, and that any proper relationship will survive on the kind of unconditional, solid, and devoted love that I offered this woman.

I am beginning to fear that I will NEVER be able to inspire that "skyrocket" feeling in ANY woman. With 40 lurking right around the corner, this is beginning to scare me to death. It is also giving me an increasing sense of desperation, which I know is not healthy. Thanks a lot, all you Moms of the world!

I am really devastated and scared by this latest break-up, and desperately wondering why I can't get a woman to stay. I guess I would like to get your comments on this unrealistic "Prince Charming" idea. — Reggie

Reggie, I'd hate for you to brand all women with the same brand. Somewhere there is a woman who is just right for you and you're just right for her. You will be her Prince Charming and she will make you feel giddy.

Desperation is not an attractive quality in a man nor in a woman. Please, calm down about your age. Men only get better with age (at least that's *my* opinion). – Queenie

♥

Dear Queenie, my boyfriend told me that he isn't in love with me after a two and a half year relationship. Our relationship wasn't bad at all, but now that I look at things I see we were lovers before becoming friends. I also see some of me faults with not being supportive on what I thought were small issues. I wrote him a letter expressing all my faults and things I could have had to make our relationship better.

I wanted to start a new, re-introducing ourselves to one another, become best friends than start our relationship over. Of course, that's not what he wants. He doesn't want anything romantic to do with me. I feel we could make a brand new life for each other and our relationship would be stronger.

I've tried to move on with my life, but this deep aching feelings telling me I shouldn't give up on him. What should I do? Yours Truly — Sylvia

Sylvia, it takes two to make a relationship work. Wanting something with all your heart won't make it happen if he doesn't feel the same way. You've tried, and he's let you know that there's no way, so it's time for you to forget about him and move on. — Queenie

♥

Dear Queenie, how do you forget about someone you've known for 15 years and end a friend and lover relationship? How do you tell them you don't want to hear from them without hurting them? — Blaze

Blaze, there is no way they won't be hurt when they're dumped. What you say and how you say it will have a lot to do with how they take it when you dump them. – Queenie

♥

Dear Queenie, I am stuck between a brick wall and a hard place. I have been in a relationship for a few years and I am not in love with this person any more. I am longing to be with someone else. I need some advice as whether to drop this person for someone else and go in for the kill, or to wait it out and deal with what I have first and then move on. — Scarlet

Scarlet, if the situation were reversed, how would you want your soon-to-be-ex lover to treat you? You get out of the relationship first, and then you go after a new relationship. It's the honorable and right thing to do. How you handle your situation pegs the kind of person you are, not just to your soon-to-be-ex but to the new person you're going after. Try to be a lady. — Queenie

♥

Dear Queenie, my girlfriend and I have always been good friends and we have had a good time together. Now that we are living together, differences between us have become more apparent. I think we always knew of these differences, but they somehow did not really affect us.

The most serious difference that we have is that I am a sociable guy that enjoys going out and meeting people. My girlfriend, on the other hand, finds it extremely difficult to meet people even though she gets on with people that she knows. We have discussed this and I have tried to help her. Despite this, the issue always comes back to bite.

Another issue concerns friends. My girlfriend has known my friends for years but somehow chooses to limit the number of people that she considers "very good friends" to a minimum. As a consequence of our move to an unfamiliar country, she believes that she doesn't really have friends and that I am the only friend that she has. This places quite a bit of pressure on me because she expects to be by my side at all times.

Recently, I have had to tell her that I need space and, for the first time in my life, I feel I need time to myself; just to be alone for a while. As a result, I have been going out without her. This has been with people from work and I have really enjoyed myself.

As a consequence, I have been attracted to another girl (who has also felt the same) but have not taken it further for the fear of cheating on my girlfriend who I care about.

She is the only serious girlfriend that I have had and I feel torn and confused over what I really want and how I should go about handling the situation. Can you help? — Ollie

Ollie, if the situation were reversed, how would you want your girlfriend to treat you? You've dated for several years, you're lived together almost a year and the two of you have moved from an area in which she feels comfortable to an area in which she feels alone.

No, you shouldn't have to be her constant companion. You need a life, just as she does. But the two of you have to work out something that is better than you being more sociable and going out to clubs alone and meeting women who make you think about dumping her or worse.

Talk to her. Tell her how you feel. Listen to what she says and how she feels. And think seriously about whether or not you'd prefer being with her or without her for the rest of your life. Your actions should be based upon that answer. — Queenie

♥

Dear Queenie, I went out with this girl for 10 months. We were good together and I now realize that this was the first time I have ever loved anyone. The problem is that she dumped me about 6 weeks ago and I cannot get her out of my head it is driving me mad, I was always outgoing and the life and sole of the party now I am always down and moody. I tried to see someone else but it never worked as I could only think about my ex. I occasionally pass by her house just in the hope that I see her.

See the relationship was fine until we went on separate holidays with our pals. When we came back we were okay for about two days then she became moody and went off sex, this lasted for about 3 weeks, I approached her about it and we ended up splitting. I am not sure if she met someone on holiday or someone here but I am sure she is seeing someone else.

When we split up she said she wanted space because she went out for a guy for five years then straight after him she saw someone for 2 years then she met me, and during our three weeks apart when we were on holiday she enjoyed the freedom with her pals. Her parting words were that I was funny, good-looking, kind, perfect for any girl and she sees me more as a friend. I got a Christmas card from her and I saw her in the pub on Friday night. We spoke as friends; she asked me to print something from the net for her and bluntly told me to post it which I have.

My question is have I a chance of seeing her again? If not how do I get over my first real love? And do you think her excuse was a lie? Because I think she met someone else. Thank you for taking time to read this as your reply will help me. — Nigel

Nigel, it's difficult to say whether or not she'll want to get together with you again. As she told you, she never had a 'break' between her relationships and now she needs the space. It's a legitimate reason and it happens more than you might think.

Whether or not she is seeing someone else, you definitely need to stop waiting for her to return and get out and meet people once again. Now that you know how wonderful love can be it's time for you to 'make yourself available' in that huge singles world.

No matter how you feel right now, she isn't the only girl who's right for you. As a matter of fact, we think relationships end for reasons that only appear later on when you meet the really right person and then look back and say 'oh, now I understand!' — Queenie

♥

Dear Queenie, I don't know what to do or where to go. My boyfriend of 4-1/2 yrs. has told me he wants to be friends now. Yes he has cheated on me. Yes I took him back.

But it is very hard to be friends. I am so afraid to even talk to him now. I don't know how to be his friend he keeps pushing me away. What can I do? — Clarice

Clarice, if he says he wants to be friends, does that mean he wants to date others? If so, since you care so much for him, it would probably be best that you stop seeing him, at least until you don't hurt so much when you're around him.

When a relationship of this type goes from lovers to friends, and only one person in the relationship wants it like this, there's going to be pain. It'll take a while but you'll be alright. – Queenie

♥

Dear Queenie, I was in a steady relationship with this girl 19 months. Then I moved to a different city for a job that I had been hired for while she stayed to finish college and work in "our" college town.

On our anniversary we had a fight over the phone and didn't speak for two days but then when we did talk she decided she wanted to break up.

Today we were supposed to meet but she never called after she said she wanted to get back together. So, my question is, "What should I do?" — Andy

Andy, it sounds like she has called an end to the relationship. You're going to have to try to forget her and move on. It won't be easy but it doesn't appear you have any other options. – Queenie

♥

Queenie, my boyfriend of almost 3 years and I recently split up. We are still very close and want to remain friends. The break up happened for various reasons, but mainly because he says he no longer has the same feeling for that he used to (i.e. I am no longer the center of his life and other things have become more important to him like finishing school and getting his degree and spending quality time with his family 90 miles away).

He says that he still loves me and cares about me very much, and we are both having a difficult time letting go to our old relationship, but we know that it's no longer working and we have to.

How do I make this new friendship with him work? I still have hopes that we can get back together in the future, as does he, but are we being realistic? — Rachel

Rachel, the break-up is too fresh for you to not hurt when you're around him at this point. My suggestion is that you stay away until the pain has subsided, until you can think of him without crying, until you can consider him just a good friend and nothing more. You dated for almost 3 years. It may take a year or more for you to put your emotions into proper perspective.

He dumped you. He probably does still have very strong feelings for you but no doubt you're trying to figure out what's wrong with you that caused this break-up. Maybe it was nothing other than he isn't ready to take the relationship into a more committed state at this time. Give him space. Get yourself cured of him, start enjoying life again without him.

Perhaps (and this is just a little perhaps) when he hears that you're doing so well without him, and if he happens to see you out and having a good time (hopefully on the arm of some great looking guy) he just might have second thoughts about you not being the center of his life. Maybe you'll still love him, maybe you won't. – Queenie

♥

Dear Queen of Hearts, this isn't a question but something for every broken hearted guy out there from a guy who knows.

Sure you loved her and she acted as if she loved you. You bought her things, took her places even helped out around the house. But in the end she just didn't feel the same way about you as you felt about her.

So what! There are too many people out there for you to be obsessing over just this one person. If you are lucky enough to have a real friendship with this person cherish it, because there is nothing in this world like a true friend one that will be there for you when you need a shoulder.

Go morn the loss of your fantasy get over it and start enjoying the friend that's right in front of you. She's going to go on with her life why shouldn't you? The only difference is that right now you have a chance to be part of her life (as a friend) forever. So stop whining about what you want and be happy for what you have.

Just think what if you had a friend like that right now?? I bet you wouldn't be reading this. — Charles

Charles, I agree with what you're saying but it's not always easy to step back into friendship-only mode when love has left a relationship. It takes time to work through the feelings of rejection, anger, depression, etc. It's also not so easy to be happy when someone you love starts dating others. – Queenie

♥

Dear Queenie, I just had a relationship end after a year and a half. We met online, wrote back and forth for a few months and then I met at her house for dinner. After a few weeks I was spending so much time with her that we decided I would move in with her (big mistake, I know!)

After about 6 months the relationship went downhill. She asked me to move out, which I did. We continued to see each other but the relationship was not the same. Then, I was dumped.

I have made attempts to get her to reconsider but she says she would like to remain friends. She has already had several 1 and 2 night stands. The news of this hurt me deeply because I am so in love with her, still.

I want to remain friends but the thought of her being with all these guys really hurts. Should I try to stay friends in the hopes that the pain will subside and I can look past her other relationships?

I love her deeply and staying friends could someday lead to a renewal of our relationship. Thank you for your help! — Chuck

Chuck, it is probably much too soon for you to think of friendship. Perhaps later, after you've healed from the dumping, you'll be able to see her without feeling so much pain. For now, my thoughts are that you'd be better off letting go, staying away, and letting her do her thing. You'll get better, it just takes time. – Queenie

♥

Dear Queenie, I have been going out with this girl for 3 years and then she left me. It has been 3 months and I still want her back but she doesn't want to she want to be friends. I have come to think that I should move to a different city where I have lived most of my life. I was only staying here for her and I live with my parents.

Should I run away from her because of the pain I'm feeling? I just think I may need to leave. Will running away to a different city help me deal with my loss. I don't know how I can stay in the same city as her. I would appreciate any advice you can give to my email. Thanks a lot in advance and keep up the good articles. — Stace

Stace, what good would running away do? The pain you feel is within you! Getting dumped is the pits but it happens to each and every one of us. You'll survive and some day you'll understand why you and she weren't meant to be. — Queenie

♥

Dear Queenie, I was exclusively dating a guy for approximately six months. We started out as friends several months before and grew closer as we spent more time together. Just before we started seeing each other, he had lost his job and was unemployed.

I volunteered to redo his resume and prepare cover letters for him as he did not have access to a computer. He accepted. So, I began preparing cover letters for him each week when the classifieds came out. However, he became increasingly lackadaisical about scanning the paper and giving me entries to prepare. I also noticed that he seemed quite comfortable and happy living off of his savings and not working.

He did however, get a part time job which he had for a a couple of months. However, his cavalier attitude about obtaining full time employment continued. He then decided that he wanted to be in the banking industry. He would only apply for jobs in that particular field. He got offers for other jobs, but he declined them saying, "I would be miserable doing that." Consequently, he was turning down full time job offers for the sake of getting exactly what he wanted.

You can imagine the stress that this put on our social interaction. We never could do anything because he didn't have any money. He was quite comfortable saying, "I don't have any money so I can't go out." However, I vowed to myself to continue to hang in there with him because he is a nice guy and I figured that things would improve once he was employed. Well, he comes to my house one day last month and says that he doesn't want to continue the relationship because he doesn't feel like a man and he's unhappy. I was blown away. Not so much because he wanted to end the relationship, but because I was so committed to hanging in there with him during his trials. I would have liked for him to at least to have talked to me about his unhappiness before making such a decision. I feel like I could have walked out on him long ago.

To make things worse, I understand that he is seeing someone else now so I feel like all of his rhetoric about not feeling like a man and wanting to get himself together was bull. I have also learned that he recently has gotten a job (in his field of choice).

It seems like I struggled with him and am out in the cold because we're not together. My feelings for him are so jumbled. I don't know what to do. One side of me wants to be with him (which may not even be possible at this point), the other side of me feels nothing but contempt for him. Any insight?? — Annabelle

Annabelle, you're angry because you feel lied to and used. You wish you'd dumped him before he dumped you. You consider the relationship unfinished because you haven't had your final say. He wasn't working when you met him, and you volunteered to help him with the job hunting. Unless you and he agreed on a fee payment for your assistance, you did it because you liked helping a nice guy.

For most men, their job defines who they are. They are a doctor. They are a lawyer. They are a mechanic. They are a banker. It is much more important than jobs 'most' women seek since 'most' women do not consider themselves defined by their career but by their status as 'wife,' 'mother,' 'friend,' etc. He was seeking a definition for himself, and it was certainly his right to wait until he found 'who' he wanted to be.

Not every relationship is destined to last. Yours was short term. You acknowledge your feelings weren't totally committed since you would have ended the relationship had you had insight into his thoughts. Consider it a learning experience.

Move on. You don't have a choice. Let go of the contempt. You might need a loan someday. – Queenie

♥

Dear Queenie, my girlfriend left me, and she told in a letter that she was hurt. I know that I made some misjudgments and I really apologized in a way of complete honesty. She is afraid that she will be hurt again and she's trying to forget me by buying things and going out with others, even another guy at this moment. It really hurts me to see this and I cannot find a way for the correct approach. What measures can I take to get her to understand that I want her back? Can you help? — Harold

Harold, you hurt her and now she hurts you. Love works that way. As far as how we each handle our hurt that varies from person to person. Some people will accept an apology and go right back, fearless of the possible pain of trusting again. Other people need more time.

Probably all you can do is let her know by a simple card, letter, bouquet of flowers with a note, phone call, or chat over coffee, that you love her, want her back, and will do whatever it takes to not hurt her again. Perhaps she'll believe you, perhaps not. Perhaps she only needs time to heal enough so that she can remember the good things of your relationship and give it one more try.

It would be a waste of your time to spend your life running after her. Once you have made your apology and opened the door for her to return and talk, you'd do yourself the most good by getting out with friends and getting involved in whatever interests you the most. If the two of you are meant to be, you will be. If not, whatever you do won't make it so. At least, that's what I think. — Queenie

♥

Dear Queenie, my boyfriend of 9 months broke up with me about 3 months ago. The only reason he gave was that the spark had gone. At the time, we both said that we wanted to remain friends. I assumed that I would have another best friend. But, as this was my first relationship, I did not realize how hard it would be. I soon realized that it would take time, and that we would both have to resolve any feelings for each other. I have done that, but I still feel strange around him. I don't know how to act around him, and, my instincts tell me that he doesn't know how to act around me either.

I have emailed him jokes since we broke up, but he believes that these jokes are an attempt to make him feel guilty and inadequate. I have reassured him that these jokes were not intended to make him feel that way. He had sent me equivalent jokes when we were going out. I even asked him if he was offended by what I had sent him, and he said that he wasn't.

I do not understand this!! I sent the same jokes to all of my friends. Now, I don't know where I stand with him. I want to be his friend, but not if he is going to misinterpret everything I say!! If he asked me out now, I would definitely say no, so I can't understand his reaction. I honestly feel that it would be a waste if we were to loose all contact. I can't understand why lovers loose all contact after they break up, especially when they have been so close. My friends tell me to cut my losses and forget about him, but I think it would be a shame. Can you help me? Thank you. — Laura

Laura, apparently he isn't ready to be friends. I think perhaps you haven't worked out all of your feelings either where you can be just a friend without expecting more.

Maybe you need to stop sending jokes, quit keeping so close in contact and let him get on with his life as you get on with yours. Perhaps sometime in the future the two of you can be friends but probably not for a while.

As for why lovers lose contact? Well, they've shared too much to be just casual friends if one still wants the intimate relationship to continue, which is the case much of the time. If both feel that the end of the "love" relationship was the best thing for the both of them and they were friends before that relationship started, then they will probably remain friends afterward. – Queenie

♥

Dear Queen of Hearts, exactly one month ago my girlfriend broke up with me. Since then we have spent two great weekends together. I thought all was fine but it wasn't. She still says let's be friends, but she won't return calls or talk to me. I don't know what to do, I think about her 24/7 and I can't stop. I never loved a girl like I love her and I'm scared.

On the second weekend that we spent together she got drunk and said a lot of "I love you" type stuff. Then she said that she didn't remember it. I have had two people say that it doesn't matter how drunk she was that she still meant what she said and might not want to admit it. I need help please I'm going crazy. — Robbie

Robbie, it doesn't matter what she says when she's drunk or when she's sober. It's what she does that will provide the answer to the way she feels.

You're hurting just like most people do when the person they love doesn't return that love to the same intensity. Unfortunately, your desperation is not an attractive quality, and could help to keep her from even approaching you on a friendship basis at this time.

Give her time and space. Get yourself together and start going out with other friends. Keep busy. Don't keep calling her. If you do something she's not expecting, such as not calling for several days or a couple weeks, she might wonder if you've learned to live without her. If she really cares, she'll make contact. If she doesn't, you need to find someone who does. She is not the only girl in the world for you. Good luck. – Queenie

♥

Dear Queenie, I recently was dumped from what I thought was a good relationship that was going to lead to marriage. We had talked about marriage several times and within the first two weeks of dating she told me that she would marry me one day. The relationship lasted almost seven months when she came over one day and said it was over. She said she wanted to date other people and have a chance to go out and explore the world and have fun.

I love her more than anyone and would do anything for her. It has been three weeks since we broke up and she has been dating someone from work for three weeks now. What should I do? Should I back off for a while and then try to get back together with her, or should I just let go. As I said earlier I love her and want to marry her. Help. — Chris

Chris, let her go. She isn't ready to settle down yet and your desire to get married has probably frightened her. She needs to do exactly what she said: go out and explore the world and have fun. If she can't do it now, when can she do it? You may not feel as though you need to, but you should be doing the same thing right now.

Many people say what they think they believe to be true when, in reality, their feelings change. Two weeks into a relationship is far too early to make a commitment to marriage. Give her time, maybe she'll return. But don't put your life on hold waiting for her to come back. Good luck. – Queenie

♥

Dear Queenie, my problem is that my girlfriend just broke up with me and I still have her in classes and see her in the dorms everyday. On the days I don't see her I do fine, but when I do all I can think about is wanting her back. She gave me the "it's not you, it's me" speech when we broke up, which is hard to stomach.

Basically I need to know how to I go about getting over her when I have to see her everyday and still love her very much. Also am I crazy to still want her back? We have had a couple bad confrontations since the breakup and I need to know how to win her back as a person before I attempt anything else. Is giving her space the best thing to do? Any advice would be appreciated! — Jerry

Jerry, when relationships don't work out, it would be best that we never see the person again so that memories wouldn't surface to remind us of the best times of the relationship, and make us sad. That isn't possible.

You're not crazy for wanting her back, but you cannot do anything to change her mind if she isn't ready to have it changed. What you can do is exactly what you said: give her space. Let her live her own life, and you live yours.

Perhaps she will decide that you were the best person for her, and perhaps she won't. In the meantime, you're going to hurt, you're going to be sad. The quicker you realize that this isn't helping her image of you, the quicker you will start to heal.

She is not the only woman in the world who would be a good match for you, even though it seems that way. Get out and start meeting people. Get involved in your surroundings.

You have a very narrow focus right now and it is keeping you from seeing the advantages of being single and available. It's a cool place to be, particularly right now for you. Have some fun! If you and she are meant to be, it will happen. If not, why are you wasting so much time being sad. Just do it! Good luck. – Queenie

♥

Dear Queenie, do you think that men and women can ever just be friends once they've been in a relationship? I've just broken up with my boyfriend, and I'm trying to be his friend, but it seems to hurt me even more.

When he sounds depressed I ask him if he's ok, and when I ask again or tell one of his close friends, he seems to push us away.

I want to be his friend but I can't if he keeps on doing this. Also, one of my friends said that guys only want to be friends if they believe that there is some chance of getting back together in the future. Is this true? This was my first relationship, so in a way I'm unsure how to act now. — Kathie

Kathie, some couples can be the best of friends. Others cannot be in the same room together. It has a lot to do with whether or not they were friends when they were lovers. If not, they probably won't be friends afterwards. If you are the one who broke up with him, it is pointless for you to try to console him. You're the reason he's hurting. Duh! – Queenie

♥

Dear Queenie, how long does it take to get over someone? I've been out of contact with the girl who dumped me (we were best friends and then started dating) for 3 months now and it's still hard. I'm so afraid of running into her somewhere. — Curtis

Curtis, a basic "rule" is that it will take half the time you spent in the relationship to get over the bad feelings. In other words, if you were in a relationship for four years, it could take two years to get completely over her.

A lot is dependent on you. If you allow yourself to feel sad about the relationship's breakup, if you allow yourself to grieve over this lost love, if you allow yourself to get angry, and if you forgive yourself and her, you will be much closer to getting over her. Good luck. – Queenie

♥

Dear Queenie, a lot has been written and said about the stages of pain and recovery for those who have been left or "dumped" in a relationship. But what is it like for those who initiate the break-up? I have read that those who initiate it actually suffer more guilt and sadness and over the break up and take longer to recover than those who were dumped and have since moved on. How true is this?

Doesn't it depend on the reasons and manner which the relationship ended? In my case, it was ended coldly, and for various reasons except him finding someone else. The rejection still hurt like hell though, even if it was due primarily to changing life circumstances, and differences in our personality and values. I have since recovered and I'm taking it slowly and surely now with someone new in my life. Yet, I sometimes wonder how those men from my past feel about what had happened.

Is it likely that these people simply feel relieved and never look back? I would appreciate your comments on this matter. — Darlene

Darlene, those who initiate a break-up do have guilt and sadness. Just how much and how long it lasts would be determined by the individual and the reason for the breakup. Just as no two people are alike, no two responses would be the same.

If you have once loved someone isn't it logical to think that at times, in remembering the good times of the past, there would be some sadness and joy, regardless of who initiated the break-up? — Queenie

♥

Dear Queen of Hearts, I was in a relationship with this great guy for over a year and a half. It started off very casual but within months we seemingly became more serious. By that I mean, we were together each and every day.

The relationship also survived a geographical separation as I moved to a different city for a while. However, shortly after I moved back, the relationship ended. He instigated the breakup with that dreaded 'I think we should just be friends' line.

I was absolutely devastated by the breakup. He started seeing someone shortly after we split up and they have been on and off ever since. During this time, I have never gotten over him. We continued seeing each other on occasion shortly after he started this other relationship.

It seemed to me that whenever they were experiencing problems, I would receive a phone call from him. I knew it was not the right thing to do on my part, but I enjoy being with him so much that I was too weak to say no.

I guess it was wishful thinking on my part that there was some hope of us reconciling. However, I knew that he is very much involved with this new person in his life. I just couldn't accept it and continued to agree to see him. Well, after a year of this it is finally over. He has decided to commit to this person once and for all. It sounds serious.

I realize that I have prolonged that painful recovery process by letting this go on for so long. I didn't have the guts to just be friends (platonic) because I was so and still am blinded by love for him. Why couldn't I have said, I love you but if you can't commit to me, then I can't be with you either.

Anyways, I'm not exactly sure if I actually have a question amongst all this blather but if I seek any advice, this would be it. This question has no easy answer, but I must ask it anyhow. What is the best way for me to get over this guy and move on with my life?

I feel so terribly empty without his presence in my life. He was and is very special to me but I cannot hang on any longer. It hurts a great deal. — Mona

Mona, of course you love this guy! And, yes, you hurt like crazy because he loves someone else and not you! He may be special but he dumped you then used you when he needed comfort during off-times with his current girlfriend. Don't you feel special being second?

Get mad, girlfriend! Getting mad will help you to get on with your life. You have a grieving process that has to take place so you can rid yourself of all those needy thoughts and hurtful thoughts about your relationship with him.

Try to go one day at a time without thinking about him. Stop thinking he'll be back. Stop hoping they'll break up. He chose her over you! (And then had the nerve to come back to you on the sly! Nice guy!)

Somewhere out there is the world's nicest guy who is looking for you. While you've got your heart buried in the sand over this guy, he's going to walk right by without seeing you. – Queenie

♥

Dear Queenie, about a year ago, my girlfriend broke up with me. She said she was confused and we were so different. It took me quite some time to recover but we kept in touch afterwards. We have been talking once in a while over the phone. The last times we talked, she said she taped some audio tapes for me. I sent her flowers and she thanked me for them.

When we talk (the past few months), she talks with the same tone she had before. However, it seems she doesn't want to go out and says she's not interested in guys now but she said she'd tell me when she was ready. I still feel strongly for her, yet I am not too sure of what she means. The signals I am getting seem to be a bit confused. What do you think is happening? Is it possible that after a year and a half relationship, she should be so burnt-out that she doesn't want any relationship with guys? — Richie

Richie, it sounds as though she cares quite a bit for you, but she has some unresolved issues in her own life that must be taken care of before she can have a successful relationship with anyone else. It's always comforting to have someone available, as you are, and my suggestion is that you continue to be a friend, if you can, but look elsewhere for romance. – Queenie

♥

Dear Queenie, I was in a three-year relationship that ended 2 months ago. Out of those three years, we lived together for two. During these two months, I have found it difficult to let go. He broke up with me, but I almost broke up with him the day before. I didn't because I was afraid that what I was finding upsetting and/or annoying was petty and wasn't worth throwing away three years for. He, on the other hand, definitely wanted to break up.

He has made multiple comments these past two months regarding my looks and being attracted to me. He also says that the things he found annoying about me when we were a couple, he didn't find so now that we're friends. How's that? Both of us have agreed that it has to be him. Meaning he was making our relationship much more difficult than it had to be.

We ride together in the same carpool to and from work everyday just as we did while we were going out. I don't know if that's the reason it's hard for me to let go of the relationship or if that's just a piece in the puzzle. He has also stated that he is totally confused and doesn't know what he wants. We have had talk after talk, but it never seems to go anywhere.

The other thing is, while we were going out, he would constantly flip back and forth with his feelings. For a few months he would totally appreciate me and treat me so wonderfully. Then for a few more months, he'd say he didn't know if he was in love with me anymore. This went on for 3 years.

My biggest problem is... I don't understand why I don't know what I want. I don't know if I want him back. I don't know if I want to be friends. I don't know if I want him out of my life. One minute, I'm fine with the way things are. The next minute, I feel like I love him more than life itself. The next minute I'm so mad at him I could almost have apathy toward him.

Is this strange, or do many people go through this? I'm am trying to find strength in God, but it only seems to work for a little while, then I'm consumed by different thoughts again. I am 23 and haven't been in many long relationships, so I'm new to this breaking up thing. Any advise you can give would be appreciated. Thanks. — Darlene

Darlene, will it help to know that what you are experiencing is perfectly normal? Who in the world told you love was easy? It's the most difficult of times imaginable! You're new to this love thing and you can expect it to not get any better for the next fifty or sixty years.

The two of you got to the love plateau that means a move to the next step: commitment. Neither one of you is really sure you're ready, and since you're both having doubts, you aren't. Incidentally, no one person is 100% responsible for a relationship not working so stop trying to analyze who was "wrong." You both were. Is that better?

You haven't been out of this intimate relationship for a long enough time to get your emotions back together, and the carpooling is not helping. You're going to hurt if he meets and starts dating someone else and he'll probably get annoyed and make a few unkind remarks if you start dating someone else. Is there a way one of you can take the bus to work or get another ride?

Personally, I think some time away from each other — some serious time way — might give both of you a chance to decide if you're ready for the big commitment: Marriage. It usually happens this way. But only if you get on with your life and let him see that you're not pining away for him. Good luck. – Queenie

♥

Dear Queenie, does anyone ever truly get over a broken heart? My ex boyfriend unceremoniously broke up our tempestuous relationship over one and a half years ago over the holidays.

Since then, I went through depression, counseling, then got back on my feet in terms of my career and met a wonderful new man. He's kind, gentle, and considerate although he has none of the passion for life, drive, and ambition which my ex had.

I feel secure and happy with my new boyfriend because he treats me with the respect I deserved but hardly got from my ex.

I just don't know why a day still doesn't go by when I don't think of him (my ex). I'm not "consumed" by thoughts of him as I was when I was depressed, but I remember him nevertheless, especially at night and during other quiet moments alone.

There are still times at night when I can't help but churn in my mind what I think went wrong, and can't believe how he could have been so cold and callous to me when our relationship began to flounder.

I thought he was my soul mate, but I was wrong and realizing this brings me sadness. Sometimes I want to call him and talk things over, but deep inside I know that it wouldn't accomplish much except to stir up emotions that are best forgotten. Not to mention, I may be betraying my new boyfriend since I'm not really sure that don't have feelings for my ex anymore.

I still want to reach out to my ex, but I don't know why, how, or if it's even worth it. Do you think I still have unresolved issues that I need to deal with, or do I just need time to help me numb the pain, perhaps forget? — Evangeline

Evangeline, you need to stop searching for the answers to why this relationship ended. Accept that it had its place in your life and that it prepared you for future relationships. Perhaps nothing went wrong. Not all relationships are meant to last forever.

Calling him would not be a good idea while you still have such strong emotions regarding the relationship. You could end up renewing your old relationship, hurting your new man, and having the old problems surface once again to cause him to hurt you yet again. This would leave you even more distressed with yourself for getting back together with him at the cost of your new, better, relationship.

It does take time. But you're not being fair with your new man. He deserves all of your friendship and love. (He sounds like he's worth it!) Good luck. – Queenie

❤

Dear Queenie, I thought she was the one. In my eyes she was nearly perfect in every way. Caring. Fun. Interesting. But most of all she made me feel good about me. We had a good time together. I miss holding her hand. I miss her smile. I tried to make her as happy as I knew how. But in the long run the time we spent together wasn't enough.

She started going out with other 'friends' and she soon found one that I guess made her happier. Was it the money? Was it something I did or didn't do? I don't know. All I do know is that she means more to me than .... LIFE itself. I know this may sound pathetic but I would do anything to get her back.

I would travel the ends of the world to prove to her that what we had in those thirteen months are worth holding on to and that I CAN make her happy. — Curt

Curt, when someone leaves us, we always blame ourselves and believe they left because of something we did or didn't do. Some relationships just don't work to the same intensity for both people. If you call her, does she refuse to talk to you? If you ask her for a date, does she say no? If she doesn't want to get back together with you, you can't do anything to change her mind except distance yourself, get new interests and get on with your life. It's painful, but so is your life right now. — Queenie

♥

Dear Queenie, I had been going out with a young lady over the past 2 months and I thought we had something. But I was disappointed to hear that she is now going out with her boss!! I felt being used and mislead over the past 2 months and doubt that I can trust my gut feelings in a relationship again. Please help and advice me how could I know that the relationship is for real. Thanking you in advance. — Tim

Tim, there is no way to absolutely guarantee that a relationship is going to last forever, nor to guarantee that it is going to be taken as seriously by both persons involved. No matter how much pain a relationship may cause when it ends before we wish it to, it is much better to have had the chance to love than not to have the chance at all. — Queenie

♥

Dear Queenie, how does one know when he is over a failed relationship and it is safe to get into another without using the other person? What if one still thinks of his ex and hopes to see her by chance or even catches himself fantasizing about reuniting? — Fred

Fred, if you're fantasizing about reuniting, you're not over the relationship. We all have different "timeframes" for moving on with our life. If she dumped you, and she is already making a new life for herself, then it's time you do the same. It doesn't mean you won't think about her sometimes, but when you do, think about the bad times instead of the good. Get busy, get involved, go out with friends, go on casual dates and don't rush into anything. Love will wait. – Queenie

♥

Dear Queenie, several months ago, my relationship with a wonderful woman ended. We had some differences, but we had many similarities as well. Since our break-up, she has refused to speak with me. I've tried being her friend. I've sent her a few letters, and called her once. Since she won't talk with me, I have no idea what to do. The only problem I know of in our relationship is that she feels we were intimate too quickly. Any advice on what I should do from here? — Dave

Dave, some people are unable to shift into friendship once a relationship has become intimate. She may be that type. She may uncomfortable and perhaps embarrassed. There is nothing you can do to change her feelings about this.

Perhaps a simple note such as "I respect your need to distance yourself from the relationship we once shared. I just wanted to let you know that I am always available should you ever need a friend to talk to."

Then, I would suggest that you stop trying to contact her. If you happen to see her, say hello, be polite and cordial. Let her make the next move, if it is to be made. Don't wait by the phone for her to call. – Queenie

♥

Dear Queenie, my girlfriend and I broke up because she needed time....two days later she started dating my best friend. Now I have lost two important people in my life. What do I do? — Jeb

Jeb, betrayal by a girlfriend is bad enough but when your best friend is the reason, this is tough to take. And now at the holidays you get to see them being happy while you remember how it used to be. I hope they're happy, 'cause you sure aren't.

I don't know how long you've known either of them but it's time to find some other friends. Try not to be bitter, although it's easy to despise one or both of them right now. Don't talk badly about them, don't try to break them up, don't try to get her back.

This is your chance to find the girlfriend you really need, the one who's been waiting for you to discover her, the one who thinks you're the greatest guy she's ever met. She is probably very shy, and you may already know who she is but you haven't given her a second thought. Go ahead. It won't be long until you will smile again. And then you'll know why your ex-girlfriend wasn't quite right for you. – Queenie

♥

Dear Queenie, my girlfriend of 2 and a half years broke up with me recently. She said that she didn't want to go out with anyone for a while. I would not be that upset with this if she had not also said that I shouldn't think about getting back together with her.

This crushed me, sending me into a world where I didn't know what was going on. I love her more than anything, and will do whatever it takes to keep her in my life.

I never want to lose her friendship, but I would like to be in a relationship with her. I am worried that if I asked to many questions or protest our breakup too much, I will ruin our friendship, but I feel that I have a right to know why she doesn't want to be with me. What should I do? — Todd

Todd, right now you can't think very clearly because your emotions are in control. Whatever I suggest really isn't going to do much good, but I can assure you that you aren't alone with feelings such as these, and I can assure you that throughout your life, this will happen again and perhaps again. The pain does not get any less but with age and experience you (hopefully) learn better ways to cope.

Most love relationships are wrapped so tightly around another person that when that person walks out of the relationship, all we see is a black hole.

It takes time and a lot of effort, and the support of friends, to make us see that the world is a bigger place than what was defined by our relationship with our lover. And, as such, when the small world of our relationship is gone, the much larger world around us opens for our exploration. It's not easy. It takes time. It takes discipline. It takes wanting to pull out of the depression and move away from the pain.

She has made a choice. Does she owe you an explanation? No. Should you try to force her back into a relationship? Absolutely not! Is there a chance for the two of you? If you get on with your life, and let her have the freedom to get on with hers, perhaps the two of you will end up back on the same path in the future. If you two are meant to be, it will happen. Life is funny like that. – Queenie

♥

Dear Queen of Hearts, you've had some really interesting and insightful comments, however, I feel I have to protest what you said when you told Todd (who was dumped) that the girlfriend who dumped him "doesn't owe him an explanation".

You bet your boots an explanation is owed when someone ends a relationship with someone. I have been on the receiving end of two major dumpings in the last few years from two women I was very much in love with, and would have been more than happy to make a life with. Right now, it's hard to describe the anger I feel toward both of them (before you say anything...yes, I'm currently in therapy for it), because they both gave me vapid, vague, or no reasons.

Anytime I have dumped a woman (which hasn't been very often), I have considered it simple, decent, human courtesy to make sure she left knowing the reasons. She might not have liked the reasons, and she might not have agreed with the reasons, but she left knowing the reasons.

To just end it with "it doesn't feel right" or "I guess it just didn't work out" is intellectually bankrupt and emotionally cruel. There are specific reasons you're ending the relationship, or something specific you don't like about the other person. Have the guts to come out with it. And it's especially despicable when this happens after the relationship has been dragged out over a long period of time, like Todd's was.

The scientist in me doesn't buy into the "seeing skyrockets", "butterflies-in- the-stomach" stuff. Generally speaking, I think it's a lot of Hollywood-perpetuated crap. I can't recall ever "seeing skyrockets" about ANYTHING in my life. But if there IS anything to that stuff, then someone should know whether the relationship is "right" or "wrong" within a couple of months.

If you come to the conclusion that the relationship is somehow "wrong", then you have a moral obligation to that other person to get out of the relationship as soon as possible, and not waste their time. The two women I have mentioned wasted large chunks of my time. Todd's girlfriend wasted a large chunk of his time. As I see it, all of these women owe Todd and I a year or two of our lives.

I hope no one thinks I'm blasting only women for this. The rules are the same for both men and women. In either case, the "dumper" owes the "dumpee"

a decent and honest explanation. I would much prefer getting briefly stung by a brutal truth than the slow and looming agony I feel now in guessing "why?"

Your own "Dumped" article says "if you can see the patterns, you can learn and make changes...". How am I supposed to find out what I did wrong...what mistakes I made...how I failed the relationship, and make the necessary changes for future relationships, if I don't get reasons why the relationship ended? How is Todd supposed to find out? I would greatly appreciate your response, and your elaborating on this. Oh, and by the way...keep up the good work! — Scott

Scott, while I appreciate your comments (they are excellent), I still stand by the comments I made regarding Todd's situation.

Do you call having a wonderful, warm, loving relationship, a waste of time? The relationship Todd had with his girlfriend and the relationships you have had were times you didn't want to end. That is not a waste of time! Do you consider reading a good book a waste of time? Or watching a good movie a waste of time? Those, too, take away chunks from your life. Or is it that you are adjusted to the fact that "x" amount of your life will be used by the book or movie and then you will take the memory of it and move on? Do you see where this is leading?

Not all relationships last forever. People change and not always in sync with their relationship partner. It is possible to start what seems to be the perfect relationship and grow apart over the years until there is nothing left but the words. Unfortunately, most times it is a one-sided need to end the relationship.

Does this mean that only one person is at fault in the relationship's demise? No. Is there something the other person could do to stop it from ending? It depends on why it ended. And here's the problem. The "why" is not always obvious to even the person leaving. Leaving is a very emotional deal for each of the parties involved, even if the one leaving does not show it. The one leaving might not be able to verbalize exactly why they need to leave. Sometimes they just need to get away to get back in touch with themselves. And that is a heck of a vague statement to make to someone you're leaving, someone who has wrapped their entire world around you!

Todd's girlfriend does not owe him an explanation because if she is unable to give a satisfactory one (in his opinion) he should not waste time dwelling on the "why." Relationships have stages, stages at which they advance to higher commitment levels or terminate. Her goals and priorities may have changed and that happens in relationships, particularly in younger couples (anywhere from 15 to 45!) as each participant is busy learning about themselves and striving to fulfill their own dreams.

If this were an ideal world, we would meet and fall in love with our soul mate, once. We would live, love, grow old and die together. There would be no need for sad songs or psychiatrists. But it's much less than ideal and we cannot control another person's wishes and desires, nor can we always be our loved one's ideal.

In a slightly more perfect world, we would hope that, after a few weeks of introspection, you could call an ex-lover and say, "Hi, I'm having a bit of a problem with closure of our relationship. Do you think you could give me a few minutes to talk it out?" And then, in this slightly more perfect world, you and your ex-lover would have one last conversation, without arguments, without blaming, without trying to set the record straight, without trying to place guilt. And, in this slightly more perfect world, this last conversation should allow the doors to close gently, preserving wonderful memories in your heart. – Queenie

♥

Dear Queenie, I just was dumped by my boyfriend; actually I caught him cheating on me. I don't know why I like him; he is such a loser anyhow. But I can't seem to let him go, no matter what he does?

He has cheated on me time and time again, but I still cling to him. He never respects me; I guess I really don't respect myself, that's why I keep coming back. How do I break this horrible pattern??? — Danielle

Danielle, you have asked and answered your own questions very effectively so far. The question is, why do you not respect yourself? You know you deserve better, don't you? Well, kick this guy in the butt (figuratively speaking, of course) and get on with your life.

Take it one day at a time without him, like breaking a bad habit. "Today it has been 3 days without a jerk fix... today it has been 4 days without a jerk fix... today it has been 5 days..." You get the picture. – Queenie

♥

Dear Queenie, I need some advice about my last relationship. I am having a really hard time getting over it. I went out with what I thought was a really great guy for about 4 months. We were very good together; we talked almost every day and saw each other about 3 times a week. I thought we were falling in love. Then things happened that I just don't understand.

The last time I saw him and talked to him we had had a wonderful time together the day before. Then one day he just stopped calling. The week before he had said that we were getting too serious and he needed to step back.

At the time I asked him if this meant he was going away and he assured me that he was not. Then his last words to me were that we'll do this again.

I have called him twice since he stopped calling but never really got an answer as to whether or not he wanted to see me again. It has now been 2 months and I keep thinking in the back of my mind that someday he is going to call.

I think that is why I can't get over it. Plus I really want him back. I just can't understand why he doesn't want to see me anymore; I thought we were good together.

I know that I must go on and realize that I am probably better of with out him because why would I want to be with a man that treats me like this. What do you think about all of this and do you have any ideas as to why he may have

decided to go away and do you think he may come back and if he does what should I do then? Please Help. — Liz

Liz, his response that things were getting too serious is the clue. He isn't ready to settle down. That doesn't mean that he might not meet someone tomorrow and be married next week. It happens to even the most uncommitment-minded individuals.

Men in particular seem to have a difficult time saying, 'well, it's been nice but I'd like to date someone else now.' So they say things like 'we'll do this again,' or 'of course I'm not leaving.' And then they leave. It's because they think that if they're honest they'll hurt someone's feelings. Since they're not honest and direct with their response they cause confusion instead.

If every good relationship between two people ended in commitment there wouldn't be too many single people in the world. In other words, not every enjoyable relationship is going to end up in marriage. Some are going to end when one of the partners decides they want to move on, just as your boyfriend has done.

Stop worrying about what you did to drive him away. You could be the world's most perfect woman and if he's not ready for commitment, he would leave. Get out and meet people and get back into the dating scene. The more you pine away about him, the less attractive you're going to be to potential dates.

Also, if you're out and about enjoying yourself, you might run into him and he just might remember the good times and want to date you again. If he does come back, play hard to get. Shy away from commitment. Tell him you've thought it over and you like the freedom of being your own person too much to give it up for a relationship with anyone. And believe it!

Dating is not a commitment for the future; it is a learning, exploring experience that could possibly develop into something more if both people are so inclined. It takes a lot of dates to find two people who are ready — at the same time — to commit to each other to the exclusion of all others, and who want that commitment to last a lifetime. – Queenie

The Not-Quite-Exes

The Not-Quite-Exes

"Is it appropriate of me to ask her to draw clear boundaries in her relationship with the ex, that is, to do 'friend' things and not romantic things like camping, or whatever?"

Old flames that still smolder can spell disaster for new relationships. You and he are locked in a passionate embrace and his cell phone rings. It's his ex, the one who broke his heart into a thousand jagged pieces. She needs help and he doesn't hesitate to run to her side despite your protests. You and she are snuggling in front of a cozy fire when her ex shows up at the front door to say he's ready to commit and sorry for everything he put her through.

Very rarely do couples split and never meet again. They may be co-workers, classmates, neighbors, or even parents bound forever together by the child they've created. Relationships end for countless reasons, some due to misunderstandings that can be repaired, and some due to errors of judgment that only need time to heal as each travel new paths apart.

How can you know if your new love will be tempted by an ex? Is your relationship solid enough to withstand intimate memories of a history that didn't include you? Are you still carrying a torch for an ex who ended the relationship you thought would last forever?

♥

Queenie, I have a boyfriend living with me and we believe we are in love but sometimes I can't understand his behavior. He had a girlfriend he loved greatly and was cheated by her and they broke up. But they still keep contacting each other. She asks if he can come and see her etc. When I confront him with it, and tell him to avoid her, he says she is a good friend and wants to see her but possibly with me.

Well, that will be the last thing I want to do since she cheated on him and don't think meeting her is a fun gathering. He will see her anyway when he has chance with or without me and it really upsets me.

I do love him and believe that he does too but I just can't keep going on with this none sense and maybe I will leave him because of this. I have told him how I feel but he thinks I am wrong...is this a cultural thing? Do western cultures adopt such insensitivity? I really wonder...tell me what you think please. — Sally

Sally, it sounds as though they still have some unresolved feelings for each other. The fact he wants to have you come along when they get together is a good thing and I would strongly suggest that you do go along and meet her.

It always helps to see how they relate to each other. If this was a relationship I was involved in I'd admit to being upset, too, because she's probably trying to get him back now that he's involved with someone else. No, it's not a cultural thing. It's a boyfriend who wants to keep both doors open thing. If he still has feelings for her it'll be in your best interest to let him go.—Queenie

♥

Dear Queen, I used to date this girl for like 3 years, we broke it off (not my choice) and went our separate ways. About 3 months later, I ran into one of her friends and we started talking and 3 months later, we had decided to get married. Well it is about 2 months until my wedding and the ex has come back into the picture. She tells me that she made a horrible mistake and that she is still in love with me. I haven't told anyone else this, but I really didn't get a chance to fully get over her and part of me still wants her back.

The "new love" is great and we have lots of fun together, but she is very controlling. I can't hang out with my friends or go anywhere without her, or she will throw a fit like you wouldn't believe. She clearly doesn't know that I talked to the ex, but now I'm really mixed up. I haven't the slightest on what I should do. Can you help me sort through this mess at all? — Clarence

Clarence, if you really want to sort through the mess you'll call off your wedding and stop seeing either girl for a while so you can decide just exactly what you want in a love partner.

There's a reason your ex dumped you after three years; are those issues resolved or is she back just because she doesn't want you involved with someone else?

Jealousy can play some mean tricks. Your current girlfriend sounds like she could make your life miserable in the long run. Breakups are no fun but neither is divorce and you're taking real fast steps toward divorce court even before you take your marriage vows. — Queenie

♥

Dear Queen of Hearts, I am engaged to be married this year. Right now I am very upset with my fiancé. Today I check his email and found out that he has been emailing his exes. He has told them that he is getting married; the part that I do not like is that he saved 2 emails from his ex where she has expressed her feelings for him. Telling him that if he comes home alone that they could get together. This is something that I did not know about.

I know that I should not have invaded his privacy, but something just did not fell right when I got home and I had to see what it was. How do I confront this or what should I do? — Sandee

Sandee, until the two of you are married, both of you can change your mind about this relationship. He may be having second thoughts. You were wrong in going through his email but now that you've done it you might as well ask him if he's thinking about getting back with his ex. If he is, then you better put the wedding plans on hold.—Queenie

♥

Hi Queenie, my boyfriend and I have only been together 5 months but known each other 4 years I know all the games he's played before me and there is this woman who he used to see but they ended up staying friends after their relationship ended they had not talked in months now all of a sudden she is calling and wanting him to come "hang out" should I trust this or is there reason for be not to. I believe him when he says there is not anything happening but still I have to wonder if I should be ok with this. — Rita

Rita, while you should forgive someone for what they have done in the past, and forget what they have done so that it doesn't cause problems in a current relationship, we think you should also learn from the past.

You know he has been a player so you know he's capable of playing. I would suggest you keep your eyes open. As far as the former girlfriend wanting to "hang out" with him — if you're welcome to "hang out" with them, if she's willing to include you in the friendship, then perhaps there's no problem. If you're not welcome, then I'd have to suspect that there's more than casual friendship involved. – Queenie

♥

Dear Queenie, I have a problem! I met my boyfriend a year ago at school and we have been living together for 10 months now. Things are going great. We spend all our time together, share every class together, and get along just fine. We even actually enjoy each other's company despite our constant time together. One problem! Before we met he was involved with this girl whom he calls his "best friend and soul mate." And though they've been platonic for about 6 years now, they've been living together for the past 8 years and had a sexual relationship in the previous years. They've been through everything together but she's married and has a kid now.

One of the reasons why he finally left her was to go on with his life. He's like a father/uncle or something special to her baby as he was there when her baby was born and helped raise him. Her husband is a total jerk and though she is married to him they are not together.

My boyfriend moved far away from her to get on with his life! We met and were friends before we were lovers so I know the depth of their relationship and his attachment to her. Neither of us intended to get together but everything just fits with us we're so much alike and at the same time so different! We're very affectionate and meet each other's needs.

Okay, back to our problem. He insists on keeping a relationship with her. He talks about doing things for her and her baby a lot and it hurts me! I thought he wanted to get on with his life! And in a lot of ways he has. BUT. . . I feel he'll never let her go! He feels bad if he doesn't call her once every week and actually would like to be talking to her even more. He says it's unfair of me to have a problem with this because they're friends, actually more like family. But she hardly ever calls him. Granted, she's usually happy to hear from him and has told him that she feels threatened by me, which makes him all the more obligated to keep in touch with her.

I don't know! Call me selfish, but I'm no fool. If their bond is so unique and strong I truly believe that they should be together. He says it's not like that but I know that I will never accept anything less than a total commitment to ME and not his best girl friend, her kid, and me!

Besides, after we graduate in 6 months, he'll (we'll) be moving back to the mainland and will be much closer to her. I feel that if I'm having problems now when she's thousands of miles away, how much more problems will there be when seeing her would be just a road trip away.

Any ideas as to what we could do? I know he's never been happier. He's told me time and again how happy he is with me and "us." He can't imagine his life w/o me and I believe it because we are so close in every way. Even a lot closer than he and his ex-lover/ best friend were. Yet, it's the scars and hurts of his past relationship that will always hold him. They are forever etched in his memory and heart because of the pain it caused and the experience it brought him.

His past brought him to me and made him the person he is for me. I just have such a hard time dealing with it and may eventually have to leave it. Any ideas? Please help me in my decision, thanks! — Carolee

Carolee, it's good and natural to have friends on many different levels. However, if a friendship threatens a current relationship, then it's time to take a look and see if the threatening friendship needs to be redefined.

In other words, if he loves you more than he loves her, he should do everything necessary to make you secure about his feelings for you. That means respecting the fact that you feel intimidated by the depth of his 'responsibility' for his ex-girlfriend and her child.

I'm curious why she feels 'threatened' by you and also why she felt she had to tell your boyfriend this. It almost sounds as though she is trying to force him to make a decision - her or you. If that's the case, and if he falls for it, then you sincerely do have a problem, one that you need to work out with him before advancing further in this relationship.

Right now, because of his emotional commitment to her, he is not able to commit entirely to you. Even if he has no sexual interest in her, the emotional ties may continue to cause you grief in the future. If you and he marry, what then with regard to his chosen responsibilities to her and her child?

There are several ways you can handle this. You can ignore the situation. You can become friends with her. You can talk to him and see if he can understand your feelings. You can end this now or later. Ignoring the situation certainly won't make it go away. Making friends with her could difuse the potential problems and perhaps let her see that you're no threat to their friendship. If she doesn't want to be friends with you because she wants you entirely out of the picture, then she is a definite threat to your relationship with him.

It's your decision, and your life. I'm hoping you can get him to understand how you feel. Good luck. – Queenie

♥

Hi Queenie, I have been seeing this wonderful lady now for 2 months. We spend weekends together as she lives 2 hours away. We became intimate after dating for 3 weeks. At about the same time, she thought there was something I should know. She told me that two days out of the month, she has to work in an office that is 2 hours drive away. She usually drives the night before, and stays over at her x-boyfriends place! She assured me that they are only friends and that there was nothing funny going on. She saw that I wasn't comfortable with the situation, and told me that she would get up 2 hours earlier and drive there in the morning. I thanked her for her honesty (as she didn't have to tell me this, as I never would have found this out.) I told her not to kill herself driving a total of 4 hours and working another 10 hours the same day.

Well last week I was talking to her on the phone. She told me her x-boyfriend stayed at her place last night. She asked me where I thought he slept. I jokingly said "in her bed"? She was very upset with my answer and subsequently broke off our relationship. She thought we had an understanding.

She said "trust" is the biggest most important thing in a relationship. She thought we were at a level which trust should never become a question. She also said, "if you didn't trust me, what were we doing having sex??"

I really didn't know how to answer that, as I never thought of trust as being a light switch. On or off. She said that her self esteem is at ground zero because of me even thinking that she would sleep with someone else.

I told her that I trust her, but if something don't sit right with me in regards to anything in a relationship, is it not my right to ask? Isn't that what we do with our partner when we don't understand something? Did she over-react or am I missing something? — Stan

Hi Stan, it's pretty normal to be concerned when exes have sleepovers on a routine basis. Can they be platonic? Absolutely! Can they be above reproach? Absolutely! However, it takes a really good natured (new) lover to be totally okay with this type of situation. Of course, since the relationship between the two of you is so new and it has not reached the point of commitment (promise of exclusivity - marriage), she has a right to do whatever she wishes. And you have the right to be at ease with her choice or a bit testy about it.

Maybe they're not quite ready to call it quits. Perhaps you'll feel better if you walk away from this relationship. What do you think? – Queenie

♥

Hi Queenie, I was dating this guy for about a week. Before me he was dating this other girl that has a child (2 years old). He was helping her out with Rent and so on. She had other guy friend helping her out as well.

I decided that I don't want to see him for the reason is that her son was sick and she wanted to take him to the hospital and asked the guy I was dating for him to meet her there.

I got upset because he no longer is seeing her and I think that why should he be concern with a sick child that's not even his. I said it is ok to visit if the child ends up staying in the hospital. I think it was an excuse for her to get him to come out there. She has a lot to lose. He was paying her bill..... So I decided I don't want to get involved in a situation like this. Did I over react? Or was it an excuse for him to go see her? — Tanya

Tanya, regardless of what her reasons were or what his excuses were, one thing is certain: if you date a guy for a week and then think you own him enough to tell him who he should spend time with and demand that he make a choice between a long term friend and you, you're going to be lonely for a long, long time.

You're too jealous to date this man. Find someone who isn't involved, hasn't been involved, and who can promise they'll never be involved with anyone else but you. — Queenie

♥

Dear Queen of Hearts: My problem concerns an old flame of mine who keeps reappearing. We have been close friends for 6 years. We have always liked each other but both were too shy to act on it. Finally, my friend met his best friend now that eventually set us up. We both had been hurt before and the relationship did not last because we couldn't get past our old wounds, so we wouldn't give and take for fear of being hurt again.

I care deeply for him and I know he feels the same way about me. It has been 2 years now and the old wounds from the past heartaches have finally healed. Should we take the chance of trying our love again and possibly losing our friendship totally or should we just let our feelings be put away and miss out on a wonderful relationship?

I know if we could get things straightened out between us it would last, but how do we learn to start trusting each other or anyone else for that matter so we can have good relationships? Since we both have a hard time expressing our feelings what would be a good way of getting around to the relationship thing again? Thanks for all your help. — Mindy

Mindy, since you need to rebuild trust in each other, slow is better as far as developing this relationship. Don't try to push it into a major commitment, let it develop upon its own.

You can spend your lifetime protecting yourself from the pain of heartache, or you can forget about the past and move into the present, opening your heart to the possibility of good and true love. Could you get hurt again? Of course! But if you don't give love a chance, you'll never experience good OR bad love again!

Which is worse? The pain of no love or the pain of love gone bad? If you choose to try again, you have a chance of it working out this time. If you don't try, you'll never know. Forget what was! Move on to what is! Good luck. — Queenie

♥

Queenie, I've never used something like this to help in my decisions about relationships but it is driving me crazy. After two great years with my girlfriend something she does has always bothered me. When I was in high school we were best friends, she was expelled from school her senior year for bad grades. Then she met a guy and they were set to be married. He goes into the service, has an affair, gets some girl pregnant and basically stomps on her heart.

A year later we get back in touch and start hanging out. We lose touch for a year again and we run into each other at a concert and we both felt something. Another year later I am riding in her car one afternoon catching up again and at the end of the ride we kiss and two year later it's still going on.

My problem is with his family! She still insists on going to his house (he does not live there anymore) and spending time with HIS sister and brother who love her so much and are very sorry about the way things turned out. Out of the blue she calls and talks to him for 4 hours on the phone. She calls it closure. I understand. Then he moves back to where we live and she goes to see him and his new wife and baby. Does not tell me about it until something told me to ask if she had seen him lately since he had moved back.

She tells me the truth. I understand. Tonight she drops every plan she, I, and her roommate had to hang out with his brother at his house. You have to understand that she is very loyal to her friends but this just seems odd to me that she would want to still have this relationship with the family who 'hate his new wife', and just love her to be around. At the end of my rope! — Don

Don, it sounds as though she's still very much hung up on him and just waiting until he becomes available again. If you like being second in this threesome, hang in there and hope she'll see what a great guy you are. You might have a better chance winning the lottery at this point. You deserve a girl who is as hung up on you are you are on her. What are you waiting for? — Queenie

♥

Hi Queenie, my girlfriend and I have been dating for 6 months. She tells me (repeatedly) that she loves me in a way she has never loved before. She writes me love poems, and tells me that she wants to travel with me. Lately, half as a joke, she even signs her letters with my last initial on her name (as if we were married) - very cute, sappy, great stuff.

In many important ways, she seems to be the perfect girl for me. There is one sticking point that keeps coming up: an ex of hers. The ex happens to also be a she, as my girlfriend had a one year "behind the scenes - experimental" experience with this one woman. My girlfriend does not identify herself as bi, but as straight. She and this person were the closest of friends for 5 or so years before their year together, and it ended 3 years ago or so. They are back to being the best of friends, but it frustrates the heck out of me that their friendship seems sort of bizarre to me.

The thing I keep saying is, "I will be ok with your friendship when it starts to seem like a normal friendship, and not like to exes." My girlfriend promises

143

me that she has NO feelings for this person (which I believe). It is for this reason that I can't understand why the other person always wants to do stuff like live with my girlfriend, visit her when she is away for the summer in another country, etc."

Realistically, I know this ex is not a threat to our relationship, but I am still not comfortable with it. I guess the ex represents a force pulling my girlfriend back to her old experimental ways. What is the deal here? What is and is not appropriate for their friendship in the context of my relationship with my girlfriend? I know that a good part of this is jealousy on my behalf.... How can I learn to fully trust my girlfriend?

Should it be a sign to me that this relationship is not healthy if I am having trouble learning to trust her even in the face of her constant reassurance that there is no one else but me (she told me a few white lies about other minor issues, which is also hanging me up)? Is it appropriate of me to ask her to draw clear boundaries in her relationship with the ex, that is, to do "friend" things and not romantic things like camping, or whatever? My girlfriend admits that her continued friendship with this particular ex has caused turmoil in previous relationships, and that "this issue has been a chronic problem."

My girlfriend is getting frustrated that this issue keeps coming up, and I am getting fed up and have to fight back the urge to just end this beautiful relationship over this stupid issue. This issue is making me think suspiciously, when I am not normally that way. This is the one issue that keeps upsetting me.

My instinct says there is nothing to worry about, my heart loves her, but a little voice in my head makes me analyze and reanalyze this one issue. How do I learn to trust, and when do I know it is time to give full trust? Whatever it is, I want this issue to stop, and I want to stop obsessing over it! Thanks. — Carl

Carl, if this other female were a man, would your girlfriend's behavior be appropriate? I, personally, see no difference between male/female, male/male or female/female relationships.

If my math is correct, she and her ex have about nine years of shared experiences while you and she have six months together. That's a lot of history on their side. Perhaps they are just friends now, but if the ex does not have a current love interest it's easy to understand your concern.

Whether or not your girlfriend says she's bi, straight or gay now, she admits to a long term sexual relationship with this woman. One night stands are experimental. Never ignore your instincts, but don't let them rule your life either. Your girlfriend has told you "a few white lies" so you don't have complete trust in her. That, too, is understandable. It will take time for her to earn your trust.

If she lets this friendship interfere with her relationships, as you indicate yours is not the first that has been influenced by this ex, then perhaps it would be best for you to back away while she decides who is the most important person in her life. Right now, it appears the ex is. Good luck. — Queenie

♥

Queenie, my boyfriend and I have been involved on an exclusive basis for a year and a half. I truly love him and he has admitted the same feelings for me while at the same time expressing how scared that made him because he didn't mean to care for me that deeply when we began dating.

He has also maintained a friendship with a former girlfriend who lives in another state. He told me previously that even if she moved here, he would not leave me for her. This week, he told me he is still in love with her but does not know how she feels. He is going to see her as she and her boyfriend broke up a few months ago.

He plans on staying with her and refuses to promise that he will honor the commitment he's made to me. A commitment which HE asked for in the first place. They have not been together for over four years but I think the only reason they really split up was that he moved too far away. I'm really hurt and afraid... please give me some ideas on how I should handle this situation? He's not gone yet, but said he intends to within the next couple weeks. — Tina

Tina, of course you're hurt and afraid. Who wouldn't be? You can see what's happening and it's not what you planned for the two of you because you believe they are going to get back together. Frankly, I think they will also, at least for a while.

He says he's still in love with her and she is very needy right now. Getting angry at him isn't going to do anything constructive for the relationship you'd like to have with him. As long as he says he's in love with her, there isn't room for you in this relationship. There is absolutely nothing you can do to change this. Prepare yourself for the pain to get worse.

Sometimes these second time relationships work out, sometimes whatever caused them to end the first time splits them up again. If he gets back with her, please make every effort to get on with your life as quickly as possible. Even if they do reconcile it may last just long enough for them to make a permanent and final split.

Regardless of what may happen, don't put your life on hold waiting for him to return. Whatever is meant to be will happen in the appropriate time. — Queenie

♥

Queenie, here is a love triangle update. I did go to the concert with this girl I've been tore down over. We had dinner and a few drinks before the show and the conversation and laughter was great. The concert was also good. We left the venue and went out to shoot some pool and drink a few beers.

Well, here's where it all started. Several beers into the evening and her true feelings started to appear. We began talking about our past. When we dated and some of the good times we had. Then the conversation shifted towards her feelings about her old ex-lover and how she hasn't been able to find anyone that makes her feel the way she did with him. Tough thing to hear, but it was honest. She cried buckets of tears throughout the whole evening. I felt bad for her because it is obvious that she still has a lot of love for this guy and he just seems to string her along. I believe she may still have some feelings for me tucked away somewhere by the way she kept bringing up things from our past. Yes, they were good times, but the unresolved feelings for her ex ruined all of that.

She was too far gone to drive home so she stayed at my place. I told her what she needed was a hug from a good friend. She embraced me, cried on my shoulder and told me how confused she is. We didn't have sex but we slept together and in the morning I took her back to her car.

I told her I would be her friend and would always be there for her when she needed a shoulder. However, this was the last time I was going to call her or ask her out to do anything. I said if she truly wants to be friends I needed to see some initiative from her. She nodded and left. She has called a few times since then just to talk and that has been good.

O.K. you have heard this twisted tale. What do you think about it and what advice do you have for me. I would still like things to work out for us, but I know better than to get between her and this other guy. That's a no win situation.
— Steve

Steve, you're smart to leave her alone. Until she gets him completely out of her system, you'd never know if she was kissing you or him.

I would suggest that you don't sit around waiting for her to get over him since there are plenty of great unattached ladies who would love to meet a nice guy like you. — Queenie

♥

Hi Queenie, my girlfriend and I have been dating for three years. Although we have gone through some difficult periods, our relationship is one that we would both like to see lead to marriage. We love each other very much, and are each others best friends. Until I did something stupid!

Three months ago, I started speaking with a long time friend about marriage. She and I dated many years ago and have remained friends (only friends) ever since. My girlfriend knew of our friendship and to her credit did not disapprove of my friendship with my long time friend. Usually I would call her or she would call me about 4 to 5 times a year. The last 6-8 months my girlfriend and I have been discussing marriage. We are both in our mid-thirties, never married, and again the best of friends.

Well, two months ago I flew to my friends' town and spent the weekend with her. I slept on the sofa and enjoyed the weekend talking about "our" future. A month later she wrote me a letter in which she mentioned how much she had enjoyed my visit and how much she looked forward to establishing a life long relationship with me.

My girlfriend read the letter. She found it in the garbage can in my house. I hurt her so much. She called my family, her family and read the letter to them all. She said she wanted other people to tell her that what she read in the letter was not what was really in the letter. Of course everyone agreed that she was in fact interpreting the letter correctly. I am so ashamed.

This happened about six weeks ago. Although we have spoken twice since then, she is very hurt and refuses to discuss reconciliation with me. I have thought long and hard about why I did what I did. I was insecure about loosing someone that meant so much to me. I was afraid that she would leave me the way my mother left me when I was a baby (my parents are not my biological parents, I am adopted). I think I have always been afraid to be abandoned by the people who care most about me. The more intense my feelings became, the more afraid I felt about being abandoned.

She never gave me a reason to believe that she would leave me. She has been my most loyal and faithful friend and lover. I don't think this was driven by anything she did or did not do during the three years of our relationship. I was not looking for sex or even companionship from my female friend. I think what I wanted out of that "relationship" a sense of security. I guess I felt like even if my girlfriend abandoned me, someone would still love me (even if she does live 2,000 miles away).

I feel that my insecurity driven fantasy and my reality have met and now I have nothing. I told my long time friend what happened. She was devastated. She felt that I used her. I feel so ashamed and guilty that I do not want to continue my friendship with her. I do not know how to apologize for doing something so horrible to someone whom I have cared for, for such a long time. I also need to find a way that I can explain to my girlfriend why I did what I did.

I recognized that I have lost all of her trust. I need to find a way to work this out. I know I want to spend the rest of my life with her. I miss my best friend. I can't sleep. I've lost my appetite.

I just miss her in my life. What can I do? I will never quit trying to get her back. I feel as if I am my own worst enemy. How can I ask her to give me the opportunity to earn her trust again? How can I get my best friend back? Thanks for the help. I really need it. — Rob

Rob, I first have to ask what your girlfriend was doing searching through your garbage. Was she trying to find something to be angry about? And was it necessary that she broadcast this problem to all of her and your family members? You may love her, but she needs to gain some maturity.

The longer people wait before marriage, the more they seem to shy away from commitment, in whatever way they can. In visiting your other friend, and alluding to commitment (spell that marriage) by talking about "your" future, you were setting yourself up for exactly what happened. It was your protection against commitment.

If your girlfriend loves you deeply, she will forgive what you have done. But don't expect her to forgive you without making you suffer for your foolishness. And don't expect her to return to you without you working like crazy to get her back.

It may be more difficult to get your friend to think kindly about you, particularly if she is in love with you and wants more than friendship. No doubt this has been an important friendship for you but it is now time for you to make a choice. After what you've done, it's doubtful that your girlfriend will be agreeable to your continuing or attempting to continue a friendship with this other lady.

Good luck. You're going to need it. — Queenie

♥

Queenie, three months ago, I met a guy in an Internet chat room. We met in person, and we very quickly fell in love. He is so sweet and wonderful. The problem is, before me, he had been engaged to this girl who had written him an Any Soldier letter.

From what little he has told me, and from what his family and friends told me, this girl was insanely jealous and possessive, and when he tried to break up with her, she tried to say she was pregnant and that she lost the baby in a car accident, and he, not believing her, broke up with her, and she married someone else.

But I can see he is hurting bad over the fact that she lied to him about something like that. He had checked the hospitals, and they had never heard of her and later, some of her family denied knowledge of any accident and hospitalization, so its not like he did anything wrong, but as a result he's afraid to let me get too close, he's holding back on his feelings. He is a strong silent type, and the info I got came from his mother.

How can I convince him that I'm not like his ex? — Jamie

Jamie, it takes time to gain a person's trust. You cannot instantly undo the damage that has been done by someone else. The relationship you describe probably started off wonderfully just as yours has. Time alone will prove to him that you are not the same type of person as she was, and that you wouldn't — couldn't — possibly do the same thing to him. Stop trying to get too serious too fast. If it's true love, it will last. — Queenie

♥

Hi Queenie, I met a girl and we started out just having a non-committal fun thing that grew into a fun and loving relationship. We shared many great moments with each other and I really began to fall for her. Things were going along great until I started to see the writing on the wall. We were spending lots of time together. She started to become more distant and eventually spent some time with an old flame that lives out of town.

I know she and this guy are friends, but I also know more went down that week than just friendship. When she came back we had a long talk and I got the lets just be friends cliché.

As I have looked back on this I know that she was starting to feel congested and that I may have pushed things a little harder than she wanted. I also feel that I may have just been a rebound for her and her old flame, and that's a hard pill to swallow.

I know that she has seen him here recently, but I don't understand why one would try to keep a relationship going at such a distance and especially with a guy who is a known dog! I also know that old flames sometimes die hard.

I think about her often and though I have dated other people they just don't seem to compare to her. I have given her distance and called her just a few times in the last two months, but she never calls me. I invited her to a concert at the end of the month and she said she would go.

Have I taken the right approach here? How should I handle the up-coming concert? What about the old flame?? Where do I fit in all of this?? — Ryan

Ryan, right now, it would appear that you're part of a triangle. As long as she has such strong feelings for this old flame, you're going to come in second best. Not a good place to be. The best thing to do? Step away and let her get her emotions sorted out. You're ready to give her all your love. Shouldn't you receive all of hers in exchange? What happens to you if the two of them get back together, which is a possibility at this point.

The upcoming concert poses a small problem. Is she going with you because she can't get the other guy to take her? Is she going with you because she really likes you? Is she going with you because she can't get a ticket for herself? Whatever the reason, you're holding your breath that things will work out to your favor and she'll suddenly realize what a great guy you are. Might happen. Or she might sit through the whole concert wishing the other guy was sitting beside her.

Why not talk with her and tell her that you care about her too much for just a casual friendship and that you'd just as soon not date her until she can say the same. If you feel badly about committing to the concert, either give her the concert ticket so she can go on her own or give her both of them and see if she asks you to go with her. — Queenie

♥

Hello Queenie, I have been dating this guy for about 2 months. We have become pretty serious, I stay at his house every night and we are together all the time. The problem is before we started dating he was in a relationship with someone for 2 years. This was his first true love. I find him sometimes almost calling me by her name. They have purchased a few things together and this gives him reason to talk to her and visit her house. I have asked him several times if he is over her and he says he is.

I don't think there is any reason for him to keep the cell phone (which is in her name only) or keep her name on the fishing boat if there is no chance of them getting back together. They have been apart for about five months. Can you tell me if you think I may be a rebound relationship or if I should give him more time to prove to me that it is me he wanted to be with? — Carrie

Carrie, he says he is over her but his actions suggest he isn't. I suspect that she broke up with him and that he is hoping she'll take him back. You know the answers more than anyone since you know why they split up and whether or not she is now involved with someone else.

You could be in a rebound relationship. That doesn't mean you have to end it. What it does mean is you have to stay alert to the possibility of them reconciling and be prepared to get on with your life should that happen. Good luck. — Queenie

♥

Help, Queen of Hearts! I am in a three year relationship and I still talk to and see my ex boyfriend. I can't see myself with my ex, he is not my type, but I enjoy being with him. My boyfriend hates that I still talk to him but for some reason I am still attracted to him. I won't have sex with him.

I need to know what is going on, I don't feel completely happy with my boyfriend but we have fun together and are very compatible. But when I hang out with my ex it's different. I still get the butterflies and I don't like that it happens.

I enjoy talking to my ex and I don't think he would want a relationship, even if I wanted one. He dates so much and we are really open with each other.

Have I fallen out of love with my boyfriend or do these feelings happen to all. Should I give up on us or break all ties with my ex, I don't think I could, I would be really upset if I had to. Help, I can't sleep, I have been feeling this way for a year and keep brushing the feelings of my ex away. — Kimberly

Kimberly, I'm guessing that you aren't over your ex quite yet. And guessing that your current boyfriend knows you still have feelings for your exm despite what you say. He knows you are still attracted to your ex, and he feels threatened. Wouldn't you if the situation was reversed and it was him in a like relationship with his ex?

Are you and your current boyfriend in a "committed" relationship? Do you and your ex include your current boyfriend in all of your activities? In other words, when you get together, do the three of you go out as buddies and friends or do just the two of you get together with the opportunity to rehash old times and perhaps "slip" into the old relationship once in a while?

A year is a long time to be losing sleep over a past love. If you can't put your feelings for him into a "best friends" mode, perhaps you need to take some time away from your current relationship to rethink what you want and need from the men in your life. — Queenie

♥

Queenie, I wrote to you a short while back about a woman I met at work and how I grew to have incredible feelings for her in less than six weeks. Well, I took your advice about listening and being gentle with my heart...it worked. I am growing to love her more and more each day. We spend a lot time together and it seems only natural that we do so.

She too, has said many wonderful things and my heart grows fondly weak at the thought of her. Perhaps it is the romantic ideal that one might meet their soul mate and know instantly that they want to marry this person.

The Situation: She and I went to work together on the bus, having spent one of the most incredible evenings ever together. When we got on her face went white as a ghost as she turned to me. It turns out her "ex" was right there.

She tells me that she wanted out of that relationship for a very long time — yet I found out later that she cried when she got to work. She felt she was mean not to speak with him. That very evening he called and told her all kinds of terrible things and when I arrived she cried again.

We spent the evening together last night again and this morning she wanted to take separate buses for fear he might be on one. I guess in a way this hurt because I would have hoped that the "us" was of more significance than the "he". I'm a little confused but I do love her dearly and am willing to do what it takes to understand. Perhaps the problem is that I find I'm not sure what that is really. I have tried to be not only myself but a listening and caring person for her as well. — Steve

Steve, you and she had just experienced an incredible emotional high when she was confronted with the presence of a man who took her to emotional lows. Of course she would have cried! She may have for a few irrational minutes thought that her life was going to revert back to the way it was with him. She may have been afraid that all the good feelings were only to lull her into a false sense of security.

You are jealous of this man which is why you don't want her to show any emotion about him. You're not unusual in this regard. But he is history and it will take time until eventually he and his memory will be mere shadows on the wall. – Queenie

Rebound Relationships

Rebound Relationships

"Stupid me thought that he would come around and that he just needed a couple of months to fully get over his past relationship."

Very rarely do relationships end because both people agree it is time to go in separate directions. What usually happens is that one person decides to move on, and the other person is stunned, devastated, and angry. The person leaving a relationship has a new direction they're going whether it is into the arms of a new love or just putting distance from a relationship that no longer has meaning for them. They're ready to accept the relationship is over.

It's much different for the person being left. They feel abandoned. They hurt. Their life has a big hole in it in which the other person used to reside. They feel incomplete and unloved. They buy into the song lyric "You're nobody 'til somebody loves you" and they rush into a new relationship without taking a break. The first person they meet who whispers tender words and holds them close becomes their new soul mate. Unfortunately, more times than not, it is not new love into which they have fallen but rebound love, and rebound relationships generally don't last very long. A sad fact of rebound love is that it will begin quickly, be very intense, and end almost as quickly.

When your heart has been broken it is too easy to think tender kisses and soft reassurances are more than what they are meant to be. When you are aching for someone to show kindness and validate your worth it is very difficult to step out of the path of rebound love but if you don't take time to move past the pain of your prior relationship rebound love can be disastrous. You'll be exchanging an old heartache for a new one, and hurting someone else in the process. Take your time no matter how difficult it seems. Slow down. Stop. Observe. There are much worse things than being single.

♥

Hi Queenie, I am in love with someone I dated. We had been sort of friends at first. We stared as rebounds for each other, nothing was to come of it but a mouth later we made it something. We stop going out after we had sex and she went to a revival and decided that we could not keep doing what we were doing. But this is not the end. Three weeks later we became friends with benefits then started dating once more. Then out of the blue she calls it off once more. Leaving me standing with my heart in my hands.

One thing she was my first she had one other person once but he had not done it right if you know what I mean. Now I am heart sick and lonely. I have tried going out with other people but I can only think of her. We talk every so often but she slips away from me. We became best friends and I miss that we help each other find ourselves. I just need some out side advice. — Jeremy

Jeremy, when you get into a rebound relationship, there's a lot of chance that whenever the pain from the other relationship breakup is gone, the rebound relationship will come to an end. It sounds as though she's ready to move on and she's been trying to get out of this relationship she began with you when she needed someone's shoulder to cry on.

You can't force someone to love you. Walk away from this relationship and try to get yourself a little more emotionally repaired before you start any more serious dating or you're going to have the same thing happen again and again. — Queenie

♥

Queenie, I have been friends with this girl for six years now. She and I have always dated other people and given advice for each other's relationships. The other night we went out to dinner and something happened. We made no physical contact, but we made some kind of connection. We both felt it. Just staring at each other with puppy dog eyes. Its crazy! She has now completely invaded my thoughts. We talked about it a couple of days later, and we were both almost speechless.

She just got out of a relationship a couple of months ago. She is confused and says that she doesn't want the complications of a relationship right now, but I can tell she still feels the same way I do. Help? Should I pursue it? Should I just give her time? This has LOTS of potential. A Leo and an Aries no less! How should I play it? — Sammie

Sammie, this just might be rebound and I would hate to see both of you ruin a beautiful friendship. Of course, it just might make a beautiful friendship even more beautiful. Play it slow....... very slow...... give her all the time she needs. — Queenie

♥

Hi Queen of Hearts, my friend of six years recently told me that she has feelings for me. She recently broke up with her boyfriend of over a year, and I have had very few long lasting relationships myself... which is why I need help.

I do like this woman very much, but she says she needs time to get over the last guy. That seems reasonable, but she broke up with this guy at least a dozen times before. Before I go and invest my feelings in this, how can I find out if this past relationship is really over? Talking to her is out of the question...she said that she doesn't want to talk. That makes me sort of uncomfortable, because I can't tell her how I really feel. How should I address this situation? Thanks for your help! — Ken

Ken, since she has a history of breaking up with this guy, I'd suggest that you give her lots of time and space to get over him before you think about starting a relationship.

You say talking is out of the question.... how can any relationship develop without communication? She's not ready for you, and unless you're ready for heartache, you're not ready for her. Walk away, date others, and give her time to either get over him or go back to him once again. Good luck. — Queenie

♥

Hi Queenie, I have been dating a guy for the past five months, starting two weeks after him and his girlfriend for two years broke up. I should have known that he would have major 'baggage' but I didn't expect anything at first except someone to casually go on some dates with. The problem is that I really started to like him and our relationship became sexual. We were talking almost every day and seeing each other about 3 times a week. We get along perfectly and he is one of the nicest guys that I have ever met and I think that he is perfect for me. He made it clear that he didn't want me to date anyone else. He also made it clear that he really likes me but that he isn't ready to jump into anything really serious (although that is what I want).

Stupid me thought that he would come around and that he just needed a couple of months to fully get over his past relationship. It got to the point, though, that I started not to feel very good about myself because I was not getting everything from him that I needed...he did not include me in things that he was doing (like he would a 'girlfriend') and was not wanting to spend as much time with me as I wanted to spend with him.

It got to the point where I realized that I needed to end things completely with him. I told him that this was not what I wanted and that I thought that it would be best for me not to see or talk to him at all and told him not to call me. He was upset about it.

It has been almost a week and a half and it has been killing me not to talk to him. I can't help but think, though, that if I give him time to get over his past relationship by himself, he will eventually be ready for a serious relationship...and that things might be different a couple of months down the road. Did I do the right thing and am I being realistic here? Thanks! — Robyn

Robyn, you have a good view of this relationship and your actions are appropriate for the circumstances. He wanted the convenience of an exclusive sexual partner but he wanted to assume none of the responsibilities of a committed relationship. Too many people unhappily settle for relationships that are this one-sided.

If he really cares for you, he will be back. Perhaps you'll still want to become more involved with him, perhaps by that time you'll have found someone more suitable. Good luck. – Queenie

♥

Dear Queen of Hearts, about four months ago, my girlfriend and I broke up. I will be the first to admit that our relationship was rocky. When we first met, I had come out of a long term relationship which resulted in a beautiful daughter and I had not quite gotten over that relationship when this new one started. I often felt torn between this new relationship and whether I should work the previous relationship out for the sake of my daughter. Needless to say, this caused problems for my girlfriend and I.

After a while, I became comfortable with my situation and decided that I wanted to pursue a relationship with the woman I was dating. However, she had decided that she had enough and ended the relationship. To this day, I find myself missing her very much.

I know that I hurt her deeply, however, I feel that we met each other at the wrong time and that if we had met, or were together at this time in my life things would be much different.

I don't know if I am being selfish, if I should try to talk her into working things out, or if I should leave her alone. In all honesty, she means the world to me. She did then and she does now. I was wondering if you have any advice to give in this matter. I really do not know what to do. Thanks. — David

David, how long has it been since you have been out of your other relationship? Has it been only a week or two or several months? Have you bounced back and forth between this lady and your previous relationship enough times that she would have no reason to believe that this is just another bounce back to her?

If you do convince her to come back to you, what long range plans do you have for the relationship? Are you serious or *serious*? If you want her in your life forever, then call her and ask her to marry you. If she feels about you the way you do about her that should at least get her attention.

If you just want her back because she's great to have around and you aren't certain about the future, casual contact once in a while to see how she's doing and a "gee I miss you" card occasionally will let her know you're still interested. If you sense that she still is interested, ask her out but don't try to push the relationship into high gear too soon.

If she is unable or unwilling to trust you because of the earlier problems, you will have to write this off to experience and move on. – Queenie

Threesomes

Threesomes

"I have two guys in my life, one who treats me bad, and one who treats me good. This sounds like a no-brainer but I'm in love with the one who treats me bad."

Is it possible to be in love with two people at the same time? Yes, it is. Is it fair to the two people who are sharing the same lover, with or without knowing they are sharing? No, it is not.

Intimate love relationships cannot be their best when the intimacies are being shared with someone else. The person who is in love with two people cannot possibly split that love equally and even if they could and did it would mean that each person would be getting half of the love/caring/sharing due them while their lover was getting twice as much.

Some people might feel that "half a pie is better than none" but in love relationships, it should be "whole pie or nothing".

♥

Queenie, my boyfriend and I have been dating for a year now. We are both 30 years old. We have a good relationship for the most part. I am, however, bothered by something. I am bi-curious. We enjoy watching porn together and I get really excited when there is a lesbian scene.

My boyfriend has discovered this and has no problem with me being interested in women. We talk about fantasies together, mine is being with a woman in front of him. That is his, too.

Today, he told me he has been thinking a lot about the fantasy that we both share and wants to act on it. He says that he has never been with two women. He wants to be respectful of me, and will only go as far as I feel comfortable with. I would like to try this, but am skeptical about ruining our relationship.

This guy is talking about marriage and family already with me. I would like to fulfill his desire before he does get married and settles down. I asked him how he thought this would affect us.

He said that our relationship is very strong and will not be affected by this. I love this guy and don't want to lose him. Help!! — Julie

Julie, you want to "fulfill his desire before he does get married and settles down"?!? I can almost guarantee that if you have a threesome the marriage isn't going to happen. I can also almost guarantee that there are very few men who wouldn't have said the same "strong relationship" line to their girlfriends (or wives) if they had the possibility of adding another female into their bed.

Here's what can happen: he decides the other woman is more his type and breaks up with you; you decide the other woman is more your type and break up with him; he wants to keep having threesomes and one is all you need to experience; you both join a swingers club and continue with sexual experimentation.

Fantasies can make sex that much more exciting. Making fantasies a reality can be a surefire relationship breaker. Proceed at your own risk! — Queenie

♥

Hello, Queenie, I've slept with my girl friend's best mate and ever since this happened I've been wanting to see her but she won't answer my calls she said she feels the same way about me, but she is now pregnant with her boyfriend. This is putting problems on my own relationship with my girl friend because I can't get her out of my head. The thing is I really want to see her again. What do I do? — Kez

Kez, tell your girlfriend that you aren't ready to be faithful to her. At least do her this favor so she can find herself a guy who isn't trying to get in bed with her friend. Past that point, you're on your own. — Queenie

♥

Hi Queenie, I have a boyfriend and a lover. I don't know how I feel about either of them. But I have a problem; my lover is one of the policemen in my town. We like each other a lot but so do my boyfriend and I. What should I do? — Marcie

Marcie, you obviously don't really love either one of them or you wouldn't be seeing both of them. This will probably work itself out when one or the other or both dump you for someone they can trust. — Queenie

♥

Dear Queenie, I found out my boyfriend has been going out with another woman for the last 5 years, and we have been going out for over 18 years. He had been lying for the past 5 years. I was blind not to suspect but I trusted him. We had some ill feeling and did not discuss them.

We have not stopped seeing each other and he does not want to end with me. He says to give him time for he cannot make up his mind. But, I am suffering and hurting. We have fights every week. He sees and spends one night with the woman. Please tell me how to end with him. When I tell him that I will start seeing other men, he will come around in 'courting' mood. I am very confused. — Lea

Lea, he has had five years to make up his mind. For most women that would have been about four years and eleven months longer than they would have put up with his cheating. I can't give you the strength to end it; you have to find that within yourself. He has two women. Is any man this good? — Queenie

♥

Queenie, will he get back to me? I had been in touch with a classmate through Internet. He told me he lives with a girlfriend and that he was having

problems with her. We started a nice friendship that turn out to be hot. I fell in love with him and he said he had strong feelings about me and that he was breaking with his girlfriend pretty soon. We e-mailed and talked over the phone for a period of 2 months. He came to visit me after he spent a week with his girlfriend. He told me that she had bought him a ticket and that he had promised her to go to this wedding long time ago, on the beginning of the third month.

He stayed at my apartment for 1 week. The first day was a dream. Then the second day his girlfriend called and he was in bad mood for 3 days. When he left said he will call me. He called me and was brief. He said that he arrived on time and had no problem and that we will keep in touch.

While he stayed at my apartment I made a big mistake of snooping into his book. I read what he wrote. When I called him he was furious about my attitude and told me that I violated his privacy and that he won't ever forgive me. I feel so guilty and in pain? Would you shed some light on this? Thanks — Kari

Kari, he wasn't looking for another girlfriend when he met you, he was looking for someone to have some intimate fun with without commitment. He's not ready to break up with his live-in girlfriend so forget about love with him. Next time, if you meet a guy who's living with someone, make sure she's his mother. — Queenie

♥

Dear Queenie, I have two guys in my life, one who treats me bad, and one who treats me good. This sounds like a no-brainer but I'm in love with the one who treats me bad. My friends and family can't stand him.

When we're together things are good. We laugh a lot, talk a lot, and just basically have a good time. The only problem is he is terrified of commitment. Every time I bring it up he goes running, but always returns. When we are around other people is when he is a jerk. That's not the side of him I want people to see. They never see the good side.

Now the other guy is new. I just recently meet him. He's nice and everything but I can't get over the other guy. I guess my question is should I wait for the first guy to come around or move on with the new guy? If the answer is move on, then how do I do that? Why can't I get over this guy? Should I listen to everyone else? — Micki

Micki, it's easy for people to give advice (and my advice also falls into this category) because they don't have to live with the outcome. So, you can listen to everyone but you should do what you think is best for yourself.

Commitment does not improve someone's personality or make them less of a jerk. As a matter of fact, consider that right now he's on his best behavior because he has you to lose if you decide you don't want to date someone who treats you badly.

However, should you marry him, he has absolutely no incentive to act any better, and he probably would act much worse.

It's your life. How do you want to spend it? With someone who treats you, your family and your friends, badly or someone who is nice? Now it's a no-brainer. — Queenie

♥

Hi Queenie, I am in a relationship and have been for about 5 years and now I want out and do not know how to leave this man because I know in my heart that he loves me and that if I leave I will break his heart and I feel sorry for him and I know in my heart that is wrong.

Well the story gets worse, see I have this friend and she has a husband and a boyfriend and she treats both very badly. Well she wants one for sex and the other for money and the boyfriend and I have become very close and I have fallen in love with him and want too be with him so now I am stuck in a very hard place. She does not love him and he stays with her because I take she is good in bed.

I do not know why he really stays with her she treats him like dirt...I do not like what too do anymore. I know that I could make this man happy only if she would let go and if I knew how too let go of my relationship I am in. but I the same breath I do not want too lose my long relationship with my friend over this man. So now can you see where I am with this...please tell me or guide me to the answer. — Cathi

Cathi, you are involved but don't want to leave him because you'll break his heart but you have fallen in love with another man who is involved with a married friend of yours but she won't let him go and you don't want to lose your friendship with her because of him.

1) Decide who you want to be with. If it's the guy you've been with for the past 5 years, then forget about this other guy. If it's the other guy then leave the guy you've been dating for the past 5 years. His heart will heal. You've already broken it so forget about causing him pain when you leave.

2) The other guy could leave your married friend if he wanted to — she doesn't have him chained in her basement. What he's getting is uncommitted sex. That means he doesn't have to worry about her wanting a permanent relationship or any of the responsibility that would bring. You, on the other hand, would demand more from him. If all he's looking for is sex, she's the better choice because there's less hassle. — Queenie

♥

Dear Queen, I've had a best friend for over five years. During this time, we've had emotional and sexual relations, but we've never dated. We've never dated because we were either seeing other people or the timing just wasn't right. The last time I asked her to date, she said she was still dealing with her last relationship and she wasn't in the right mind frame. Later, I fell in love with another woman and my best friend backed off with her friendship. 1 1/2 years later, my best friend and I had an open-hearted talk and concluded we were still in love with each other...even though we were dating other people.

Since then, we have had sex, sent each other love notes, and have told each other how we plan to grow old together, etc. (We live in separate States, so please add long distance into this situation). I couldn't stand lying to my current girlfriend about my best friend, so I was planning to leave and move closer to my best friend.

When I approached my best friend about my intentions via email, she has completely ignored me and seems to be backing off more and more. She simply won't talk this out with me.

I've tried calling but realized that I can't make her talk to me. I think all of this is too much for her to handle but I'm not sure, since she won't even talk to me. I don't think she has told her current girlfriend about us and now I'm not really even sure where her heart is (even though I'm afraid to admit I may know the answer).

My heart is breaking and I feel so confused. Should I call her? If so, what's an appropriate waiting time? Should I wait for her to call me when she's ready? Should I just give up and move on? I just feel like I was a perfect partner as long as I was chase able. As soon as I began to speak seriously, my best friend went into hiding. I'm really trying to do the right thing but it looks as if I'm in it alone. Thanks for your help. — Lynn

Lynn, it sounds as though you and your best friend have been cheating on each of your current girlfriends and now that you want to make this relationship more legitimate, she's not ready.

This isn't any different than any other messy triangle (or perhaps this would be considered a quadrangle since there were four people involved at one point) that doesn't work out the way at least one of the players wishes it would.

I don't have any suggestions other than you need to get over her because apparently she's not ready to leave her current girlfriend to make a solid relationship with you.

Maybe, if you leave her alone and stop pushing for a committed relationship, and stay out of her life, she will realize how much she misses you and will end her current relationship and invite you back into her life. Maybe. And maybe not. Good luck. — Queenie

♥

Queenie, is it o.k. to love two girls at the same time?? I'm confused!! I love my girlfriend but I also have strong feelings for another girl could it be LOVE?? — Enrico

Enrico, it's okay with me if it's okay with them. As far as whether it's love, well... it might be love as you know it but it isn't the 'two people who are committed to only each other as soul mates' kind of love that leads to long term commitment. — Queenie

♥

Hello Queenie, about a month ago, this guy that I was friends with and I starting sleeping together. We both decided from the very beginning that it would never go beyond friends. Well, I have fallen for him. I haven't told him this for fear of jeopardizing our friendship. I introduced him to my friend.

Since then, she and him have been talking alot. She knows how I feel about him and how I feel about him and her. I do not like the fact that they talk. But then again I have no right to be jealous because he and I are not together.

The other night he called me and asked me if she would go out with him and if there was anything that I could tell him about her. Little did I know, she was there listening to everything I said.

Then he lied to me telling me he was alone. But finally they came clean. I told them both that I was mad, and all they said was that it was a joke and they were trying to make me mad.

She said she just wanted to see what I would say. Should I just forget anything ever happened, and let them continue to be like they are.

She knows I don't like it, she swears nothing is going to happening between the two of them, but I don't know now if I can trust her. Also, should I continue this sexual relationship I have with him? — Gina

Gina, I personally think you should stop having sex with him until the time you and he are in real, true love. Right now, you're having sex for all the wrong reasons and without even having the title of his 'girlfriend.'

If he wants to date your girlfriend and hang out with her then he isn't too 'in love' with you. If she is busy hanging with him and playing stupid jokes with your mind, then she isn't too much of a friend of yours.

If you feel you can't trust her, maybe you should at least trust your feelings. Their little joke was mean and dumb. Maybe they were trying to send you a message.

Whenever you start having sex with someone it should already have gone beyond being 'friends.' If you don't both love each other, what good is 'making love'? That's what human beings call the physical act that you and your boyfriend have been doing. And it's a beautiful thing when both people are in love (with each other).

Something you might want to understand about some guys is that they don't have to be in love to have sex. They could have sex with a toaster oven and it would be great sex to them. In other words, if it is available, and sex is an option, they'll do it. And having sex doesn't make them fall in love with whoever (or whatever) they're having sex with.

Sex, for most girls, is a different matter. They see it as a special sharing between them and a guy. They believe that having sex with a guy will lead to more serious things such as commitment and marriage some day. Most times it doesn't. — Queenie

♥

Dear Queenie, I am a 21 year old woman and I am in love with someone who is engaged to someone else. I've known him for a very long time. He still

comes and see's me. He calls me she knows nothing about it. He tells her he through my number away over a year ago.

To this day he's still my best friend we talk almost every day. Still he says he loves her, and is going to grow old with her. The last time we were together he kissed me. I don't mean just innocent pecks we kissed like animals. I had my hands all over him. He hesitated so we stopped.

I want him heart and soul. Just not if he loves her. After that he went and lay done on the ground and I went and lay next to him. If he's really my best friend how can he hold me like that knowing how much I long to be in his arms. He say's he loves me like a sister how many men lust their sisters? — Michelle

Michelle, you're not his sister so he isn't lusting his sister. He is lusting after a girl who has very little respect for herself if she would settle for being third in this relationship that is meant for two.

He tells you he loves this girl. He tells you he's going to grow old with her. How much more does he have to say for you to understand that he doesn't love you the way he loves her? Not that, even with the scope of the love he says he has for her, he still cheats on her. But you make it easy for him to cheat. You're willing to settle for whatever he is willing to give.

If you believe that he loves you more than he loves her here's how to make him realize it too: stop seeing him. Tell him it's over, you don't want to hear from him, see him or have any contact whatsoever. Tell him that as long as he is engaged, he is out of bounds, off limits. Then stick to it.

If he finds that he just can't stand not seeing you and calls begging to see you, don't give in. If he breaks up with his fiancee, then you can see him again. Of course, you may then not be too trusting, knowing that when he was telling her he loved her, he was making out 'like an animal' with you.

If he doesn't break off with her, then you know he cares less than you do, and what future is there in it for you? Lying next to each other on the ground is not the same as sharing the same household as a married couple. It's much easier, and can be done with virtually anyone who's willing. — Queenie

♥

Queenie, two weeks ago I allowed a girl to join my lover and myself on a weekend trip. The idea was to have a threesome as a gift from me to my lover. She and I discussed what would be o.k. with me and what would not be.... shortly into it she broke our agreement.

Later in the trip I got emotional and jealous with my lover and he was quite put off by this, so much so he seems to have all but ended our affair. There is a large age difference between us, myself being quite a bit younger than he, and therefore there are limitations on our future beyond a couple of years. I have been realistic about that from the start. My problem is he seems to be pursuing her now, and its driving me nuts! We all work together, which makes it harder. I have spoken to her and she says she is not interested in him in the way I am, and yet she flaunts the attention he gives her in my face.

I am currently keeping to the old saying of keeping your enemy closer than your friend, but I just want her out of the way! I was extremely happy prior to this and want things to return to the way they were before. Any suggestions on getting rid of her? — Nichole

Nichole, things cannot return to the way they were, your threesome took care of that. Since you didn't expect this relationship to last very long, consider it over and move on. As a matter of fact, since seeing him chasing her is bothering you, I'd suggest you move on in your job, also. And, the next time you want to give a lover a gift, make sure it's something inanimate, like a book. — Queenie

♥

Dear Queenie, I have met a wonderful guy he is everything I want in a man (except for looks) which I can ignore because his inner beauty blinds me. His cousin is my sister's boyfriend and he goes to my church, so he would come around periodically.

I knew he was interested in me but I also knew he had a live in girlfriend. At first he would join in with the family for different outing, then it started turning in to just me and him going out. However, I told him I was not interested, because of his situation, but he was very persistent.

He and his girlfriend decided that maybe she should move out and both should start seeing other people. He has been in a relationship with her for 5 years. Well to sum it up my feeling for him has grown and he also cares about me a great deal (and yes we have been intimate).

He tells me he still has very strong feeling for her, and how she was with someone before and it almost destroyed him. He also tells me how wonderful she is and they had set a date to be married but they both backed out. She still comes over periodically and they still see each other. I also know she thinks this is her punishment for what she did to him and is willing to wait. However, he wants to see me every chance he gets and is willing to drive quite a way to do so, or when I'm in his town he makes it a point to see me.

I don't want to be in the middle, nor do I want to be hurt if he decides he wants to work things out with her. I care about him a lot, and it is very hard to let go. Help!!! — Angie

♥

Angie, their relationship probably wouldn't have lasted even if you had not been in the picture. That being said, you need to be assured that he won't bounce back to her periodically until he's sure he's made the right decision with you.

I'd suggest you back away until he and she are definitely over and done and he knows it as well as she. Good luck. — Queenie

♥

168

Dear Queenie, I am currently re-involved with the man that cheated on me over a year ago. Regardless of the fact that he cheated I still loved him very much. He and I share a special, spiritual type of connection. He contacted me a few times and asked me to marry him and each time I told him that things weren't right with us if he was looking somewhere else. I later found out, only two weeks after his last plea with me to marry him, that he was engaged to the girl he cheated on me with. I was so hurt and angry that I lost all desire to continue in school and work. I pulled myself together enough to get back in to my work and maintain an outward appearance of being fine.

Then I saw him again and he had changed so much. He told me how much he loved me still and how he didn't want to marry this girl, but he had proposed because he felt I was gone forever. Well, we have since decided that we are going to try again. The problem...the other girl. He still lives with her, though the relationship is over. He says that he just can't seem to leave her. He has an apartment of his own, and he has told her that he doesn't love her. He is in counseling to try to understand why he is an habitual liar and can't seem to get away from her.

He says it has to do with his father who was very abusive. She reminds him of his dad and he struggles for her approval so he can fill the void that his father left. She still treats him awfully, and he says all the time that he desperately wants out and to be with me. I have tried to be patient and loving and understanding, but I have reached my limit. I still love him, and when I attended his counseling session with him his counselor said that we could be very happy together if he could get over this.

Have you ever heard of a situation like this before, and if so, how do I help him through this and build our relationship from there? — Karen

Karen, there aren't any new stories, just new players. It's a dead end for you at this point. You can't control him and what he does, but you can control your life. How do you want to spend it? Waiting? Or living? Your choice. — Queenie

♥

Dear Queenie, I have been in this relationship for 11+ years off and on. We have been friends and have supported one another through everything. He recently told me he met this cyber queen girl and is getting married. He continues to call me at all hours of the night. I don't reject his phone calls, but this past weekend, I went to visit him. The chemistry between us was so strong it took everything I had to not fall for him again. Now I'm sad and lonely, hoping that there might be a chance? We love each other, but can't seem to stay committed to each other for longer than a few months? I miss him desperately, What should I do? — Tracee

Tracee, what do you want to do? Do you like being his girlfriend instead of his wife? If so, keep on in this relationship. If not, wish him well with his marriage and say goodbye. If he loves you and you love him enough to commit forever — without anyone else involved — then go for it. It's your choice. — Queenie

♥

Queenie, help! My boyfriend is a great guy but he's attracted to his best friend's girlfriend. Worse, the little strumpet knows it and has a tendency to try to get in the middle of things. I didn't know this until rather recently. She likes being the center of attention. Why she doesn't simply focus on the best friend whom SHE pursued is not relevant, I suppose.

My problem: I'm in a VERY delicate situation. Since I only figured her out recently, since she can be quite manipulative, since my boyfriend is used to women using/hurting him and since he really cherishes his friendship with her, how do I keep my sanity?

He swears he'd never cheat on me but I know this b*tch is going to try and wear him down. She tells him about her sex life, sexual preferences, she's tried to tell me things about him which he's not told me yet, and twice she's called me saying he might dump me which of course freaked me out. Then when he called all was fine. To his credit, he warned me that if she and I got to be friends, she would meddle. I just had no idea.

Help! How can I handle this? So far, I try not to pursue him and I try to remember that he sleeps with me, not her. Still, I'm getting paranoid and jealous and there was a time that I did confide in her (though luckily not too much). Furthermore, I know she's cheated on her boyfriend at least once with yet another guy (she told me herself, the idiot! I did not tell either of the guys this). Luckily, I think my boyfriend has enough decorum (and has been cheated on enough himself) that he would not get together with her while he's dating me.

Please help me out of this mess. No matter what I do, I'm done for, right? She has no girl friends close to her age really (I wonder why?) and sees nothing abnormal with having this one guy who's obsessed with her accompany her and her somewhat desensitized boyfriend on romantic weekends out of town!!!

My boyfriend and that fellow and her and her guy all went out of town together once and it nearly killed me. He said he couldn't afford to pay for me and she said that's a huge lie. — Nora

Nora, some people would enjoy being in a situation like this as it would give them enough material to write 15 or 20 successful novels and when they had exhausted the story possibilities, they'd take some of their royalties and go into deep analysis.

Perhaps you'd be better off walking away from this whole scene. If he follows, and remains with you on your terms, then you might have the start of a solid relationship. If not, there's nothing for you anyway. — Queenie

♥

Queenie, I like this guy but yet at the same time I have a guy I work with who I like and is Gay too, just like me but I don't know which one I should date

170

first or what I should at all. The thing is I can have more fun with the one I work with because I will see him more often and he is out to a few people. The other guy is not out to anyone at his front as the guy I work with is out at home.

Well I don't know what to think the one I work with is nice and Sweet, but the other one who I like and want to be there boyfriend is kind of immature.

I just wish I knew what to do and who to choose and try and be there boyfriend better yet just date for now you see I need some help figuring this out. I just wish I could choose one and get it over with, without having any hurt feelings at all. Well I do need help. Signed, Confused

Well, that makes two of us who are confused, however, I say choose the one who makes you feel the best about yourself, the one with whom you have the most fun.

Since there are two of them and only one of you, and if they both like you, once you make a choice, someone is going to have hurt feelings. They'll get over it. Good luck. — Queenie

♥

Dear Queen of Hearts, I've liked this guy for about 4 months and i've been with him a few times. I also have recently made friends with a girl who I have also been involved with. She is also bisexual and has been with the guy I like! Last week we shared him and it scared me to see him enjoying her as well as me! she liked it and said she could do it again. All I seem to do is cry about it.

I have been told in the past that this guy likes me too but I have never heard him say it himself. I can't share this guy with my friend. I could bare giving up on him but I am scared that they will be together. I don't think I could handle that. — Cheryl

Cheryl, I can't help you with this problem. I certainly don't suggest sexual encounters of this type, and particularly don't believe they should take place unless all parties are consenting adults, which is obviously not the case in your situation.

In today's world of AIDS and other STD's, I'd strongly recommend that you save the sex for someone you love, not someone you "have been told" likes you.

If they want to get back together, there's nothing you can do to stop them. You're going to have to learn that you are the only person over which you have control. — Queenie

♥

Hi Queenie, I have fallen in love with two men. One is younger than I and the other is older. They're both sweet, lovable, caring individuals. The both know how to make laugh and treat me like a queen. I've known the younger one longer than the older one.

I have so much in common with the both of them this is what's making it so difficult. Please I need your advice. I asked your advice on another subject in

which your response was great. I just wanted you to know that I took your advice and they were right. — Rhonda

Rhonda, do these men know about each other? If they don't, your situation will be decided for you when one learns about the other. There is no reason you can't have two boyfriends — unless you are considering commitment with one or the other. If you are, you'll have to decide which one makes you the happiest.

Here's where I usually suggest that someone make lists and, as much as I hate grades, they can work as tie-breakers in situations such as this. You're pretty lucky. Most people are looking for just one person such as this! — Queenie

♥

Dear Queen of Hearts, why do I always want what I can't have? It seems like a silly question. One man I am dating, Joe, is very loving and caring. Tom, this other man I met I feel so strongly about. He is shy and tells me he is afraid to call me and I'm so old-fashioned (but still in my 20's) that I don't like making the first call. Tom and I have so much more in common and are also caring and loving when I see him. I have met up with Tom four times (by chance) around town. Each time he has always come over and stayed next to me. We've sat up talking about everything until 3am.

My friend gave me a book to read called "The Rules" which I enjoyed but would not fully institute into my life. The book does make a good point about men who take the initiative to call and find you and who make an effort toward the relationship. Which Joe has definitely done. The book states that these are the men that are going to make women happy because they know how lucky they are and appreciate what they have.

Joe is a great guy but nothing that I could see myself with long term. Tom however has stuck in my mind and the person that I feel I could grow old with. Sticking with my old-fashioned ways... Tom has my phone number but I don't have his therefore even if I did break down and decide to call I couldn't. Tom is always on my mind no matter where, when, or what I am doing.

Am I wasting time thinking about Tom? What can I do to get him to call? Should I just convince myself that he is not the one, even though I have never felt this way about anyone - ever? Taking chances in love and romance is not my strong point. I am just getting back into the dating game after two years of avoiding it at all cost due to a really bad relationship and having him stalk me. So, I'm fairly nervous about making any move.

Why does Tom seem so right? I know that he is divorced (an apparent ugly ending), age 32, loves his family and friends, and works a lot. He tells me that all of his friends keep telling him to call, he has told all of them about me but I still have not heard from him. Any and all advice will be helpful. — Victoria

Victoria, you have a couple options here. You can keep waiting for Tom to make the first move or you can get your courage up and the next time you see him, ask him out. If he has told all of his friends about you, and they keep telling him to call, it is not out of line for you to suggest that the two of you go out for a pizza and to a movie (or something similar). — Queenie

♥

Dear Queenie, I was in an 8 yr relationship with Conway which ended 1 yr 1/2 ago. Then three months after it ended, I started dating someone seriously (Dan) for the past year. Dan wants to get married. I still have feelings for Conway. What I liked about Conway that I'm missing in my relationship with Dan is passion and he was more protective, which I liked. What I like about Dan is that we get along really well, but we do not have many common interests. — Maria

Maria, if the relationship with Conway has ended I don't understand why he seems to still be an option here. You're comparing Dan to Conway and that is unfair to Dan since he is not Conway. I'd suggest you hold off marriage until you are truly in love with Dan, if that ever happens.

Did you start dating Dan on the rebound from Conway? It sounds as though you need to finish mourning the loss of your relationship with Conway and free yourself up for Dan or whomever else you might meet who could become a suitable companion. — Queenie

♥

Dear Queen of Hearts, a little over a year ago, I met someone who does the same work I do but for a different company. Our work takes us to various cities so while we are not co-workers, rarely does a day pass without our seeing each other. There was no initial attraction and as I got to know her I found that she and her boyfriend had recently moved here trying to get started so there was never any interest in her on my part. She always spoke of her boyfriend very negatively, but, other than sympathize, I did nothing.

Come last winter we began to really get to know each other well at work and I thought I could meet her boyfriend, thinking it would be nice for us all to get together. The first red flag (which I ignored) went up when she told me that he was the jealous type and didn't want her to have any male friends or even to go out with female friends where she might be picked up. Our friendship would have to be a secret.

Then he got a job which kept him out of town for weeks at a time. You see where this is going. I didn't. I just thought I had just made a great new friend. Then I realized how very much we had in common, and after a few months of phone chats, lunches, movies and fun, it hit me like they say it can, like a thunderbolt. I was in love.

I told her how I felt, expecting her to have me back off. She never really acknowledged my feelings but she would not let me go. Since then the two of them have bought a house together so it has always been clear to me that she is not going to break it off with him. However she has become increasingly sullen and desperately sad about her relationship, while I suffer terribly during those times they are together and we cannot meet.

Finally she admitted to me that she loves me but feels trapped and that she can't leave. I have decided this must end but am at a loss as to how to deal with the fact that I cannot help but see her at work. I avoid her when I can but that has the added effect of making me think about her constantly. Plus if she knew that I did that it would hurt her terribly and I would not hurt her for the world. I cannot quit my job. What are my chances of either successfully getting over her in this situation or of her deciding she may want to take a chance with me? — Jerry

Jerry, she currently has two boyfriends. She could choose you over him but she doesn't want to. She is an adult. She is not trapped by poverty or lack of education or ethnic barriers. She is not married (or is she?). If she truly loved you, she would do whatever it takes to leave her boyfriend and make a solid relationship with you. She doesn't want to. Period.

Don't worry about hurting her. She has two men to lean on. Worry more about him. Can you sympathize with him? He loves her and probably has no inkling whatsoever about her relationship with you. Or perhaps he's been through this before.

When the pain of this relationship exceeds the pleasure you're getting from it, I assume you'll wake up and move on to someone who will be willing to love you exclusively. When you wake up, don't be angry. Just be glad you didn't waste more of your life on someone who cares so little for you. Words are a cheap commodity. Actions are the true expression of love. — Queenie

♥

Dear Queenie, a year-and-a-half ago, I met Jay. We worked together and when I first met him on his first day of work, I knew that I wanted to get to know him. When business was slow we would talk about anything and everything. He told me he had a girlfriend, but he rarely talked about her and when he did, he said the relationship was practically over. He flirted with me constantly, and basically led me on all summer.

When I realized that he would never break it off with his girlfriend, I used another boy to take my mind off Jay. I was in love with Morris, but I was in love with Jay too. And I'm sorry to say, I loved Jay more. Then Jay broke up with his girlfriend and my hopes were high, but when he told me about his feelings towards another girl, my hopes crashed to the ground immediately. This girl was a very good friend of mine and she and Jay have been serious for 6 months now. I broke up with Morris a few weeks ago and being with Jay is all I think about.

When I talk to Jay lately, it seems like he is starting to lead me on again. His gif told me that he did have feelings for me last year, but what about now? He trys to cheer me up alot and he thinks that my depression is due to the recent break-up, but my pain is caused by this unrequited love. I want to pour my heart out to Jay but if I do, will I lose his friendship? Will I lose Wanda's friendship? Even if they break up, would it still be morally wrong to let myself fall for Jay?

174

I can't imagine a life without Jay. He is truly my closest friend, and I don't want to lose that. But my feelings for him are so incredibly strong! I can't get into my schoolwork or any of my extracurricular activities. Please help. I am so alone and I feel like there is no escape from this pain that I have endured for nearly 2 years. — Bambi

Bambi, Jay may care about you, but not in the same way in which you care for him. Who knows what would happen if you confide in him. Perhaps he feels the same way, perhaps not. Life is full of gambles, some you win, some you lose. Weigh your options, decide if it's worth losing him completely if you confide and he doesn't feel the same way. I would have to think, though, with the current relationship that he has with Wanda, and his prior relationship, he and you are not meant to be.

Try to enlarge your circle of friends so that you don't spend so much time with Jay and Wanda. If they were a brick wall, would you continue to hurt yourself by running into them all the time? — Queenie

♥

Dear Queenie, I was seeing a man for a while. He was a great lover and a great friend. After almost a year together, I broke off our sexual part of the relationship. I had been getting feelings that he just wasn't happy. As soon as I broke it off, he started seeing "Linda". We remained as close as a man and a woman can get without sex. Then, after about 2 months, he started saying that he was thinking about me in a sexual way again.

At first I put him off. Then he moved in with Linda. We have mutual musical interests, so one night he came over and one thing led to another...yes! I gave in. Now he is leaving Linda and he wants to continue seeing me. But he says that he's not going to break off the relationship with her completely yet. He's afraid of how she will react.

I love this guy. He is really a very nice, gentle and sweet man. But, I really have feelings for him. How can I tell whether or not his feelings for me are genuine? — Chelsea

Chelsea, I hope you are using protection. It might also help to put some latex around your heart, too, as this guy is going to cause you a lot of pain in the future. He cheats on her because you enable him to do so, now he'll cheat on you because you and she enable him to do so. It sounds like the great male dream come true. If you're happy, I'm happy. – Queenie

♥

Dear Queenie, I have a boyfriend "T" who I've been with since last December and we had gone out for about 6 months before that but I broke up wit him because I wasn't attracted to him anymore.

After about 2 months we decided to try it again. He has been very bossy lately and telling me I'm slow and to hurry up and laughs when I don't understand something.

I finally got fed up with it and told him "Then don't wait for me if I'm slow just leave!" He said "Fine I will!" and then left. I love him very much and I don't want to break up with him b/c I'm just not one of those types of people who can see people heart broken. Well, since that little incident I have been hanging out with his best friend, "S", and told him about what was going on between us.

He and I had gone out before but it didn't last very long because he was still getting over his last girlfriend and I didn't want to commit quite yet. He is the type of guy who flirts with about anyone. Since I've gotten to know him pretty well and I have been able to tell him my problems and have him listen I think I'm starting to like him more then "T" and I think he likes me too.

I don't know what to do, I've tried to tell myself that I'm just imagining it but I can't stop thinking about "S"! I don't want to hurt "T", because I love him too and when we broke up before he was devastated but I like "S" too! HELP!!!
— Barbie

Barbie, it sounds as though you aren't really ready to settle down with "T" or "S". You say you love "T" but you can't stop thinking about "S". This is normal because "S" is treating you better than "T" is treating you right now.

You've already broken up with "T" once so despite your not wanting to see someone's heart broken, you are capable of saying 'goodbye.' I'd suggest you say it again to "T" and tell him it's because you like "S" a lot.

You can expect that "T" will get upset with you and with "S" and possibly "S" will get upset with you for getting "T" mad at him, but somehow I think that's going to happen anyway. — Queenie

What's Age Got to Do With It?

What's Age Got To Do With It?

*"I am in love with a woman who is 12 years younger than me.
She is great and we have a good time, but I am worried that
when I am 70 and she is still in her 50s, I won't be able to, uh,
keep up with her."*

There's much to be said for dating someone whose age is close to yours. The two of you will likely have the same reference points regarding past and current events, tastes in music, and a plethora of experiences that someone much younger or much older would not be able to relate to.

Becoming involved with someone within your age bracket should ease the worry about aging since the two of you probably will age at about the same rate and neither of you will look out of place on the other's arm. In a perfect world the two of you would live out your twilight years together. But then, we all know this isn't a perfect world.

Love doesn't ask "how old are you" when it hits. That question comes up later. Should it really matter how much older or younger you are than your lover? As long as each of you is of legal age, no it shouldn't.

But what do you do when your family and friends put in their two cents about the "old guy" you're dating or making wisecracks that your girlfriend is young enough to be your daughter? And when is too young *really* too young?

Maturity can come at any age and that is the biggest key to whether or not age is going to be a problem.

♥

Hi Queenie, I am 17 years old and I have a huge problem. I have known this guy for about two years. He is 24. We would like to date each other but there is one problem, my mom, she thinks he is too old for me.

I have tried to talk to her, but she won't listen. My dad would allow me to date him though. He is a honest, good person. What could I do to change her mind? Thank you. — Andee

Andee, sorry, but I'm on your mom's side. He is too old for you. If you really, really want to date, I think you need to wait a few more years until you're at least 22 or 23, maybe older. At that point I doubt your mom will have any objections. If he's really an "honest, good person" he'll wait. — Queenie

♥

Hi Queenie, does age matter? — Jaxson

Jaxson, age usually always matters with fine wine, various cheeses, and sometimes with love. It depends upon the people involved, how they feel about each other, how they feel about themselves, their emotional maturity, and whether they're both of legal age. Of course my feeling is that if you have a question about it, then maybe it does matter. — Queenie

♥

Dear Queen of Hearts, I am 33 years old and the man that I am dating is 48. He treats me better than any man I have ever dated before and he is always thinking of my kids. The problem is he worries about our age difference because he thinks that later on in the years I will want someone younger as he gets older. I don't believe that this will happen because I really love him. I have never felt this way about anyone before. So, what should I do? I feel like he is my soul mate and that we were meant to be together. Do you think that age should be an issue in a relationship? — Blondie

Blondie, the only time the age difference is important in a relationship is when it bothers one or both of the people in that relationship. It bothers him so it is a big deal. As far as him worrying about the future, he's wasting the present while he worries about something that may never happen. — Queenie

♥

Queenie, I'm almost 21 years old and have been in love with this guy for 7 years, he is 12 years older than me. I lived out of the country for quite sometime, so we didn't see much of each other. I consider myself loud, sincere, and forthright, I just seem to buckle up and lose any sane thought in my head whenever I see him. I feel this connection, with him, but he's shy as well and I just don't know what to do anymore.

I just feel as if my life is passing me by and that my best years are being spent without this man. He gives me signs that he's interested, but I feel the problem is with the crowd of men he hangs out with: divorced men who trample over the sanctity of marriage, even though everyone has a free will, peer pressure is still alive and kicking in your 30's. I did a little each time I see him, because I know that once again I'm not going to be in his arms tonight, and that loneliness is kicking into 4th gear. — Luce

Luce, it sounds as though you've been making this guy your fantasy boyfriend since you were 14. Isn't it time that you stop dreaming and start dating real men? If you don't you're going to look back on all the years you could have had a life and wonder why you never even tried. — Queenie

♥

Hi Queenie, I just meet someone three weeks ago and we have only gone out a few times, but I feel in love with him. I never have felt this way so quickly about anyone. He tells me he feels very strongly about me. The problem is that he is five years younger than me and is only visiting the USA for two months. I am afraid to tell him how I feel about him because I know he has to leave. Should I tell

180

him how I feel? I am being a fool for hoping that we can be together? I am so sad could you please give me some advice? — Michelle

Michelle, no matter how you "feel," true love takes longer than three weeks and a few dates to develop. If it is a meant to be relationship the distance won't stop it from developing further. Tell him too soon and you may scare him enough that he'll be glad to put an ocean between the two of you on a permanent basis. — Queenie

♥

Dear Queen...I have found my perfect match, but I can't have her. It's a long story so I'll get started. First of all, she is 11 years older than me. We met when I went to work at the place she works. She had had a boyfriend for about a year at that time. After about a month of working there we started spending a lot of time together. I saw her at least 4 or 5 times a week, outside of work. This is all while she was still dating her boyfriend. Another two or so months went by and I realized I was madly in love with her.

One night, I worked up the nerve to tell her how I felt. I drove down to her house as I had planned to tell her in person, but couldn't get myself to leave my car. So I called her from my cell phone and confessed my unconditional love for her. She was shocked, and flattered. She said that I had brought out things in her she hadn't felt in a long time.

We continued to see each other on a more-than-regular basis, and we just got closer. We'd do things like watch sunsets at the beach, go out to romantic dinners, and watch movies on her bed. Things that couples do, aside from the kissing and the sex. My feelings grew stronger, everyday I fell more in love. Apparently she did too, because not long after that, she broke up with her boyfriend, I finally had my chance.

I could tell she wanted me, because she kept hinting like, "So, take me out on my first night being single." But I guess I'm either too much of a gentleman or too shy to make a move because I lost it two days later when she agreed to get back together with him. She later asked me why I hadn't "made a move" when I had the chance and that she wished I had.

I was extremely disappointed but I am an optimist, so I kept my hopes high and continued our friendly relationship. Then, her boyfriend moved about 3 hours away and a few months later he ended the relationship saying he had never been attracted to her. I was the shoulder to cry on, and she came to me with her problems, which brought us closer. Our relationship continued but without any sex.

A week later she told me that her ex-boyfriend wanted to talk to her. I advised against it but she got back together with him. I was crushed. I got upset and started crying right there in public. I didn't speak to her for two days, which felt like an eternity. We "made up" and started hanging out again. Everything was back to normal. For a few months we became closer than ever. Just when I thought everything was about to turn my way, she calls me one night. She says her boyfriend doesn't want her to see me anymore. I couldn't believe that she would accept his demand, but she did. And we didn't speak for nearly two months.

Two weeks ago, she emailed me at work. We corresponded over email the rest of that week and she was talking like she wanted me back. We made tentative plans to get together over the weekend, but she never returned my call from Friday night. On Monday, she emailed me, saying she was with her boyfriend. When I asked her what the deal was with them, she said, "The same thing that has always been." I told her I couldn't talk to her until she and him were through and she agreed.

Two days later, I caved again. I said I couldn't stand not talking to her, so we started talking again. Over the next week, I tried to get her to leave him for me. The thing is, she knows she's in a mediocre relationship, but for some reason, she doesn't think there's anything better out there. I guess my question is, how do I get her to realize how much happier she could be with me? I know that we were meant for each other, do I just wait for her to come around? Thank you for listening to me. Sincerely — Matt

Matt, there's nothing you can do to "make" someone love you, but you can do something for yourself. I'm not going to harp on the age difference because eleven years might not be so much of a difference if you and she were in your 50s or 60s, but it is a big difference now. You don't have the world experience you need to handle a situation like this. She has the experience and that's why she can keep stringing you along so she has someone who makes her feel good when the relationship with her boyfriend turns bad.

You need to stop caving in to what you think is true love and tell this woman goodbye one last and final time. There are plenty of young women who would be thrilled to meet a guy like you but you're never going to find them while you're wasting your time on someone who plays with your feelings. — Queenie

♥

Hello Queen of Hearts, I'm in a relationship with a man 12 years younger than I am. we've known each other a little over two years — went places together as friends off and on for over a year. I've always had stronger feelings than friendship for him but was very hesitant to make them known because of our age difference. As a result, I am very insecure in this relationship. We first had sex together after I'd been away on vacation for a week. Since then, we've had sex maybe 5 or 6 times. It's always wonderful — lasts forever and I just feel so satisfied and close to him then.

But — and this is my problem — he says that sex is not that important to him, that it's more important that we are friends. He says that before me all his relationships were just for the sex — and they never lasted. So this time he wants it to last and doesn't want sex to screw it up. He says that I am very desirable and that my age does not matter.

I sometimes feel like a fool — I should be happy with a man that wants something other than to get in my pants all the time. At other times i wonder how he can care — be around me for days at a time and sleep in the same bed — and

not want to make love with me. I've never felt this way about someone before and I just am so confused. Is it possible for a man to just get burned out on causal sex and lose interest in sex even with someone he says he cares about? To me, sex is a part of a caring relationship. — Deborah

♥

Deborah, I doubt there are too many couples who are always on the same level as far as their sexual or emotional needs. My personal feeling is that a relationship may have difficulty if the sexual aspect is not fulfilling for both partners. In your case, it would appear that he doesn't have a very high sex drive — not a problem if it doesn't cause problems for you. It does, so it's time to decide what you need to get from this relationship.

Since he doesn't want to advance this past the 'intimate friends' category (which I don't think is a good relationship for you), you need to decide if you can return to being just friends (without the sex) so you can free yourself up to date other men who will want to enter into a complete relationship with you.

Talk to him about your feelings and let him know that right now you're unhappy and you're going to be making some changes so that you can enjoy the friendship once again. If he only wants to be a friend, then he shouldn't have a problem with you dating others. If he wants you to be exclusively his, then he should be ready to move to a more committed relationship.

If he has a sex drive that is incompatible to yours, you certainly should think twice before trying to make this a permanent 'intimate' relationship. Of course, that's just my opinion. — Queenie

♥

Dear Queenie, I'm 30 years old and met a 38 year old woman. She's nice, creative and fun to be with. We are going out on a date this Saturday. What I'm concerned about is the age difference. I do not know whether she will be my life partner. I heard from friends that for a woman to give birth at an age close to 40 may result in a child born with deformities. It is also dangerous for women as well. Please advise. — Stan

Stan, it's far too soon to be thinking about babies considering you haven't even begun dating her yet. As far as the age matter, perhaps you need to do some actual research on the matter instead of listening to what friends have to say. — Queenie

♥

Dear Queenie, my surgeon invited himself to my house for a drink (before the operation). I said we should wait until after the operation, he agreed. Yes, it is unprofessional. But he has a reputation as a great doctor. I know nothing about his personal life except that he is single and age 34 and I like him a lot! I am an attractive single 45 year old.

Never has a man been so aggressive about showing so much initial interest in me. I like this a lot right now but have so many questions about the age difference, i.e. does he want children? (I don't have any)...and I can't get involved sexually without commitment. I feel the awkwardness of a teenager but I have most of my life in back of me instead of ahead of me. I really had just given up on ever having a lasting relationship when i met him! — Coral

Coral, slow down a bit! You're thinking about sex, commitment and children and you haven't had the first date with this dynamic doctor? He *must* be aggressive! You've already said he's unprofessional, even though he has a reputation as a great doctor.

Why is this wonderful man still single at 34? He obviously isn't shy about going after a woman he wants, so maybe before you get too much more emotionally involved, it's time you do some checking into his personal life.

I'm suggesting this because you're talking about having a lasting relationship with this man. Can those words describe past relationships women have had with him? Perhaps there is something that creates sparks between the two of you, but maybe he is a master at flattery also. Is he genuine or is he a gold-plated heartbreaker?

As far as the age difference, it isn't significant if you and he are both emotionally mature (or immature, for that matter) and neither of you have problems with the age thing. Good luck. — Queenie

♥

Dear Queenie, I'm 25. It seems really weird that the only women lately that seem to be attracted to me are the ones that are like 18, 19 or 20. Not that that is a bad thing. I recently met someone that is 18 that I'm attracted to.

My concern is the age difference and is it a normal thing for a guy my age to have a relationship with a woman that much younger than I? What is your advice on how to approach this situation? — Tommy

Tommy, women mature faster (generally speaking) than men. That means that 18, 19 or 20 year old women may be very well suited to you. Anyone younger than that is too young. Good luck. — Queenie

♥

Hello, Queenie, I am sure this will be an awkward situation, but I will tell you anyway. I am 18 and am attracted to a young woman of 22 and she is attracted to me as well. This is the first time anything like this has happened to me and would like any advice you could give me regarding the situation concerning if I should pursue a relationship or forget about it (not likely).

I would like to know what a young woman of the age group would enjoy. I know that sounds pretty general but anything would help. What should I do let her know that I share the same the feelings as she does? From her friends I have heard that she is one that will go to a man, and then leave him, and then come back to him. Do you know what I'm talking about? I would really like any advice could get on what I could do to aid this relationship and what to maybe expect as an outcome, lets say the classic of flowers and chocolate. What should I be prepared for, a challenge or something else? — Mark

Mark, it sounds like she has much more experience in the ways of love than you do. The only way you'll get the experience to handle situations like this is to plow right in and get your heart broken like the rest of us.

If you want to date her, ask her out to a movie or suggest some other activity that isn't too expensive or intensive. If she wants to go, she will. It's way too early for flowers and chocolate. And, yes, it'll be a challenge. All love pursuits are. Good luck. — Queenie

♥

Queenie, please help me. I am in love with a guy for sometime now and he seemed to be Unfortunately my parents who didn't like him because he was 29 and I was 19 found him and humiliated him in a number of ways. In addition they told his employer lies and got him fired. He was still friendly to me until I had a big fight with him since a so called friend of mine told me that he was telling things about me. I found out later that this was untrue; my so called friend admitted that she lied to me. Now I don't know what to do with this man, I am madly in love with him. Help me. — Nicole

Nicole, if you still are living with your parents or dependent upon them for your livelihood, then I don't see how this man would be able to be a part of your life, if your parents still feel the same way about him. Sneaking around to see him against their wishes would be inappropriate and not very mature on your part. When you are on your own will be the time to see if he is still interested in you. Until then, it would probably be best to leave him alone. — Queenie

♥

Queenie, here are the facts: I'm 20 and she is 29. She was engaged for the last 3 years until he broke it off. I knew her before and after that breakup, and after several months of hell for her, she seems to be becoming herself again. We are friends (as opposed to acquaintances), but I want to be closer.

The main problem (other than her past breakup) is that I get the vibe (99.9% sure) that she views me as this little kid who never enters her mind as someone to take seriously. This frustrates me since we will be having a great meaningful conversation and out of nowhere she'll say something about how "old" she's getting or how unusual it is for someone as "young" as me to think about matters of any substance.

On the one hand, that could be good since she (possibly) sees that I'm NOT a little kid, but on the other hand, she says it as though she's utterly shocked to find out that I think about such things.

I do not want to put her in an uncomfortable situation (and risk our friendship) by doing something that is too bold, but I have to do something.

I do not know how to "play games" or "drop hints," since I prefer direct communication, but is either of these a wise move? The two most obvious choices to me are to either: 1. ask the direct question or 2. Wait and hope that she will have some kind of epiphany and that no one else will come along. Any ideas would help. Many thanks. — Alex

Alex, women are much more aware of age differences when a man they're with is younger than them. It's almost a stigma to be romantically involved with a younger man. Some women feel this more than others. It will be even worse if she looks her age or older, and he looks his age or younger. More than one woman has been asked about her "son" by less enlightened acquaintances.

Think of it this way, when she was 20, you were 11. It makes the difference more obvious, doesn't it? Okay, so when you're 41, she'll be 50. Not so bad. But at that point, she'll feel at more of a disadvantage because the normal aging process will be kicking in and she'll see more lines and wrinkles and gray hairs than ever when she looks in a mirror.

Women are like that. Their eyesight magnifies their own flaws and diminishes those of women younger than themselves. And it won't help that as you mature you'll be looking more handsome than ever and attracting fit and firm 20 and 30-somethings.

Depending upon her career, her coworkers, bosses, and others with whom she has to deal may view her less credibility for having a romantic relationship with someone younger than herself. Why? Envy, perhaps.

At any rate, it's highly acceptable in our society for a man to date a woman much younger than himself. But the reverse is rarely true. And it's the woman who takes the most flack in the relationship.

So, perhaps you could (1) ask the direct question in such a way that she has an easy out if she's uncomfortable with taking this relationship to a different level, (2) depending upon the answer, you'll know whether you need to wait for her epiphany. Good luck. — Queenie

♥

Dear Queenie, my fiancé and I recently moved to the same city to go to separate universities. We moved in together and have no roommates. She says I never want to go out together or spend quality time with her.

I love her and realize that I am guilty for this but I do not enjoy going out to the bars or places with large crowds. She also says that I used to be fun and outgoing now I am serious, I tried to explain to her that the reason I am serious is because we have responsibilities such as bills and academic deadlines to meet.

Before we moved we spent every day together she lived at her house and I lived at mine. Now that we live together she can't understand that it has to be different. She is 19 and I am 23 I have been a lot of places and she has led a sheltered life with her mom and dad. Please help. — Jonathan

Jonathan, even though you spent every day together before you moved, you and she had your own "spaces" at your individual homes. Those spaces have now been eliminated and you can expect that your basic differences will make living together more difficult as time goes on. You see what just a few years can add to a person's experience level? You understand responsibilities and she hasn't had any yet.

The goal is to give her some sense of the need for responsibility in her life. Not an easy thing to do when moving from the security of mom and dad to the comfort of a boyfriend who's always there, even if he is no fun.

If you can, you should probably move into a place of your own and give her the space she needs to learn to depend on herself instead of others. Not an easy lesson but one that serves well for all of life's future surprises. — Queenie

♥

Dear Queen of Hearts, I met a 21 year old woman at university and we have been seeing each other for six months. Her life is filled with social engagements; work and university studies whereas mine, I have chosen to slow things up a bit and 'smell the roses' so to speak after a medical shock some years ago.

I am confused with my motives for wanting to spend more time with her and I feel that I am being too demanding to ask her to spend some more time with me. She tells me that she is sick of the stress of 'pleasing' everyone, and studying all the time.

When I organize a picnic or a stroll along the beach she turns into a different person, so serene and relaxed and she tells me this is the place where she wants to be all the time. She is an incredibly intelligent woman and works exceptionally hard to achieve a high standard of academic work, and she is possibly the most beautiful woman I have seen. I like this woman very much but I don't want to feel that I am just 'slotting' in to her life when it suits her. Am I being too selfish? — Darryl

Darryl, this young lady is just getting started with her adult life. She is building a strong academic foundation for her future. This is an important time in her life when she is learning about herself and the world around her. If you are trying to get her to slow down to fit more into your life style, you are probably making a big mistake.

It is your choice to slow down just as it is her choice to strive so hard. Those little times away from the stress are enjoyable to her but she knows that life isn't one big picnic or stroll along the beach.

It is natural to want to spend time with someone we care about, but it does not mean that the other person must give us as much of their time as we want or need.

If you are demanding that she give you more of her time than she can comfortably give to you and still maintain her studies and other commitments, you are not thinking about what's best for her but rather what's best for you. And that is selfish. If you need more than what she can give, you need to find someone who is more like yourself.

She doesn't have the need to "smell the roses" yet because she hasn't yet finished planting her garden. — Queenie

♥

Dear Queenie, it all started about 3 weeks ago. I'm a camp councilor and I work with this guy who, for the record, is 21, I'm almost 17. Not that that matters. So, we've been working together, and I've been interested in him for some time...3 weeks ago, he told a girl, that we both talk to, that he was interested in me, but that he was shy, and that he wanted to take the time to get to know me better, because he doesn't like rushing into things.

When she told me the news, I was floating on air! The next day, he gave her a friendship necklace, to give me...and told her he thought I was pretty etc...and that he was very interested...okay, I told her I was interested also, and to ask him, if he would come talk to me...well, he would never talk to me one on one...always through this friend of ours.

What do you think? When I confided in my friend that I really thought I was interested in him...she went and told him I was in love with him...no I suppose he thinks I'm shallow, but that isn't what I said. I feel like we need to clear things up between us...but I don't want to make him feel uncomfortable by asking him to talk with me about it...would you feel uncomfortable? How should I approach him?

I know I should figure this all out on my own, but I'm so frustrated now...I'm at an end...I even wrote him a note, explaining that I didn't know how to reach him, to get him to talk to me...he never said anything about it. Jenny has gone and told lots of other councilors about us, so they are all bugging him about it...I know that's my fault, but how was I supposed to know Jenny had a big mouth? Are you confused yet? I am! DO you think you could help me out?? — Crystal

Crystal, the age thing does make a difference here. You're 16. He's legal age. If something developed betweeen the two of you that went farther than "just friends" he could end up in jail.

You say this guy is saying really sweet things, but you're getting everything second hand through someone else. The reality is he might not be saying anything at all. Are you sure your girlfriend isn't making a lot of this up?

I think you should stop trying to make contact with this man. He seems to be making it plain he doesn't want to get involved, no matter what you keep hearing from your girlfriend. Find yourself another boyfriend, one closer to your age. — Queenie

♥

Dear Queen of Hearts, I am in love with a woman who is 12 years younger than me. She is great and we have a good time, but I am worried that when I am

70 and she is still in her 50s, I won't be able to, uh, keep up with her. I am 43 now. Should I go for it, or suggest that she find someone closer to her own age? I would be crushed if she left me for a younger man. — John

John, why are you worrying about something that "might" occur 27 years from now. Let's assume everything happens as you are projecting, you have 27 good years and then she leaves you. Come on! There are thousands of marriages with these age differences and more with both partners still devoted to each other — many despite problems that may limit their physical intimacy. Maybe she won't be able to, uh, keep up with you. And, heaven forbid, you leave her for a younger woman.

If you love her, you should "go for it!" Marriages don't survive just because the physical aspect is so in tune. It helps, but in loving relationships, there's more, much more — friendship, companionship, caring, sharing, laughter, tears — partners are comfortable, happy, and glad to be with each other even without sex. If sex is the whole enchilada, it isn't much of a relationship. — Queenie

♥

Hi Queenie, I'm 23 years old and I'm in love with a woman who has the age of 32 years old. The problem is that she finds me too young — I told that the age doesn't matter but she doesn't understand that. Well, it's like one of my friends who is 33 years, he goes with a girl who has 18 years old and I told her that, and she says it's not the same thing.

Why? Is it because the guy is older or what? Please help with that. Thank you. — James

James, you have told this lady that her being older doesn't matter. It apparently matters to her and in this situation, that's what counts. Society has always accepted older men with younger women more than the reverse. Most older women/younger men matches work because the man is more mature than his physical age. And all of the matches in which there are age differences work because the differences don't matter to the people involved.

This isn't what you wanted to hear, is it? I'm sorry. Both of you must want to have a relationship, and then if there's a problem you both can work on smoothing it out.

You are not getting any encouragement from this lady so I suspect that she definitely isn't interested in making the two of you a twosome which is why I suggest that you keep looking for your special love and let this lady keep searching for hers. — Queenie

♥

Queenie, I am a 21 year old male going to college and I have been dating a 30 year old woman for over a year. Everything is great and I never have felt better. But my problem: is this a normal relationship? — Mark

Mark, you're in a great relationship and you've never felt better? This would not seem to be a problem. Are you worried about the age difference? It shouldn't make any difference if the both of you care greatly about each other. If outsiders or family are imposing their feelings about the age difference into your relationship and you are foolish enough to listen to them, then you may not be mature enough to handle this great (in your own words) relationship that you and she have together.

If it was the other way around, if she was 21 and you were 30, would you be questioning the normalness of the relationship? Times have changed. Enjoy what you have. – Queenie

Not Ready for Love

Not Ready for Love

*"I told her I needed space, and that really hurt her. I'm not
even sure if I mean that anymore. Sometimes I want to be with
her, but other times I just want to hang out with my friends."*

One of the realities of true love is that it does not always happen
to both people in a relationship--or wanting a relationship--at the same
time. What do you do when you have searched desperately for that one
perfect person, and then you find THE ONE but they're in love with
someone else?

What if they insist they could only be a "friend" and nothing more?
Or your potential soul mate claims he or she loves you but they don't know
if they're ready to settle into the exclusive, committed, lifetime type of
relationship you see the two of you having?

Wouldn't you think that your soul mate would be just as ready for
commitment as you are when the two of you meet for the first time?

In a perfect world, that's how it would happen.

♥

*Dear Queen of Hearts, here's the situation. About 2 months ago I went
out on a date with a girl I then worked with. She is 22. I'm 26. She and I hit it off
pretty well. I took her out to dinner and a movie. We asked each other a lot of
questions, and discovered we had a lot in common. We laughed a lot, too.*

*At the end of the date, I dropped her off at her apartment and asked her if
I could kiss her goodnight. She blushed, said she was sorry and that she likes to
take things slow, so we hugged instead. She thanked me for asking though, because
"other guys would not do that."*

*Fast-forward two weeks later and she called me at home. She said that
she doesn't think it's a good idea that we date anymore because she still is not over
her ex. She thought she was, but she said she still thinks about him, and thinks it
is unfair to me that she dates me while her head is elsewhere.*

*Her ex was her only love. (She is a virgin, too.) She doesn't think too
highly of herself (in level of attractiveness.) I was hurt by this letdown. She gave
me a cool birthday card two days after she told me about not wanting to date right
now. I had flowers delivered at work for her and though she kept the flowers on the
counter so people could see, for a week I heard no response. When I saw her last
night for the first time since all of this, she took my hand and told me thanks and
that they were lovely.*

Through other people, I know this much:

*1) She told a mutual friend that the date between her and another guy
(me) went really well. She has no idea that our mutual friend knew it was me.*

2) Last night, before I arrived at the party, she was asking about me.

*Now, I realize that she has gone through a world of hurt. It reminds me of
my first letdown. But, I'm not sure which way to go throughout all of this. I kind
of feel like there is a glass wall (instead of ceiling) between her and me. I don't*

know if I can ask her out again. I'm afraid of pursuing, or even hinting that I'm pursuing...because I know that can scare a girl, and that's not what I want. We laugh a lot when we're together, and I feel we have a good chemistry, but I don't know what do next.

Is this a lost cause? What should I do? Thank you for your time and consideration, and I look forward to hearing from you soon. — Bo

Bo, everyone heals although at different rates. Perhaps time is allowing her to see the nice guy you are and she's trying to drop subtle hints that she'd like you to ask her out again. Why don't you? A date doesn't have to mean you're serious or committed. It's just a date. If she says no, it's simply because she's not ready. Nothing more. If she says yes, well, there's your answer, too. — Queenie

♥

Dear Queenie, I've been seeing this guy for about a month, everything was going great, I mean he told my best friend that he really liked me, was awesome, was really fun to be with, and that he's never got to know any girl like he's getting to know me. But lately he's been telling me that he'll call me after he got out of work, but he hasn't called me or paged me.

This has been going on for 3 days I and don't know what to do. I really like him a lot and don't want to lose him. Please write back and give some advice. — Toby

Toby, it sounds like he knows you as much as he cares to so he's putting skids to this relationship. This is where you make it known you're not holding your breath waiting for him to call or page and if you really want to play the game right, you'll start dating other people and not being home when he calls.

You can't lose him if you don't have him and it sounds as though he's either leaving or gone. — Queenie

♥

Queenie, I'm an American woman who's been working in the Orient for a year. My boyfriend, whom I met several months ago, has recently been talking about marriage. Cultural differences aside, I'm at a loss as to how to handle this. Half of me wants to jump into the idea, and the other half wants to run the other way. He has many wonderful qualities which I admire, but lately I've begun to pick out things which really bug me about him.

Maybe I'm becoming hypersensitive to his faults because I'm afraid of moving deeper into commitment; or maybe these are warning signs that I should stop things where they are now before it's "too late."

One issue that bothers me is where we will live. Since I speak his language, and he doesn't speak mine, it seems more natural for us to live in his country. I love the country, but also love my family back home. I feel like the very idea of marriage is forcing me to make an impossible choice. I realize this is a long and unfocused question, but maybe you have some advice. — Trina

Trina, if you're really and truly in love, he'll have no faults and you'll be blind to the difficulties you might encounter with such a marriage. There are many marriages between cultures that work extremely well.

Dating is the time that we tend to gloss over faults and flaws of the person we love. Faults that bug you now will be incredibly overbearing after marriage. Having to make choices that involve leaving family and friends can create very real ill will as the marriage wears on.

From my view, you really need to step back and evaluate exactly how much you love this man. Can you live with the cultural differences, etc., that will come from making this "impossible choice"? I, personally, think your warning signs are pretty intuitive. Love is difficult enough when everything is even and you can't see the reality of the situation. — Queenie

♥

Dear Queenie, I have a friend who I care for deeply and he said he cares for me to. We've been friends for over a year and we've gotten really close like a couple, but every time we get too close he backs away, which makes me defensive and I start getting cold with him.

About a month ago he finally told me that a few years ago he was in a relationship which turned out to be devastating to him. He was even going to marry this woman but she turned him away. Well he still loves her and she hurt him really bad.

I am the first woman he's let this close to him but he is scared of getting hurt. He also said he was leaving for college soon and he feels that if we get to close he might end up falling in love with me and he won't want to leave. He's gone this far and only has two more years to go. He is 33 years old, holds a full time job, goes to school part time.

To be honest I am in love with him and don't want to loose him but I don't know what to do. I could use some advice, please thank you. — Mandy

Mandy, if he's still in love with her, then you can't lose him because you don't have him. I think you need to back away from trying to get him to commit. He has his hands full with his job and education commitments right now, and since he's still hung up on her, your demands will only make him keep backing away.

You might want to suggest to him that since he's not ready for commitment the two of you should date other people. Perhaps, if he thinks he will lose you to someone else, he will rethink his feelings. — Queenie

♥

Dear Queenie, my girlfriend and I had been dating almost 1 year. Everything was always perfect and we were also best friends. In fact, we used to talk on the phone almost every night for at least an hour (she made the calls).

Three weeks ago the calls stopped, and my calls and pages weren't returned. She finally told me that I'd scared her off because in a very intimate moment, I told her that I wouldn't want to go on living without her. She says she

doesn't want to be the center of someone's universe because her exes felt the same way and they wound up stalking her or trying to kill themselves.

Hell, I'm just a normal guy who thought he was paying her a wonderful compliment. I told her I didn't realize the impact my words had, or which button I'd pushed, and asked for a fresh start. To my shock, she refused. We hugged goodbye and I haven't heard from her since that day two weeks ago.

She told me she loved me, and had even told her friends that she'd finally found a good relationship with a nice guy. I miss her not only as a lover but as my best friend and I want so much to write her a letter — nothing heavy — and tell her so. In my heart,

I don't think she wanted to break up, but she's at once turned on and terrified of commitment.

If it's significant, she was recently diagnosed with Epstein - Barr virus so she hasn't been feeling well, and the illness may be affecting her behavior. Please give me advice! — Thomas

Thomas, yes, her recent illness may be affecting the way she looks at life. She may want some time alone to consider her options. I don't want to blow this into monumental proportions but everyone reacts differently when they've been labeled with an illness or disease.

Why don't you send her a simple bouquet of her favorite flowers or a cute gift such as a little teddy bear, with a note to the effect that you miss 'your best friend'? Perhaps she will respond and perhaps not. It's worth a try.

I think you paid her a very nice compliment; too bad it didn't have its intended effect. — Queenie

♥

Hi Queenie, I've been in a relationship with a girl for nearly 9 months now. I'm a senior in college and she's a sophomore in a neighboring college. Things were great for a long time, but now that I am looking for a job which may be far away, problems have arisen.

Now we often fight about stupid things. I told her I needed space, and that really hurt her. I'm not even sure if I mean that anymore. Sometimes I want to be with her, but other times I just want to hang out with my friends.

My question, is it possible to have a healthy relationship even when the future is so uncertain? She wants to take it one step at a time while I am really worried about what's going to happen.

I think that's the reason I keep hurting her and causing her to cry herself to sleep, but I don't know. Just need some advice. — Alec

Alec, young love (and if you aren't 35 or older, it's young love--at least in my view) can cause a lot of pain because you're both constantly changing. It's difficult to make a commitment for a lifetime when you haven't had a chance to really experience a lot of the options that are available, or when you don't have your career fully on track.

I believe in taking everything slow. Particularly when you don't really know which way you want to go. If it's true love, the two of you will get together. — Queenie

♥

Dear Queenie, I got together with this woman who was dating a friend/ co-worker, We went out and had a great time, well we ended up with a hot passionate night of love making, she was worried that I wouldn't call, well I have been calling and have only seen her once since then, (in three weeks) I call her most every day, and she seems upbeat and talkative, But always too busy to see me.

She says that she needs to get over her last relationship. She almost never calls me. I get a lot of mixed messages, and am pretty confused. Am I wasting my time? or should I give it a while? — Nicholas

Nicholas, I think if you're trying for a repeat of that hot night, you probably are wasting your time. She may feel she made a mistake in getting so personal so fast and she may want to slow this potential relationship down. Let her have some time and space. She's being honest about getting over that other relationship (it's only been three weeks according to what you've written). It takes time. She doesn't want to make another mistake. — Queenie

♥

Dear Queenie, I have been friends with a female for about a year now. We slowly started to hang out and have our "make-out" sessions on the living room floor. We lived nearby at the time, and she would make surprise visits to me which I really liked. Neither of us are too open about our feelings. We have never talked about our feelings for each other. 2 months into it, her ex-boyfriend (they had recently broken up) died in an accident.

My response was not to pressure her into anything and just become supportive in any way. Her response was withdrawal (which I understood) and natural depression. She still refers to him in the present tense, and has pictures of him all around. I am confused because we have been hanging out a lot more together, in groups and in one-on-one situations and seem to have grown closer.

I feel like I did in the beginning, and need to tell her that I care for her. I truly adore this girl. But I am afraid if I do then it will screw up our friendship. Can you help? — Brandon

Brandon, she mourns this ex-boyfriend because some issues that needed closure were left open when he died. Perhaps she has some guilt about the breakup, or other issues that needed to be resolved. Death has a way of making even the less perfect of people 'saints.'

There is nothing you can do except let her know you're nearby should she need someone to talk with and share a warm hug. Go slow and easy and let her work it out. — Queenie

♥

Dear Queen of Hearts, I have been involved with this man for the past several months. Everything was fantastic until he started training for a new job. For the first few months it was really difficult, he was always studying and we very rarely had quality time together but I was happy just being with him. These last few months have been really difficult and we have spoken about the relationship, or lack there of numerous amounts of time.

He tells me that he doesn't have time to nurture the relationship and right now he needs to be by himself to concentrate on what he needs to get through. He assures me that he still loves me and doesn't want the relationship to end, just to be put on hold until everything can return to normal. He feels he is not being fair to me and doesn't want to hold me back from anything. I assured him that I love him and I only want to be with him, so if we need to deal with this by not seeing one another until he graduates than fine. I don't know if he is trying to let me down easy but when I ask him if it would be better off for him if we just ended it he tells me no.

I don't know what to do. My heart tells me one thing but my head tells me another. I was engaged to a man a few years back and then he became a police officer and changed completely and we broke off the engagement. I don't know if I am being naive and holding onto something that is just not there. — Hanna

Hanna, true love finds a way... it doesn't sound as though it's "true love" for him. Listen to your head. Continue on with your life. If he's "the one," you'll find out soon enough. If he isn't, why waste another day waiting for him? Good luck. — Queenie

♥

Dear Queenie, I have known this girl for four years. We have always been close friends, nothing romantically or sexual. Lately, I have a different feeling towards her and want to go further into a relationship.

We have always got along good and she enjoys being with me. However, she got involved with a deadbeat guy about three years ago and had a child to him. Never married and they were only together for a short time. Matter of fact, he has not been around for over a year now. She says it is over with him, but I think differently. I asked if we could start a relationship, and she said she is not ready, and doesn't know if she will ever get into another one.

She says right now she can only feel for me like a brother, actually more than a brother, but that is all. I get along good with her and her child, as well as her parents, but am confused. Tell me if you think I should continue with pursuing her, or if I should give up? — Danny

Danny, she has told you how she feels. It is up to you to believe her and act accordingly. You can't force someone to have feelings for you. — Queenie

♥

198

Dear Queenie, I met a young woman recently who works in a company that provides a service to my company. She works very long hours. I find her very nice, intelligent and bubbly and wanted to establish a friendship/relationship. She said that if I wanted a relationship, I was wasting my time as she wanted the time now to establish her career and find out more about herself. She's 25 and I am 30.

I explained to her that career and relationship can be managed at the same time. I understand that she broke off with someone 6 months ago after a 2 year relationship. I do not know how this would turn out (i.e. nothing, friendship or something more than that) and told her that I will go slowly to know her better. I also understand that her parents are divorced and she is staying with her mother. My question is do you think that I am pressuring her or should I just take the "hint"? — Richard

Richard, why not tell her that you think she's a very nice person and that you'd like her for a friend... no strings, no obligations, no romance. Once in a while invite her for a casual lunch or other light social outing. Get to know her, and let her get to know you in this type of unthreatening, non-pressure environment. If there develops an attraction both ways, that's the time to take the friendship another step. — Queenie

♥

Dear Queen of Hearts, you may not remember me from earlier postings in the year, but you have given me wonderful advice. Since last I wrote to you, the man I wanted to become romantically involved with did just that. Before I left for graduate school, he told me he loved me and he wanted to marry me when I finished school. He said, "So this is what love is," and was very happy. I was ecstatic, but sad because I was leaving.

We now communicate with one or two phone calls a week and cute cards and letters to express how we feel. Everything was going fine for a while. We even looked at rings (the solitaire diamond kind) the last time I was home. That was his idea, not mine. He has plunged headfirst into a romantic relationship, and for a while, I was deliriously happy, happy that the man I'd loved for five years had finally given his heart completely to someone...to me.

Lately, though, I feel the strain of graduate study in my life and the possibility of not being able to balance a musical career and a marriage or a family. I had dreams of my career long before I met this man. He says he will support me, but being married someday would still put limits on how much I could perform. And I'm not even sure I would want to get married right out of grad school. I barely know him as more than a friend; I couldn't marry him without taking time to know him romantically as well as platonically.

Not only that, I'm also very lonely. Most of my friends in grad school have constant dates every weekend and I think, "I could have that," but I am reminded of my boyfriend several states away.

I don't want a serious relationship with anyone else, but I would like someone to take me out, show me a nice time, acquaint me with the city, and be a good friend. It is very difficult for me to be so young and yet not be living the life

I want to live. I feel I am not ready for this level of commitment, even though my boyfriend is, and I don't know how I should tell him without shattering what fragile bonds we already have. He would make a wonderful husband someday, and I don't want to lose him completely because I know there aren't many men out there that could be all that he is to me.

We haven't spoken and I am beginning to wonder if he too is having doubts about our relationship. He had promised to call earlier in the week. I'm preparing myself for a breakup, because I don't know if he could ever understand my life as a performer.

His silence is worse than the most hurtful words he could say. I have never been in a long-distance relationship before and I have no idea how to deal with the many emotions I am experiencing. Please help me. — Tamara

Tamara, isn't it sad that what you wanted you got and then you didn't want it any more? Perhaps this is why your boyfriend held off so long before falling in love with you — he was afraid you'd do exactly what you're doing. How sad.

You're going to have to help yourself with this. If you recall, I tried earlier to suggest your course of action wasn't necessarily the proper one for you to take. I can't tell you what the best thing is for you, you have to make that decision. Make a list with the pluses and minuses of the relationship and see how they add up.

Loneliness can be combated by going out with friends — girl friends who don't have dates and guy friends who are just that. Romance doesn't have to be a part of the picture if all you need are companions for non-romantic outings while you're in school.

I would hope your boyfriend would understand that you can't stay just in your room and go to class while he's not around.

No doubt he has sensed the distress you're feeling and it is causing him distress also. You need to talk with him about your current feelings, let him know that it isn't something he has or hasn't done but rather your need for freedom before you commit the rest of your life to a relationship. He may be feeling the same way or he may be fearful that he will lose you. He might. And you might lose him, whether you want to or not.

This is why I originally suggested that you not make any commitments until you were through with your schooling and had a chance to explore the world on your own for a while. Maybe someone else will learn from your experience. — Queenie

♥

Dear Queenie, I just told my friend of 5 months that I have feelings for him more than just a friend. He got mad. I was very shocked about his reaction. He said the quickest way to get rid of someone is ask for more than friendship.

Also that relationship is not important to him at his point in life, that he's "been there done that". Yet he tells me his problems his worries, he only lets me see what's wrong in his life.

My question, is it so possible a man can be so hurt just by an X that he totally gives up on love? I care about him so much, I am willing to stick around just as a friend, but I feel that I can't help him...What can I do? — Lana

Lana, apparently he needs a friend more than he needs a lover at this particular time. Not only that, he may always consider you a friend and never be interested in making you more than that, despite your feelings for him (he does get a choice in this matter). Not such a bad thing if you can handle it, since good friendships can last a lifetime.

Your statement that you feel you can't help him if you stick around as just a friend is curious. He trusts you enough to confide in you... don't you think this is enormous help to him right now? Or are your personal needs getting in the way? If you need more of a relationship than he wishes to give, then I'd suggest that you search for someone else.

And, yes, it is possible for a man (or a woman) to be so hurt that they give up on love... for a while. — Queenie

♥

Dear Queen of Hearts, I'm a 23 year old guy and am in love with a girl 4 years younger than me. We've known each other for more than half a year. We've been going out and I help her with a lot of things. But, the problem is I'm studying abroad.

When I last went back for vacation, I voiced out to her some of my feelings for her. She paused for a while and replied that we're quite different. But, later she told me that she need to consider. I 'pushed' her a bit because I'm leaving for study again and she finally replied that she doesn't wish to get into any relationship yet. What she desires now is just friendship.

I was depressed at first. Before I left, I still go out with her and still continue to care for her. She still accepts my help and present. She also continues to voice out things to me and remarked that my advise is always very valuable to her.

Now I am back for my study and am hardly in touch with her because she's quite busy. Do you think there's still hope for us? Could it because I'm away that she can't accept me? — Vinny

Vinny, both of you are just embarking on the greatest adventure you'll ever have — becoming full-fledged, independent, responsible-only-to-yourself adults! She's discovered the magic of this time and isn't ready to be restricted by a committed relationship. That doesn't mean she won't be ready in a few years.

She's offering her friendship. Life doesn't always give us everything we want when we want it. She wants friendship. You want a relationship. Which one of you should get your wish? I like to think you'd grant her wish for now.

There's always hope. And probably the distance had nothing to do with it. She simply isn't ready for commitment at this time. Don't sit around waiting for her to change. You're only going to be this age once. Make the most of it! — Queenie

♥

Dear Queen of Hearts, I have felt in love with this 25 years old girl about 3 months ago, at that time she was just breaking up with her boyfriend. And she told me that she is scared to get involved in another relationship, she just wants us to be friends. I didn't give up, sending her flowers and gifts. She liked my flowers and gifts and was going out with me about once a week, but couple weeks ago I try to be more close with her, just on words, not even touching. She reaffirm that she want us just to be friends.

Now we are back to friends and going out about once a week and 3 phone calls a week. I send her cards, gifts, flowers once a week. I think that I may be over giving. So far she had bought me a tie, for my birthday, and a mug for me. She told me that she's afraid that I am expecting something from her since I gave so much to her.

During the date, I have paid most of the time but sometimes she would pay and she's on time most of the time. But I am the one who's calling most of the time, she only calls me to say thank you after she received the gift, flowers.

Is she interested in me? Does she like me? Shall I keep going or give up and find someone else? What should I do now? Thank you for your advice. — Jon

Jon, it is sad that when we find someone to love, they don't always feel the same way about us. It would seem that you are a very nice person who cares very much for a very nice girl who is not ready for another serious relationship right at this time. She says that she just wants to be friends.

You must understand that if she had deep feelings for her ex-boyfriend, it will take time to clear her emotions so that she can begin a new relationship. It isn't easy to erase deep feelings for a person when a relationship ends! You wouldn't want her to fall in love with you and then fall in love with someone else so quickly, would you?

Most people need time and space when they are getting over a failed relationship. She is being honest with you about her feelings. It is nice that you want to give her gifts and take her out, but perhaps you are doing too much, too soon. I would think she must like you, or she wouldn't go out with you or talk with you on the phone. But liking you does not mean that she's ready to love you!

If you must have a girlfriend now and you are unhappy with the way things are going between the two of you, then perhaps you need to tell her so and look for another girlfriend. Is there a reason you and she can't be just friends, even if you date others? If she's as nice as you say she is, isn't she worth having as a friend for now? Talk with her. And good luck! – Queenie

Trust and Forgiveness

Trust and Forgiveness

"How come I can't get over the fact that my boyfriend of
1 year and 1/2 cheated on me with one of my best friends? He
claims he was drunk, but I don't know if he was for sure."

It's easy for me to tell someone they need to trust their lover and forgive their betrayal. I know that forgiveness strengthens relationships and trust is imperative if relationships are to survive for the long term. Forgiveness allows a couple to begin again, to move past the pain of betrayal, to rebuild trust. Most relationships are going to have rough spots. He makes a mistake and she forgives. She makes a mistake and he forgives. But what happens if he or she can't forgive and won't forget?

When a lover is genuinely sorry for cheating the betrayed partner has a choice to forgive or not. If there is no forgiveness the relationship ends either immediately or when one or the other decides there's no reason to prolong the inevitable. "I don't want to be hurt again" is the reason some lovers give for splitting up. "How can I trust him (or her)" is the question uppermost in their mind.

My measure for a relationship is simple: When the pain exceeds the pleasure, end it. Put another way: is your life better with or without your lover? That's where forgiveness and trust come into play. Forgiving someone their betrayal does not mean you forget what they've done, it simply means you don't keep bringing up the past and holding it over their head. And what if you forgive and they cheat again?

I'm not one of those "three strikes and you're out" people. I think forgiveness is appropriate for a first offense but a second offense may signal a pattern that will continue for as long as the relationship lasts. Forgive a second offense? Some people can because they've not quite reached their pain "threshold" but the trust levels certainly may suffer.

Each of us knows our limits, that "final strike" that signals the "you're out" for a relationship. Until you reach that point, forgive for your own peace of mind, and trust for the future of your relationship. What's the worst that can happen? You're betrayed again? You'll survive. And what's the best that can happen? Your love grows to a higher level? It can't happen if you don't take the chance that forgiveness and trust are the right moves right now.

♥

Queenie, is there a way to learn how to trust? I have a hard time to trust my partner, and this without reason - I go crazy, somehow I learned how to mistrust and now I want to learn how to trust again. Please help. — Jason

Jason, it takes time and more time. What's the worse that can happen if you trust again and he or she misuses that trust? You hurt again. So? You're hurting right now. Pain is pain. If life is good right now don't ruin it by worrying about what might happen again. If it does, it does. Then you can hurt, when it's justified. — Queenie

♥

Dear Queenie, my boyfriend of 10 years had been cheating on me for the past year. I knew he was but he always denied it. He finally came out and told me that he was cheating on me and that he had fallen in love with her. But that he realized that he had made a mistake and did not want anything to do with her anymore. He said that she came into his life at a time when he wasn't feeling to good about himself and she made him feel good. He wants to get back together and try again.

He says he is going to change and that he will never cheat on me again. The problem though is that she still wants him and she claims she loves him. This is the only time he has ever cheated on me and besides this affair our relationship was fine. I'm not sure whether I should take a chance in letting him in my life again or if I should just move on. Please help! — Mika

Mika, if you love him enough to give him another chance, then forgive and forget. If you can't forgive and forget, then let him go and find someone else. She may still love him, but if he isn't in love with her, then she has no chance. If you do give him another chance, and he fails, write him off. — Queenie

♥

Dear Queen of Hearts, I'm 29 she's 26. I've been dating this woman now for almost great 3years and she broke it off about a month ago now. It started off kind of bad; I dumped her for another girl on a ski trip after seeing her for a month. I dated this other girl for about a month and then started missing her so I went back to her and she accepted me back. Before I met her I was kind of promiscuous and she knew it. I've settled down and changed a lot since then and I'm madly in love with her, never wanting anyone but her.

We moved in together after about a year into the relationship and we recently moved back home to our parents' places, as I went back to school fulltime, it's been 3 months now. I quit a good paying job sold my new car, and I didn't see her everyday; I gave up a lot.

Now I have nothing, although, I don't regret going back to school. I'll admit our relationship got stale since moving out, as I wouldn't do outdoor activities as much as she wanted. We had our mild arguments and I seemed to forget about the problem when she kept thinking about them. We should have worked them out right then and there, but I was lazy.

Every waking moment has been thinking about our relationships demise, and I found a number of things I was doing to push her away and didn't know it until she was gone. I noticed that we didn't resolve many of our problems, I put more weight on my opinions, I didn't take her birthday as serious as I should have, sent her flowers much, some inconsiderate situations, pressured her into some things I thought was a good idea. There are more, but they all were little things that built up and I can see now how they might have been pushing her away.

I wrote her a huge a-mail explaining to her that I see all these things in hindsight and want a second chance, well a third chance. I guess I had to loose her all the way to see this new outlook I have on us working out. I think she doesn't think it's possible for me to change, and eventually I would go back to my old self, but I've had a revelation. It's been a real eye opener and a kick in the ass.

I've tried to give her time, but my heart won't let me. I've tried to see her after her class and have asked for another chance; I've sent her emails, and roses to her work and house. With my optimism and impatient I stupidly called her at work to see what she thought. She said no again and sent me an e-mail saying that we should cut ties until after Christmas; I was sad. I think she's mad at me, and losing some respect for me, lowering my chances of getting her back.

My heart says still fight, but my head says give her more time; I know absents makes the heart grow fonder, but I've got it in the back of my head that she could be out looking for someone else, and if I don't act now I will loose her forever. I think that she still loves me too. She was so much apart of me, it feels like I lost a leg since she left me.

I've remained faithful to her and told her that I'm going to wait for her. I can't see myself with any other ever and wish she believed that, and I think that she thinks I'm out chasing women. I screwed up in cheating on her the first time and I'm not going to screw up now, even she told me not to wait. How much longer should I leave her alone? Should I confront her and tell her how I feel now? Does she want to see me fight for us? Do you think she thinks once a cheat always a cheat, and if so what can I do or say to convince her I couldn't? Should I ask her to go to counseling? I know there is a lot of questions her but could you answer them to the best of your ability? Thank you! I need her back! — Signed, owner of a shredded heart

Dear Shredded, when you break someone's heart, you can expect to get a lot of heartache back when they get enough courage to call it quits. Maybe she's through with you, maybe all she needs is a break. Either way, she needs some space and you're not giving it to her by sending her notes, calling on the phone, and emailing her. Cut all ties and let her have the space she needs and has told you she wants.

I have no way of knowing if she buys into the "once a cheat always a cheat" line of thinking but you have a lousy history and she's smart to be cautious. You're talking a good game, but actions will speak volumes more and your actions until she left haven't been saying the right things about your feelings for her.

Send her a nice teddy bear with a little heart locket or something else sentimental for Christmas along with a nice card. Don't call, don't drop by, and don't send her email. Just send a nice little romantic gift. Maybe she'll give you a chance to talk. — Queenie

♥

Dear Queenie, I have been going out with my girlfriend for almost a year now. The thing of it is that I am 21 years old and that she is my first real relationship. In the past I just didn't bother having a girlfriend. I was too busy going to parties and going out with the guys. The problem that I am having is that she and I say we love each other and have sex quite often. These kinds of things are kind of new to me, and I'm having a big fear of her cheating on me. I don't know if I'm just being a little paranoid, or I just don't want to be hurt. We spend a great deal of time together, almost all of our time.

For some reason when I heard how she had sex on the beach a year or so before we started going out I got all kinds of depressed and sad, and had the fear that it could happen to me. I heard of this about 4 months ago and it still bothers me. I really would like to know why that is. I also would like to know why I am so afraid of her cheating on me. Thank you for taking the time to read this, I hope you have some kind of help or solution. — tbone

Tbone, why are you worrying about something that happened a year before the two of you got together? That was then, this is now! You certainly didn't tell me anything in your email that would indicate she had cheated on someone else before she met you so why would you think she would cheat on you?

Love means sometimes you'll get hurt. Relax; enjoy the love the two of you share. Have a good time. Being depressed and sad sounds like a person I wouldn't want to be around. Why do you think she'd enjoy it? Forget about the past. It didn't concern you then, it shouldn't concern you now. — Queenie

♥

Hi Queenie, I've been living with my boyfriend for 4 years. Sometimes I am madly in love with him and there are times I ask I myself why I am with him. He is a good person 75% of the time; he helps with laundry, cooking, cleaning etc, and is a good lover. But there are times he says things that really hurt me like: You want me to leave so you can find someone else. And do you love me? I wish he would be more secure. We are always together and hardly go out apart, by choice.

I do not cheat on him or plan to; I do love him and believe in for better or worse... I just want to know....How can I get him to believe in me and quit being so insecure. His insecurity may stem from his first wife cheating on him. We get along really good most of the time and do talk a lot. I tell him how much I love him and need him just about everyday and he tells me. We laugh a lot and we enjoy each others company. I know everyone has their little fights. It's just his insecurity and stupid remarks that get me so mad and upset. Can you please help me understand why a person can love someone but can't believe in them? — Anna

Anna, it can take a long time for someone who has been betrayed by someone they love to learn to trust anyone completely. Hopefully, within time your boyfriend will learn that you are not his ex-wife and he will trust you as much as he trusted her before she betrayed him.

You are paying the price for her betrayal and he doesn't understand that. Unless you have experienced the pain of adultery in marriage, you cannot know the fear a man or woman will have that anyone they love deeply will betray that love. Give him time, give him lots of assurance that he's the only one and that you love him completely. — Queenie

♥

Dear Queen, about 9 months ago, my boyfriend cheated on me. The girl he cheated with was supposed to be a very very good friend. At the time that this happened, my boyfriend and I were having problems. We had just broken up the day before it happened, and he was supposed to move out. This girl took advantage of him. She fed him lines like, "I would never treat you like she treats you" or, "no matter what, I would always love you." Being that he wasn't hearing the right words from me, the things she said enticed him.

It takes two to tango, so to speak. He had his role in it too. We talked and talked about it, and I realized that I was not ready to lose him. I confronted the girl. Most of the things she told me were lies. She was trying to make me think that he had cheated on me in the past, which I knew he never did. My boyfriend and I ended up getting back together again. This girl started causing problems. So he called her and told her that his name better not come out of her mouth again. A few weeks later, she ended up going out with his brother-in-law.

Now I am pregnant, thinking that all is fine. But it's not. My feelings of anger are aroused. He has not done anything but be nice. He spends all his free time with me, makes me feel good, and is the man that every woman would kill for. I am very confident that he adores me just by how he treats me. I've gotten a lot better too. I am no longer abusive towards him; I listen to him, and show him affection. Our relationship is at its best, it's like the incident was a turning point in our relationship. I am very confident that he has not cheated on me since.

I thought that I could forgive and forget, but I can't let go of what happened. I am afraid that I might get revenge on him and make him feel the same way he made me feel. I feel so betrayed for what he did. I have confronted the girl again, about 2 months ago. She apologized, and admitted she shouldn't have lied about things, and should have stepped away in the very beginning. We are not friends, but we are no longer enemies. First thing I want to know, what is the percentage of men cheating again on the same lover? Second, just some friendly advice about my situation. — Monica

Monica, I have no idea about percentages or other cheating data — I'm not really aware of any serious studies that have been made of this situation. And I'm not sure why statistics would help you in this situation. Betrayal is a terrible thing. It takes a long time to build back the trust once you have been betrayed.

From what you have said, your attitude and treatment toward him helped drive him to someone else. Too bad it was this 'friend' who had a lying problem on top of everything else. That doesn't excuse what he did, because she certainly didn't force him to do something he didn't want to do. And, if he was unhappy with you, he should have left you first and then started something with her.

However, you say that this whole incident brought the two of you closer together. Okay, consider the good that happened, forget the bad and give this man, the father of your child, a whole lot of forgiveness. Start again, with a fresh slate, and forget the past since it can't be undone. But don't forget that if you abuse this relationship, you're asking for trouble. — Queenie

♥

Hi Queenie, I am in a relationship that is pretty great except for one thing. My boyfriend lives two hundred miles away from me and he's in the military which is not a problem other than he wants our relationship to go further, and get a little more serious.

Here's the real problem. I feel that I can't trust him. He's very sweet and caring, and is really into me, he told me he can see himself with me for a long time. But I feel that I just can't let myself believe him? What can I do for myself, and what can I say to him that might make this better? — Tiffany

Tiffany, why don't you trust him? Has he cheated on you in the past? Is it the distance and the fact that you can't be there with him every day?

If you love him, forget about the worrying and the distance. Which pain would you rather have? The pain of him being gone? Or the pain of the distance? Or, is it that he wants more intimacy and you aren't ready? If that's the problem, hold off until you're more comfortable with the situation. Don't force anything. — Queenie

♥

Queenie, do you think I'm crazy that I gave my girlfriend another chance because she cheated on me? My friends think I should dump her because once they cheat they do it again. I lost lots of friends because I stay with her. — Anthony

Anthony, it doesn't matter what I think or what your friends think. It matters what you think and whether or not the two of you are in love. If you have lost friends, they weren't true friends. It is not true that everyone falls into the "once a cheater always a cheater" category.

Some people learn what's important and never cheat again. Trust your girlfriend until she does something to prove she isn't deserving of that trust. — Queenie

♥

Dear Queenie, my question to you is: When you fall in love with someone. Should one fully trust the other person unconditionally, until that person gives you a reason not to? (This is how SHE feels) or should they have to earn that trust through ones actions and communication (I feel this way. I am also not the jealous type or do I care if she has a few friends that are male). Please help me if you can. — *Stan*

Stan, you trust until you have reason not to. In other words, you start off believing that the person is honest and true. Would you trust that someone wasn't a thief or would you make them prove that they weren't? Are you the type of person who believes that women can't have male 'friends'? If so, you're going to have quite a bit of difficulty in life and love. — Queenie

♥

Hi Queenie, I wasn't totally honest trying to end a relationship, got involved with someone else fell in love, they resent me for lying to them, I love them dearly and now they don't want me, no communication whatsoever, What shall I do to have them in my life to get them back my heart is broken, after I owned up to the truth, now they don't think they can ever trust me. I'm very sorry this happened. My heart is now broken, what shall I do to keep them in my life. — *Benjamin*

Benjamin, they aren't obligated to give you a chance to hurt them again. No matter how heartbroken you may feel, their pain is worse. Maybe they don't consider you to be worth so much pain to them. If that's the case, there's nothing you can do to get back with them.

Consider this to be a lesson in the consequences of dishonesty in relationships. Perhaps, if you are a quick study, you won't have to go through this type of heartbreak too many times. — Queenie

♥

Dear Queen of Hearts, I have experienced adultery with my friend of 4 years. As a result have been very insecure about his activities. I have expressed on many occasions about my trusting him again. We both have promised to try and let the other know what we are up to. Especially when something unexpected occurs. I have noticed that sometimes he would call me or leave a message about his whereabouts. My problem is when he claims friends unexpectedly call, he never leaves a call or leave a message about what he is going to do. Could this be because he is lying or just don't care about what I think or how I feel? Or should I stop letting him know my whereabouts? — *Carole*

Carole, I don't know his side of this relationship and from what you say, I'm not sure if he would tell the truth about his feelings toward you. But it isn't my happiness on the line here, it's yours. Either you trust him or you don't. If you don't, why be in the relationship? — Queenie

♥

Queenie, how can I learn to trust my mate again after he has cheated on me? And also how do I get over it and stop throwing it in his face? — *Paula*

Paula, if he cheated once, he deserves another chance, without being reminded of his mistake. Why destroy a good relationship over one mistake? If he cheated more than once.... dump him and move on. — Queenie

♥

Hi Queenie, I'm in a rather unique situation and I don't know what to do? I left home (and my boyfriend) to take a job for overseas for several months. While I've been away my boyfriend has cheated on me (more than once with more than one person). . . . I don't think that he would have done this if I was still home but that doesn't excuse it either! I thought that we were committed enough to one another that we could be separated physically for this long and still be together?.

He still loves me and he swears on his life that he will do everything in his power to spend the rest of his life with me. . . . And I believe that he will do that but I'm not so sure I should let him.

I do love him and I know that he is a good guy. . . . . He's been my best friend for 5 years and my boyfriend for 2 years. . . . . We're in love but. . . . . . . I don't know. . . He says that our love should see us through this but I believe that our love should have been strong enough to have never created this mess? But I do still love him.

Please. . . a little help would be greatly appreciated. My heart tells me to work things out but my heart also said we would never have a problem like this. Thank you for anything you can tell me. . . . . It's good to have an outsider's opinion on the matter. — April

April, if you love him and are planning on spending the rest of your life with him (marriage, kids, the whole route), forget this ever happened. Trust him. If he breaks that trust in the future you can take the appropriate action then. Listen to your heart. — Queenie

♥

Queenie, I am a very jealous person and I do not trust my boyfriend because of certain situations. I have tried every thing from therapy to anti depressants and I am almost to the end of the line. My boyfriend and I fight constantly and I'm afraid our relationship will come to a bitter end. Do you have any ideas on how to help me get through my jealousy and untrust? — Tanya

Tanya, if those "certain situations" mean he has cheated or is cheating, then perhaps he isn't worthy of trust. If you mean that he has cheated in the past but says it's over, then, unless you've got some *very* strong evidence that he isn't to be trusted, you should forgive and forget.

Which hurts worse, the pain from trusting and finding that trust was misplaced, or the pain of not trusting and losing his love forever? If you trust, you have a chance of getting hurt, but you also have the chance of having a good relationship with him. I think the risk of a broken heart is a small price to pay for trusting someone. — Queenie

♥

Dear Queen of Hearts, recently my relationship with my girlfriend ended because I was worried about her safety. See she and I chat in this chat room on the internet, and I was trying to protect her by telling her that he was a cheater, and that he only wants women for sex. I was trying to protect her that was all. I never meant to hurt or upset her you know? I really love her lots and would do anything for her. See she lives in Canada and I live in the United States. He lives in Canada too, but she and I are in love. I was suspecting he was trying to get with her, so I was worried about her and stuff, I was watching where she was going, I mean I trust her, but not him.

She had to keep explaining herself, which I never wanted her to do, I love her so much and I lost her, everything that her and I had. I saw her in Canada at the beginning of January and it was the most romantic time. Then when I got back home, she wasn't the same, she didn't talk to me as much and she chatted with him more than me. She and I knew each other for a year or more, she only knew him for 2 months, so you would think she would understand where I was coming from! How I want to protect her from perverts, why? Cause I love and care for her. She and I used to talk for hours before I saw her, everyday and all night we used to chat. I would call her and stuff.

See she never had a relationship, but she is in love with me. She broke it off with me cause she said that she had to think of school, work etc. I accepted that. I am so upset, because I'm thinking her and him are together, for I caught them in a private chat room and I saw his post to her saying "IF there is an us" which is making me think they are together, which explains why she doesn't talk to me as much, and why we broke up. I don't want to come to conclusions though. I love her, but I don't know if she still feels the same. She said because of all of this trouble between her and I she cries at night. She also said that I'll always be her first true love and all that. In her last letter to me, it made me think that its all my fault.

I'm thinking maybe if I go to the person I used to be, then she will love me again? I'm not sure if I should date again right now or what? I mean this girl is perfect, she is my dream girl, everything that I could possibly want in a companion, I'm so in love with her, but I don't know whether I should set her free. I want her to be happy, not upset ya know? Well thanks for listening; I hope to hear from you. God Bless! — Norman

Norman, you say you trust her but you don't trust him but what you really mean is you really don't trust her. If you trusted her you would know that in order for him to take your place, she would have to let him. In other words, he can't *make* her do anything she doesn't want to do. So, if they are together, don't blame him, it is because she wants to be with him.

I'm not sure what you mean by you were doing certain things to try to protect her from him or even how you know that she was in contact with him when you live so far apart. Are you saying that you figured out some of her passwords and have been tracking her online activities? If so, you've gone past the line as far as caring is concerned.

When you grow older you will understand that you cannot tell someone else what to do, and you cannot control someone else's actions. You'll also understand that no matter how long you date someone, the length of time does not mean you own them.

Love means respecting each other's space, not trying to take that space away. Good luck with your next romance. — Queenie

♥

Queenie, my boyfriend cheated on me 2 years ago. I can't seem to trust him and it is pulling our relationship apart. I love him so much and I really need to put this behind me but I don't know how. It affects everything, it is so true that without trust a relationship is nothing, we are only holding on to hope. — Carole

Carole, either you want to love him or you don't. Trust him again. Forget what happened. How can you possibly hurt more than you already do? If he breaks the trust again, walk away. — Queenie

♥

Dear Queenie, my girlfriend once done drugs with her long time friend. And I told her, that person is a bad influence. After couple month she started talking to her friend again. Which she didn't tell me about, that I have to find out from someone else. After I found out she were talking to this person and confronted her, she said "I didn't tell you because you will get mad." And I'm really piss off not because she talk to this person, but because she not been honest with me. What should I do? — Rick

Rick, what do you want to do? Honesty is very important in any relationship. If this is a one time lapse, perhaps you want to calm down and give her another chance to be honest with you.

If this is something she does a lot, you might want to rethink how serious you want this relationship to be. Good luck. — Queenie

♥

Hi Queenie, I have been dating my boyfriend for seven months now. He has been talking about us getting married (not in so many words, he hasn't come right out and asked me) and every time I try to draw him out, he clams up. The problem is I'm beginning to think he's cheating on me.

He's started to stay away from home overnight, which he didn't use to do. The last time he stayed away from home was last Saturday night. He said he went to a football game with his friends and he says they got home around 11:30 p.m. but he got a call that his uncle was in the emergency room at the hospital. He called me around 7:00 Sunday morning.

I have only been seeing him for about six or seven hours a week, and there are several other things that I can't quite put my finger on but they just don't feel right. He says he bought me something that will prove to me that he's serious about me but it's my Christmas present. He says he's not seeing anyone else, that he is not even interested in seeing any one else, and that he loves me and only me. Should I trust him or trust my instincts that are telling me something is wrong? — Danielle

Danielle, if you don't trust him, trust your instincts. He can say anything. It's what he does that counts. Incidentally, since you're close to being part of the family (since he's been talking about getting married), it would seem the "family" thing to do would be to call one of his parents and inquire about the uncle's recovery. — Queenie

♥

Queenie, I am single. I got a girl that I do not love because I think she do not is worthy of me. I do not trust her, she said she loves me but I don't believe her. — Jamal

Jamal, if that's the situation you need to get another girlfriend and let this one find someone who will trust her. — Queenie

♥

Dear Queen of Hearts, I was engaged to a guy about a year and half ago. We had been dating for 4 months before that and we were deeply in love. I was having personal problems at the time and couldn't fully open up to me about everything that was going on, so he ended up finding someone else and moved out (we had been living together for 6 months) with no notice. He moved in with this other woman and lived with her for about a year and a half. Meantime, I never talked to him, just went on with my life.
About 4 months ago, his girlfriend moved out on him with no notice and he found out my phone number from a friend about a month ago and we have been talking.... he wants me back, says he still loves me. I'm not involved with anyone and have always thought about him over the past year and a half and of course am still in love with him.
I want to know if you think this could be a rebound relationship (me) or if he could really mean what he says. He has apologized about what he did which involved me and I have forgiven him. Or, maybe she was the rebound relationship?? I just don't know and I don't want to get hurt again the way he hurt me before. — Shavon

Shavon, it appears she did to him what he did to you. I'd suggest that if you decide to get back together with him that you take your time. Just remember how badly he hurt you the first time. It's acceptable to forgive him once, but don't go so quickly that he'll get a chance to do the same thing a second time. — Queenie

♥

Queenie, how come I can't get over the fact that my boyfriend of 1 year and 1/2 cheated on me with one of my best friends. He claims he was drunk, but I

don't know if he was for sure. I hate the fact that I can't trust him anymore. Will it ever get better between us???? Will I ever forget???? — Gina

Gina, very little causes as much pain in a relationship as when one of the partners cheats on the other. In this case you had double pain because one of your "best" friends also betrayed your trust in her. Being drunk is not a valid excuse.

Restoring trust takes a long time. If you believe him, if you will forgive him, and if you will forget that it happened, it will help pave the way for a better relationship between the two of you. It's not easy. You are probably afraid that if you do trust him he will cheat again, making you seem to be a fool for believing in him. Maybe he will.

Trust him anyway. Give him the benefit of the doubt. Forgive him this mistake. Put it out of your mind. Learn to enjoy being with him, the way it was before this happened. History cannot be changed. If he cheats again, give him the door. — Queenie

♥

Hello, Queenie, I have written before but never got any advice. Anyways, this is my problem. My ex boyfriend and I had been going out for 2 1/2 years. A year and a half ago we started having problems. To keep this simple I started feeling insecure because he and another girl started talking to each other everyday. He would flirt very openly with this girl in front of all of us. Well I asked him to please stop talking to her and he told me that he thought of being with her sexually if we didn't stop fighting.

Naturally I was upset with this comment and I broke up with him. Well he came back to me saying that he did not want to lose me so he would stop talking to this girl and we could work our problems out. After that I thought everything would be fine again. Approx. 4 months later he started to talk to her again. I found out three months after he started to talk to her. He had been having lunch with her, going to her house after leaving mine, e-mailing her, and phoning her.

Again I was pretty upset and broke up with him. He came back asking for another chance and promised to stop talking to her. I took him back but I was very skeptical. It turns out that they started talking again. Naturally I was upset and broke it off.

The problem is that he claims he wants me back and it is over this other girl. Supposedly they have stopped talking since we broke up. I love this guy with all my heart. I want to give him another chance but I am afraid to get hurt. He says he doesn't see his life without me in it. What should I do? I want him but I can't trust him anymore. Please help me!! — Nina

Nina, trust is critical to the success of any relationship. If you take him back again you must be prepared to trust him. Are you? Are you ready to give him one last chance? To forgive and forget? To believe him when he says he cares only for you? If not, tell him it's over and start dating others. — Queenie

♥

Hi Queenie, I am 27 years old and I have been dating my girlfriend for 10 years. We have been together since she was a frosh in high school. I am at the point now that I want to move on. She on the other hand is not sure if she's ready because she's never really been on her own. I don't have a problem agreeing to take some time off except the friends she hangs around are bad influences.

Last summer I asked her to marry me and she said she couldn't because she wasn't ready. We took some time off after that and then I left the relationship. About 3 weeks later she came back saying she was sorry and she wanted to get married. After long discussions I found out she was cheating on me.

I really love her and I wanted to try and work things out. I have forgiven her and I feel that I'm ready again. I haven't asked her again because she mentioned that she may need some time for herself. I know that time off with her friends will only mean going from club to club, and her cousins talking to every guy they see. So do I take the time off and hope our love is true or am I setting myself up for another broken heart? I love her and I want to try but I don't know if I'm just being blinded by love. — Fred

Fred, I told one of my male friends about your situation and asked his advice. He first stated that you should dump her before she dumps you. After a bit he decided that wasn't an adequate response and said it appears that the relationship won't work because there's too much "baggage" and not enough life experience by either one of you.

From my perspective I have to agree with him that neither of you could possibly have enough experience in dealing with matters of the heart to be able to have the type of commited relationship that will survive the long term. You say you have forgiven her, but you surely have not forgotten what she did to you. This appears to be eroding the relationship all on its own. You don't trust her out of your sight with her friends, and trust is an important component — perhaps the most important — of a marriage or any committed relationship.

Neither one of you has experienced life enough to spend the rest of your lifetimes successfully together. If you have been with this girl for the past 10 years you are a perfect candidate for "male midlife crisis" when, at 40 or so, you look in a mirror, see a few gray hairs and wrinkles, and gasp because life is passing you by and you haven't experienced all that life has to offer! Get out and do it! NOW! Let her do the same! If the two of you are star-crossed lovers, meant to have that fine and true relationship we all yearn for, you'll come back together. If not, don't waste any more time! Life's too short! – Queenie

How to Leave Your Lover

How to Leave Your Lover

"I'm currently engaged to be married. I no longer wish to go
through with the wedding. I've tried numerous times to tell
her how I feel but I just can't do it."

In a perfect world love would last forever. This isn't a perfect world and even the most perfect love can turn sour leaving no option but to break up. Breaking up is a painful process that should not be attempted by those who are cowardly. Unfortunately, the acts of cowards make breaking up more painful than necessary.

The best way to end a relationship is by leaving alone. That means don't start a new relationship before your old one has ended. No matter how badly breaking up will hurt your lover, betrayal sets an extremely high pain level that will be very difficult to overcome. Leaving one relationship to run to the arms of a new love is the supreme act of a cowardly lover.

If you must end your relationship, do it without involving other people. Don't discuss it with friends, family or coworkers to get their opinions and their support. There's nothing worse for an ex to learn than that everyone else knew you were leaving long before you walked out the door. It's embarrassing and humiliating and you don't need to add that to your list of break up sins.

To minimize the trauma for your soon-to-be-ex, don't end your relationship on a day of celebration such as Valentine's Day, Christmas, Easter, their birthday, your birthday, or any other day that has special significance. If you can't stay in the relationship any longer, pack up and leave well before a significant date or holiday.

If you're serious about ending the relationship, do it. Don't leave and return, leave and return, leave and return. No matter how much your lover hurts, you're only giving them false hope by returning just to leave again.

Most people ask "why" when a relationship ends even if they're afraid of what they'll hear. If you can provide a sensitive and logical answer, give it, but don't get drawn into painful debates or angry name calling. Leave the relationship the same way you entered it but close the door tightly on the way out.

♥

Hi Queenie, I left the US some years ago and have lived with a man out
of the country since. We have a small business that has supported us. I am getting
older and my better judgment says it is time to leave but I'm afraid of the unknown,
where to live what would I do.

Where and how does someone in my situation begin to make sensible
decision to begin a new life? As for my relationship I believe there is no future and
time is running out. — Carly

Carly, yes, time is running out. The decision to leave is the hardest part. Once you make the decision and do it, you'll take each day's challenges as they come. It's not easy but it is rewarding. Each day that you wait is one less day you have in your future. — Queenie

♥

Dear Queen of Hearts, I don't want to date my boyfriend anymore. We had dated for 5 months three years ago, then I started dating this guy who I became engaged to and I dated for 2 1/2 years. Then I broke up with him and started dating the guy from three years ago. We have been dating for 3 months again and I know it is not what I want. He lives in another state which makes it more difficult. He doesn't respect what I say and so in return neither do I. We don't have that mutual respect for each other that relationships should have. Also, he doesn't want me being friends with my ex and told me to choose my ex or him, and I told him not to do that, I told him not to force me to choose a friend over him.

He will be here in 5 days and I don't know what to do, because I don't want him to kiss me or anything. I thought about breaking up with him when he came up here, since his plane ticket is nonrefundable but I don't want to be with him, because he is very dramatic and will make a big scene and cry and beg me, and all this crap and I don't feel like putting up with it, I don't know what to do, especially since he keeps telling me I am the only positive thing in his life right now. So please help and give me some good advice. — Rhonda

Rhonda, you broke up with him once and you broke up with your ex after being engaged to him so you must have your 'break-up' skills pretty well defined. Not much I can suggest as far as how to do it other than just do it. If you don't want to 'put up' with the big scene then call him or write him or email him and tell him it's over and give him some decent reasons why the two of you just aren't couple material.

Or, since you dated him and probably told him how much you loved him, etc, etc, and gave him some hope that this was the one true love, at least resign yourself to listening to him beg and plead and try to change your mind, reminding yourself that it'll soon be over and you can find someone else to fall in love with. Sure he'll cry and beg and make a scene. But he'll get over you just like he did before. This time, let him leave for good. — Queenie

♥

Dear Queenie, I've recently graduated from college and I am currently using my degree in the field that I studied. About a year ago, just before I graduated, I met this girl. I haven't had a girlfriend since high school. This one was nice and I liked her a lot before I knew she was a leech. Before I knew that if she could get me to be next to her that she would never let me leave. She's a psycho. I must have told her 6 times already that I wanted to leave. She doesn't listen.

I've tried talking things out with her, but things just get worse. She's told me on countless occasions that she doesn't know what she'd do without me, and that she just couldn't go on living without me. I can hardly stand it any more. on top of all of this, she's a feminist. I think she truly believes that it's my duty to go to work and make money to spend on her.

She's going to school right now, but she has still managed to be home every day when I get home. We've been living together for over a year now and I don't know what to do. She's to a point where I think someone is going to have to just leave before I can have one bit of happiness. I think one of the reasons why I can't stand her is because her parents have a lot of money. Her Mom has no respect and doesn't care where the money comes from. But it's not her fault. She never had money her whole life and now she's got more than she would ever need. So she has a warped view of money.

She's told me that she doesn't know how much money goes through our house. We run out of money every paycheck. I'm down to ten dollars in my bank account right now and I can't take it anymore. I get paid on Friday or Monday. I hope it's Monday just so that I can maybe have a little more later.

I make plenty of money, but she spends it all. It's not like she takes my card out and spends it all on whatever she wants either. She's gives some to charity and she asks me if she can buy something or other in such a way that I am an asshole if I say no to her. We are never going to have anything if we keep going on like this. I'm going to blow. I feel locked up. Last night I was hoping that a spaceship would come along and aliens would abduct me.

Weeks before, I came pretty close to jerking the steering wheel into oncoming traffic. I don't know what to do. I can't talk to her. I need to get away from her more than anything and she wants me to be near her more than anything. Please, please, please help me.

I need a change of scenery. I can't take this humidity anymore. Helpless, hopeless, running out of time (I feel like I'm about to be converted into a ball of mush through a painful process of her life). — James

James, what is keeping you from leaving her? Is there a child? Do you have a legal arrangement? Are you afraid of hurting her feelings? Are you spineless? I fail to understand why you don't pack your bags and walk out the door. Even if it's your apartment, do it and take control of your life.

There are times during your life that you'll need to make some difficult decision and then put them into play. This is one of those times. — Queenie

♥

Dear Queenie, I recently broke up with my boyfriend of 6 months, He was very upset and did not know how he was supposed to cope with it. I told him that I did not have the same feelings that I had in the beginning. I also told him that I had no interest in him anymore. Was I harsh? I told him over the phone, but I wanted to tell him in person.

I felt bad that I had to tell him that way. He told me not to bother seeing him when I go back home for spring break. After talking to him for 2 hours on the

phone he made me promise to go and see him so he can hold me for the last time. I don't know what to do. Please help me? — Arial

Arial, I can't help you, this is your promise. I always try not to make promises I can't keep. In my opinion, that would be a worthwhile goal for you to make, also. — Queenie

♥

Hi Queenie, I've been dating someone on and off for about a year and half now. Before this, we dated in high school and broke up under very bad circumstances. A year later, we reconnected and that's when our present relationship began. Since then, it's been a constant string of broken promises and shattered hearts as a result of some selfish and self-absorbed behavior on his part. Recently he realized that he may have lost me for good and worked hard to win me back. We decided to begin dating again. It just felt right.

For a short while, our relationship was heavenly and I found myself falling in love with him all over again. But over the past couple of weeks, my feelings for him have changed drastically. This is of no fault of his own, however. He is still a reborn angel. For an unknown reason, though, I don't feel the same level of passion and love for him that I once did.

We live four hours away and only see each other every few weeks which doesn't help the situation. I do know that I love him despite any pain he had caused me. I'm not sure if past heartbreaks are standing in my way or that I am outgrowing him. I can't imagine letting go of him but at the same time, I can't help but think that it's time to move on and find someone else.

The prospect of this breaks my heart and no matter what he has done in the past, I cannot find it in my heart to hurt him in any way. He has made it very clear how deeply he loves me and has walked to the ends of the earth for me again and again since I took him back. Please offer any suggestions as to how I can sort through these feelings that I've been having (or lack thereof) and what course of action I should take in light of them. Thanks so much for your help. — Kandi

Kandi, as people mature, their needs change. That is very true in relationships. I think you have identified the situation and know the answer. It's difficult to dump someone you care about, but the pain will go away and eventually, if you do it right and with caring, they will return as a friend.

You are not obligated to love someone because they love you. Your first obligation is to yourself and finding the person who makes you the happiest. Throughout your life, there will be many relationships that don't work perfectly for one or the other of you. Learn now how to end them as gently as possible. Good luck. — Queenie

♥

Dear Queenie, I just broke up with a man whom I have been seeing for over 11 months. Why? Because I fell out of love with him and now I am beginning

to see another man. My problem is that my heart still aches for this first man. He loves me so dearly and I can see that. I know that I do not wish to be with him. So why does it hurt so much? I am in my mid twenties so I have had experience with break ups but for some reason this one hurts so much? Did I do the right thing? Will the pain ever go away? — Darlene

Darlene, I have no way of knowing if you did the right thing but if you fell out of love with him, I have to think you did. Who knows why it still hurts. Maybe you have a super case of "guilt's" because he's such a nice guy. I'd suggest that you stop having contact with this man so that he can heal and you can get on with your new relationship. It is the best for the both of you. — Queenie

♥

Queenie, I'm currently engaged to be married. I no longer wish to go through with the wedding. I've tried numerous times to tell her how I feel but I just can't do it. The main reason is that she is extremely sensitive. In her previous relationship, she attempted to commit suicide. This worries me because I still care about her and I don't want her to hurt herself.

I understand that she will be seriously hurt emotionally but I want to prevent any more than that as much as I can. So my question is what can I do for her and how should I tell her? I'll do what ever it takes. Again, although I don't have intimate feelings for her, I still care about her very much. — Alan

Alan, breaking up is always going to hurt someone. How you do the breaking up can soften the hurt, but not by much, it's still going to hurt. In this case you have the added problem that she may be emotionally unstable. For this reason, I'd suggest that you seek counseling for yourself to understand how to deal with her and with your feelings at this time.

Perhaps the best way to get help for her would be if you tell her that you want to go into couples counseling or marriage counseling. Then the two of you go together and each of you express your feelings openly and honestly. This is a situation that needs more than I can offer. Good luck. — Queenie

♥

Dear Queen of Hearts, I've been dating my current girlfriend for roughly 9 months. Things, however, are very much not going well. I knew she had some problems when I first started dating her, but I didn't know what I was up against. She is obsessive and likely co-dependant over me. I did like her to start with, but she is also a very crude and aggravating person. I can barely stand her. I would just break up with her if it weren't for the fact that she is a diagnosed and unmediated manic-depressive who may just try to kill herself again. — Stephan

Stephan, does this mean that you have committed your lifetime to her? Because if you haven't, you're going to have to break up with her some time. You said "who may just try to kill herself again." Has she made the attempt before when you tried to leave her. If so, how serious was the attempt and why didn't it succeed? I don't have the training to counsel you properly. You need to find someone qualified to help you. Good luck. — Queenie

♥

Hi Queenie, I am in an engagement of 5 months. Since we have been engaged, it seems like we are going in two different directions. It also seems like so much of a struggle to find things that we both like to do. I have tried to tell her how I feel. She gets very defensive and ends the conversation. The next day, it is like nothing happened. I don't know if she is in denial or what.

My question is what is the best way to end this relationship knowing that I have more than once told her how I feel about things (I have even told her that we need to really think about continuing with the relationship.) Thank you. — Mac

Mac, the best way to end this is quickly and with as little harm as possible. Clearly the two of you have fallen out of "sync" with each other and things will only get worse from this point on. This sometimes happen when the "total commitment" of marriage is made.

Tell her something such as: you feel that the two of you are not ready to continue the engagement, that you love her, respect her, and want a lifetime of happiness for her, but you feel there is something missing in the relationship. She isn't going to be happy. As a matter of fact, the tears, shouting and all the emotions that will be released may just bring the two of you closer together or may make it clear why this won't work. — Queenie

♥

Hi Queenie, a male friend of mine wants to break up with his present female relationship because his former lover is now in the picture — this is someone he still loves and who now has revealed that she loves him, too.

This guy is a "nice Guy" and wants to find a low stress/non-hurtful way of breaking up with his present lady. Any suggestions? — Caroline

Caroline, there is no low stress/non-hurtful way of breaking up with someone who loves you. There also is no low stress/non-hurtful way of staying with someone when you don't love them anymore. To cause the least amount of pain to her, he needs to explain the situation and beg her to forgive him for the pain he has and is going to cause her.

Watch how he does this so that when he dumps you later on for someone else you'll know the drill and be able to have more empathy for her feelings. You are the "former lover" aren't you? — Queenie

♥

Hi Queenie, I have a problem. I broke up with my boyfriend 3 years ago. He tells me he still loves me and I was his first love. I don't love him anymore. He keeps visiting me and looks for excuses to talk to me. It is annoying because every time we are having a conversation, he starts talking about how much he loves me. He asks me if I want to sleep with him. I told him no because I want to go on with my life. I stopped talking to him before but then I felt bad. I would like to keep his friendship but I feel uncomfortable every time he talks about us going back together. We talked about it but he says that he can not change. I broke up with him because our relationship was not healthy. — Audra

Audra, there are some people who cannot be "just friends." It doesn't matter if you hurt his feelings at this point. Tell him that because he cannot change his behavior, and because his behavior is hurting you, you do not want to see him anymore. Good luck. — Queenie

♥

Dear Queen of Hearts, I have been involved with the same guy for about 5 years, and I care about him very much. However, I am realizing that I have feelings for someone else. The problem is, the someone else is one of his very good friends. I don't know what to do. — Juli

Juli, have you grown bored with your current relationship? It sounds as if you have or that it doesn't fulfill all your emotional needs. Do you want to marry your boyfriend? Would you like to spend the rest of your life with this guy? If not, make a clean break and then let it be known that you are no longer involved and are available for dating.

If his good friend picks up the clues and asks you out after the relationship has ended the problems are much fewer than if you start something while you're still dating his friend. To make a play while still involved with your current boyfriend might have some unpleasant complications and you might lose not only your current boyfriend but this potential new guy as well. – Queenie

Cheaters and Cheating

Cheaters and Cheating

"I have cheated on him with three men (all one night stands).
After the first one, I confessed, and he forgave me. I never
intended for it to happen again."

Why do lovers cheat? The reasons are probably as varied as the creativity many cheaters use to cover their tracks. Regardless of the reason given, cheating is certainly one of the most painful things a lover can do when they're in a committed relationship.

Can cheating ever be justified? Most cheaters can come up with any number of excuses, even placing blame on something their partner has done or is doing. "You made me cheat" is a phrase heard by many heartbroken lovers once a betrayal has been discovered.

Can cheating be forgiven? Forgiveness takes time and a lot of cheaters expect their partner to be quick with forgiving and forgetting. "Okay, yeah, I'm sorry, I'll never do it again," is expected to wipe out the pain of discovery. It is supposed to put the trust back into the relationship.

Can a cheater be trusted to never cheat again? Some relationships will be repaired and be stronger than ever after a betrayal. Some relationships will be weakened.

Whether or not someone will cheat again will depend a great deal on their reason for cheating the first time. If they've cheated more than once, there isn't much more that needs to be said.

♥

Dear Queenie, I was away on a trip to see family and my boyfriend cheated on me with my sister. He is sooo sweet and I thought would never do anything like this and he said he was not going to call her (there friends) until he got back with me. I don't know what I should do. — Shelby

Shelby, I would dump him so fast he wouldn't have time to zip his pants. — Queenie

♥

Queenie, I am engaged and love this girl with all my heart...One of my best friends for 13 years hit on her and me and him no longer talk. They still talk once every now and then (only on the phone) do I have a reason to be upset? Plus she has changed our date to get married 3 times?

Does this mean that she is not ready or she doesn't want to marry me. I am 26 and she is 23. She set the date for 2 years from now, should I wait the 2 years or is she just playing a game. She tells me I am her everything and she loves me. What is a guy to do...I need some advice. - Charles

Charles, obviously she isn't ready to get married. Perhaps she has doubts about you, maybe she has doubts about herself. Whatever the reason, rushing into marriage now would most likely guarantee a trip to divorce court a few years from now. If you love her two years is not too long to wait to make sure that this is the right move for the both of you. — Queenie

♥

Dear Queen of Hearts, last year "He" worked for a company and traveled out of state some times for days sometimes weeks,1 or 2 months at times. This relationship is in its 18th year. I missed him so much when he left, at first I couldn't wait for him to come home. Then he started picking fights, arguing, lying. I heard him in the bathroom talking on his cell. "I didn't hang-up, come on" he says he was just playing to mess with me.

I jotted down my birthday on the calendar to remind him. I see it whited out a few days later. Then I see "J's b-day" noted a few months later. He says he hadn't noticed. He sends for me while he's traveling to make up for all the trouble lately. When I get back a week later I call him and a woman answers, "you're not his girlfriend anymore I'm his new girlfriend now." He says he was in another room. She was with someone else.

Now he always proved he loved me, always proved he was loyal. I've told him not to call me. He still calls. I've gone through lie after lie, disrespected, I've talked to her, and still he denies everything. Why not just go if he's found her, why keep dragging me through this. Because I let him. Well, why doesn't he just be happy with her since he went that route? Why hang on to me.

He doesn't like confrontations yet doesn't avoid it, makes plans w/me yet she shows up, then denies all knowledge. Why not be slicker if he's just going to lie. I know if he cared he'd at least spare me and be more discreet but he's not too bright. But why keep me hanging if he's got someone better or just new. I keep going back because I love him. What's his excuse for calling me and not letting me go? — Lady

Lady, he knows that no matter how badly he disrespects you, you're going to come right back to him. He doesn't need to be discreet or honest or respectful of your feelings. No matter what he does, you're going to take him back. Too bad you don't love yourself as much as you love him. If you did you'd tell him to take a hike. — Queenie

♥

Queenie, my boyfriend and I have been going out for two years now. One night he went out with his friends to the bars. Unfortunately, I couldn't go. One of his girl-friends got really drunk, and she started touching anyone she could get her hands on and, from what I heard, my boyfriend was sitting next to her.

She started rubbing my boyfriend's legs and back. My boyfriend being drunk too rubbed her legs and back. My boyfriend didn't remember what happened 'til the next day. The girl didn't remember anything at all. It took my boyfriend about three weeks to tell me what happened. He felt that he didn't cheat on me, so he didn't tell me sooner. Do you think he cheated on me? — Trina

Trina, it isn't important what I think but I think the loss of memory excuse is a bit overused. What do you think? If getting drunk and forgetting what happens while he's drunk is something he does as a routine, I certainly hope that he uses, and you use, protection.

So much for words of caution. Until you're married, the both of you are 'fair game' for other people who are attracted to you and to whom you are attracted. Just my opinion, of course. — Queenie

♥

Hi Queenie, my girlfriend and I recently broke up. She initiated it. She still wants to keep in touch. She lives in the U.S and I am stationed overseas for the next several months. It was not a bad break-up. No yelling or shouting or name calling. Just talking things out and crying. But now I have reason to believe she was cheating on me. So my question is: what is the best way to confront her with it? — George

George, now you're at a point where you have a need to confront her and place blame for this breakup? Not all relationships last forever. If she did meet someone else in whom she developed an interest isn't it better that the two of you break up? Love triangles are most dishonest relationships and always guarantee at least one person and sometimes all three will get hurt.

If it's critically important, and you have a need to vindicate yourself as the reason for this breakup, ask her if she was cheating on you. This won't help your future friendship with her, and it won't accomplish anything worthwhile. Some relationships work, and some don't. Yours didn't, not at this time. If you think the future might be better for the two of you, keep in touch as friends as you meet and date others. Good luck. — Queenie

♥

Dear Queenie, I met this guy over a year ago and he indicated that he was attracted to me. But I wasn't ready to get involved, he was going away and I was wary of long distance relationships.

I spent time with him while he was in my area and visited him in his home, but I kept the relationship platonic. I wanted to wait and see what develops upon his return here. He used to be so sweet and accommodating during my first two visits. Prior to my third trip, I casually mentioned to his nosy best friend that I wanted to get to know someone better before I would get horizontal with them. Things have spiraled downward after that. He was still friendly but distant.

We kept in touch by e-mail but he always had some excuse not to see me whenever, I went down for a visit. He only got in touch with me 4 months after he got back here (a week after he found a job). We never had a chance to get together, but I thought it was because of work pressures. It turns out he had affairs with three different women. Now I'm jealous, and I realize that I really like this guy. What am I to do? — Dana

Dana, you wanted a relationship that meant more than sex and you told his nosy best friend this (why hadn't you mentioned it to him? these are the topics of conversation between people who are developing relationships, not their nosy friends), and so everything cools down, but now that you know he was going after sex while being platonic with you, you're jealous?

I'm not really sure what type of relationship you really want, or perhaps you just want to know you're as desirable to him as the other three women he bedded when he didn't bed you. That, in my opinion, isn't a good base to any relationship, except a casual one. Don't you think you deserve better? I certainly think you do. — Queenie

♥

Hello Queenie, about 9 months ago, I noticed an acquaintance of ours getting more flirty to my boyfriend. He and I had some stresses and since he also found her attractive, I told him of my insecurity and he promised to not put himself in any position that would allow the opportunity to lead to anything further.

Not even a month later, after coming back from his visit to this girl and her boyfriends' house, he comes, I ask if the boyfriend was there, he says no then says, this guy that was there also gave her a ride ... immediately I knew he was lying, I felt it. I went out to the car, the passenger seat was reclined, a cigarette butt lit but the ashes were the entire cigarette, lit, and then forgotten. He gets very angry, jumps into the shower and later, can't even make love to me. He said it's because I didn't believe him.

My gut still feels a lie. What should I do?? Do I trust my gut or do I believe his story? The girl, who I ran into months later, had a totally different version of the version of that night.

My guy says that he'll leave me if I don't move past this. He wants me to accept that it was totally innocent, even though she said "He knew you were going to get mad about giving me a ride, but just said she'll have to deal with it."

I haven't been able to get past the feeling that he is lying. I love him, do I stick by my gut, which is usually right, or is there a possibility that I am wrong? Please respond, we're just about to split over this situation. Can I forgive when I feel he's still lying? — Louisa

Louisa, when in doubt, it's probably better to "trust your gut". The possibility certainly exists that nothing serious happened between the two of them and that he's trying to cover because he knows you'll be mad so are you willing to let this go and take a chance that he won't get into a similar circumstance again? If not, walk away. If so, forgive and forget. — Queenie

♥

Dear Queen of Hearts, my boyfriend just broke up with me because he doesn't think he is ready for a serious relationship and thinks that all of the problems we have had are due to this. We are still in love and beside this we were the perfect

most loving couple. He says that when he has sorted his problem out that we will get back together and every thing will be as it was or better. Do you think this could happen?? — Min

Min, it depends on the problems the two of you had whether he was just looking for an acceptable way to break up or if he was afraid of getting deeper into a commitment. Sounds like it's time for you to focus on yourself and not sit waiting for the phone to ring. If he is telling the truth, both of you will benefit from time away from each other. — Queenie

♥

Hi Queenie, I have been with my boyfriend for 6 yrs. We do consider ourselves a "married" couple because we both felt that since we have been together for so long, it was like we were already married anyways - but without a piece of paper to prove it.

We had a great relationship during this time and I really had no complaints - in any area. But he recently went out of state for business and left me in charge of our business. During this time I found out he had an affair with one of our employees. I don't know when exactly it started or how long it lasted, but she turned up with a baby. She had it while he was away. He says it may not be his and plans to get a paternity test. He has not even seen the baby yet.

I had my own infertility problems during our relationship, but am now pregnant. I also lost another baby 2 yrs ago and had to get emergency surgery because of it. I desperately don't want hers to be his baby and don't know how I will handle him going off and having a baby that wasn't mine. We do plan to stay together and probably get counseling, but I can't bear the thought of what he did and if it's his baby, how I am going to deal with it. Please help me. I don't have any close family or friends to talk to. — Desperate

Desperate, I hope you now understand the importance of that "piece of paper to prove it". If I were to find myself in such a situation I'd get counseling to get my emotions under control so that I would have the strength to deal with this man and his problems, and I'd make sure that legally I was protected regarding my personal situation as well as with regard to the business. Good luck. You have a lot of things to deal with all at one time.

Please don't misplace your anger - your employee may be just as trusting as you are and her baby is the most innocent pawn in this whole mess. — Queenie

♥

Dear Queenie, if you know that your lover is seeing other people do you confront him or ignore the fact? — Terry

Terry, ignoring the fact does not make it go away. If you're fine with being one third of a relationship then do nothing. Otherwise, do something to cut the numbers from three to two being aware that you may not be one of the two. —Queenie

♥

Hi Queenie, I'm 23 and have been with my boyfriend for nearly 4 years now. I thought I loved him and, although we are very different, believed we had a brilliant relationship. However, over the past year we have lost our original closeness and I met someone else with whom I have also been having an on/off relationship. My boyfriend has never found out about this but broke up with me because he claimed he wanted to have 'more fun'. However, when he found out I was dating other people he claimed he'd made a terrible mistake so we got back together. I keep telling myself I have to break it off with one of them because I hate this deceit and it would be awful if either found out. But does the fact that I am doing this to both of them mean that I can't be in love with either? — Anna

Anna, I personally think it's possible to love two people at the same time. However, it is not possible to have a committed relationship with someone if you're involved (and in love) with more than one person.

Are you ready to commit to one person? Do you want to get married, have children, etc? If so you'll want to choose one of these men and let the other go or let them both go and continue on with your search for Mr. Right. Deception is a terrible foundation for any relationship. — Queenie

♥

Dear Queenie, I am a 19 year old female who has been seeing a 29 yr old male for almost seven months now. We have lightly touched on the idea of marriage, and although I love him, and feel more for him than any other man I have been with, he is also the only man I have cheated on. I have cheated on him with three men (all one night stands). After the first one, I confessed, and he forgave me. I never intended for it to happen again. I don't want to lose him, but I don't understand how I could have done this to us--if my cheating a sign that there is something wrong with me, or my relationship? Should I end it, or reaffirm my commitment to making this work? — Lola

Lola, three one night stands in seven months while you're involved with someone you "feel more for" than anyone you've ever dated tells me you aren't really serious about commitment with this man. I don't know what your cheating is a sign of but if you really do think you might have a future with this man I'd suggest you get some counseling and try to find out why you're bent on destroying this relationship.— Queenie

♥

Dear Queen of Hearts, I have known this guy for 7 years and we've been close. We have been on and off 5 times. Now we both have been out of school for 2 years and both matured, well at least I was already mature; he had lots of growing

up to do. We both love each other. Well this time around we started dating in March and its now July. He talks about marriage all the time. He says he is in love with me. We have been getting along so well this time around. I love him and I'm happy.

There have been 2 big problems. He had this lying problem. He's never had a 'real' relationship and never been good with sharing feelings till now. All my friends say I can do so much better and that he doesn't deserve me. It's probably true but it doesn't change the fact of how I feel for him. So back in June I was really sick and it was our three month anniversary. I had asked him to come down that day because I didn't feel good at all. He said he was helping his dad but if he got time he would come down.

Well he never called or came down and the next day I asked him about it and he said that he went out to the movies with a girl (friend). I was pissed!! I was like you lied to me. He had these plans for a week and kept it from me. Right before he left for vacation he told me and looked me in the eyes cause I told him I didn't trust him anymore and he looked at me and said you can trust me I don't want to lose you and he cried.

I tried my best to believe him while he was gone. But I couldn't. So just this past Saturday I found a piece of paper with a meeting place, time and describing a girl with her name. I asked him about it and he said it was a joke. Come to find out he had plans on meeting a girl off the internet while he was on vacation! He said that he didn't meet her cause he had something really special at home, but I can't believe him. He's lied too much.

I walked out on him and he cried all night. This guy never cries. He is now saying that he realized when I walked out that door that I am the girl for him and he can't live life without me. How can I believe him! — Jess

Jess, you believe him until he does it again and then you let him cry and talk you into believing him again until he does it again and then you let him cry and talk you into believing him again until he does it again... do you understand what to expect in this relationship?

Who cares what your friends think, it's not their life. But it is your life and right now he seems to have very little respect for you. Oh, by the way, be sure you're practicing safe sex if you're having sex with this guy. — Queenie

♥

Dear Queenie, my boyfriend and I are at a very tough time right now. He has been away in boot camp and was not there for the birth of our daughter or the pregnancy. I have been faithful until about a month ago. It felt so good tell him that I had been faithful all that time and now I feel so bad to lie.

Does that mean that I am falling out of love with him or needed to have sex? I cheated with one of his friends. Knowing that he has cheated on me many times even when I was pregnant makes me feel he deserved it. What do you think am I falling out of love or do you think I was trying to get him back?

Could you tell me some hints on catching your lover cheating? — Suzi

Suzi, neither one of you seems to know the meaning of true love. I can give you a hint: cheating isn't part of it. Neither is getting even on his cheating by cheating on him with one of his friends. You're right, Jerry would love this one. I don't have his phone number but you might want to give him a call. —Queenie

♥

Dear Queen of Hearts, my boyfriend cheated on me about a month ago. The way I found out is that he contracted an STD and gave it to me. We've been together for three years and have one child. I found this out a month ago, right after we moved in together and bought all kinds of furnishings together for our home. I decided to give him another chance. Can this relationship work? Or are we doomed? Is there such a thing as men who only cheat once? At this point, I'm not sure if he will do it again or not. I still am not ready to trust him, and he doesn't do anything to try to regain my trust, maybe because we have such poor communication. I'm just tired of my emotions riding a rollercoaster. Please help.
— Niki

Niki, it takes a long time to build trust back once someone has cheated. Can this work? Yes, if the two of you are willing to work at it together. Are you doomed? If he can't be faithful, or, if you aren't able to forgive and forget. Are there men who only cheat once? Probably, the same as there are probably women who only cheat once.

My feeling is that no one is perfect and everyone deserves the chance to be forgiven when they do wrong. That doesn't mean that I think you should continue to forgive him if he continues to cheat. But he does deserve a second chance. After that — do what you have to do.

Get those emotions off that rollercoaster. Settle down to being in love again. Don't waste this precious time with suspicions and mistrust. If he never cheats again, you're wasting time and energy worrying about what might happen. If he does cheat again, take care of it then. Good luck.
— Queenie

♥

Queenie, I am a 24 year old guy and I have been dating an 18 year old girl for three months. When I met her I said to myself that I was going to marry this girl, but not for her looks although she is cute. To make a long story short she in one month cheated on me 3 times, and one of the guys thought that he was her boyfriend. She spent almost all of her time with me. She even spent all of her money on me, took me out to nice restaurants and bought me gifts. Great sex too.

I ended up busting her at her other boyfriend's house. After I caught her, I got her to admit all of the horrible things that she did. I still care about her but I have way too much pride to date her again. The ironic part is that she is head over heels in love with me (I'm positive) about that. I want to know who in their right mind would do that and why. Was it the sex, or just that she didn't know what she wanted, or was it her age, or was it that she met somebody that actually cared about her (me). It doesn't make any sense how she could spend all her time and money on me, but then screw the next cute guy that came along.

It seems as though it probably would have continued If I had never caught her. Do you think so??? I need all of the answers to my questions or I'll go crazy trying to figure it out myself. Do you think that I should give her a second chance if she is truly sorry, or is it too late for that? — Eddie

Eddie, I can't give you all of the answers. You're living this life, not me. I do think that three months is a pretty short time to get so serious and I certainly can't feel that she's as in love with you as you think she is if she's dating other guys at the same time. Incidentally, if you're not practicing safe sex with her, you're leaving yourself open to AIDS and several other ugly diseases. Actually, that goes for anyone you might be sleeping with.

Why is she spending money on you and buying you gifts? I'm pretty old fashioned, of course, but as you being the older guy here shouldn't you be doing the spending and her be doing the receiving? Maybe that's why she dates the other guys.

My take is that she's young, insecure, and isn't ready to settle down. I include insecure because of her not being faithful to one guy. — Queenie

♥

Hi Queenie, my boyfriend and I have been together for four months. I'm 20, he's 26. And I am in love with him. My problem...I baby-sit to earn extra money, and the father — unmarried — has always been a bit of a flirt. Well, during a brief time my boyfriend and I were apart, I ended up having an affair with the guy I baby-sit for. It was a stupid thing to do, and I realize that I love my boyfriend.

I can't live with the guilt. My girlfriend says I'm out of my mind to tell him, but I can't look him without thinking of how I betrayed him. He has always been honest with me. And I think I should be the one to tell him what happened. How do I break it to him? He knows something is bothering me, I've told him personal problems. He was my first real love. And I know that I will never do this again. How do I convince him? — Stella

Stella, I have to agree with your girlfriend, although I don't know the complete details. If your "affair" occurred when you and your boyfriend split up, then I don't see where you were obligated to remain loyal to him at that time, just as he had no obligation to remain loyal to you.

If you want to tell him just to be able to get rid of the guilt you have, that's definitely not a good reason. You think you hurt because of what you've done, but it's nothing compared to how he'll hurt knowing what you did.

A lot of people do things during breakups that they wish hadn't happened if and when they get back together with a serious love. Unfortunately, there isn't a way to go back in time and undo what now turns into a perceived "betrayal." You convince him by never doing it again, whether or not you decide to tell him about this time. Good luck. — Queenie

♥

Queenie, I don't know what happened with me that now I can't even stop going to my girlfriend's friend house we practically go every day and I flirt with her a lot and I know that's wrong but my girlfriend doesn't get mad and neither does she. I know that's wrong but it's too late now I'm so attached to her I can't stop talking to her but what is really sad and is hard for me because every time I would hug her or something she wouldn't say nothing that's why I feel so bad and she told my girlfriend that for her to tell me that she felt that she was disrespecting my girlfriend because she was letting her self like for me to hug her and she would flirt back with me and know I don't know what to do because I'm so attached to her and so is she but she told my girlfriend to tell me that she doesn't want me to hug her or flirt with her anymore and it's hard for me and that's why I'm asking for help. — Jose

Jose, first of all, you're going to have to write shorter sentences, or at least learn to use punctuation. Either you flirt and hug this girl and get into trouble with your girlfriend, or you don't. If you love your girlfriend, you won't do this. If you don't love your girlfriend, you will.

Life will continue to be full of temptations. If you don't know how to say "no" to some of them, you are in for a lot of heartache in the future. Good luck. — Queenie

♥

Dear Queenie, I recently wrote to you about the three guy triangle I was in, boyfriend out of state and two others guys bothering me. Well that situation has been taken care of. Now another situation has come about, and I am not quite sure what to do. See, I care for my boyfriend a lot, but the distance is starting to take its toll. I recently met up with a good guy friend, and we had a lot of fun together. The problem is, I have liked this guy a lot since I have known him, which is longer than I have known my beau. This may seem as a no-brainer, but being I live here with the guy I like, and my boyfriend lives away, a little friendly advice would be nice! Thanks! — Anna

Anna, the best I can tell you is, from what I'm reading, you don't appear to be ready to settle down with just one guy. I'd suggest a nice little heart-to-heart with the guy who's out of state, explaining that you're just not ready to commit to him or anyone right now. Let him know that you'll be dating others. Don't expect him to wait for you, and don't expect that you won't break his heart. No matter what you do, you're going to hurt this guy but be out in the open about it. Good luck. — Queenie

♥

Queenie, I've been dating this really great guy for a while now. A few months ago things really weren't going all that great and we were constantly fighting. Entering the picture is a guy friend of mine, someone that I could really talk to and who I always have a really great time with. For about a week I was really down and upset about my boyfriend, and my guy friend thought that maybe the best thing I should do was to break up with him because he was making me so unhappy.

One night my friend came over to watch a movie and he had his arm around me. I thought this was normal because this is how we usually were. That night he kissed me, but the thing is I kissed him back. I felt terrible, and avoided this friend for a while.

My guilt turned in to me being really short and having an attitude towards my boyfriend. I broke up with him. A week later we got back together and have been ever since. Things are wonderful and we've really learned how to appreciate each other. But I always have this friend in the back of my mind, because I never told my boyfriend that this happened.

My question is do I tell him? He has said things to make me believe that he already knows. I feel horrible for what I did. — Cyndi

Cyndi, you kissed a friend when you were down. What's to tell? You are feeling guilty about something that is less than you're making it out to be. Forget it. Give it the insignificance it deserves. — Queenie

Moving On

Moving On

"My question is if I still love this girl, how do I get her out of my system so I can have meaningful relationships with other women that suit me and respect me?"

Why is it so difficult to walk away when a relationship is over? Why must some people hang on and on when their ex clearly has no further interest in maintaining even the smallest friendship? Is there a defective gene that blinds lovers to the truth? Or, will hanging on eventually wear a former lover down to the point that they realize the person they're trying to avoid is the one person in the entire world that completes them?

Perhaps relationships wouldn't fall apart in a perfect world but this world of ours is far from perfect so relationships do fail and it does no good to cling to the tatters of a relationship that clearly has no future.

How does one know when it's the right time to move on or the better time to hang on?

♥

Dear Queenie, first, let me inform you on some of the hurt and pain this man has inflicted on me. He's cheated on me, humiliated me like I've never been before, has treated me like I wouldn't ever dream of treating anyone else. This man has done the un-thinkable to me so much wrong.

Here's my question. I live with anger and rage everyday because of him. I'm mad at myself and hate him with every bone in my body. I still have to keep in contact with him, it's been a year later and I still have the hate in me. Should I try and be civil and try to put this in the past? Or, what's the best revenge on him?

Please, I need some kind of advice; I don't want to live with the hate anymore. Oh yea, he's a very successful man and nothing ever knocks him down. Help! Help! What should I do?? — Jeannette

Jeannette, you are obsessing about destroying this man. You are past simple anger. You need professional counseling to get past the hurt. As long as you continue to hate him so much he will have control over your life. Once you stop obsessing you will begin to get back the control you have handed over to him. — Queenie

♥

Dear Queenie, I am a bit confused about the way things have been going on in my life lately. My girlfriend and I broke up about 2 months ago. She called me about a week ago and told me that she is very happy with a new man. Lately she has been calling 4 or 5 times and day and still insists that her heart is with him. She called me on her cell phone while I was at work and the song "How do I live" was playing on the phone. She then called back and told me that she was thinking about me. I then got a call and she was in front of my work and talked to her for a few minutes. She called me again and I told her to leave me alone and she said that I was mean.

I just want to move on but it's hard when she keeps calling me even when I tell her not to. There has been a lot of jealousy on her part, and it ended up with some physical violence. I really don't know what to do about her, because I still love her and don't know why. Please help! — Tony

Tony, unless you want to resume this relationship you will have to be extremely blunt with her when she calls. Tell her that you don't want her to call you at work as it could have a detrimental effect on your job.

If she calls you at home, either use an answering machine and don't return her calls or tell her that you're busy and can't talk then hang up each time she calls. Unless she's incredibly stupid, she should get the message. — Queenie

♥

Dear Queen of Hearts, Love Hurts! What happens when you've dated someone for 5 years and they want to end the relationship but you don't?

It's so unfair especially after so much time and energy has been put into it. How do I live without him, not to sound so dependent, but he's been part of me and I don't want to imagine life without him.

Is it true that all I can do is maintain a friendship? What if out of my own selfish anger I don't want to be friends because that would mean giving him what he wants.

Also can you give me some tools on how to get over someone you still love deeply? What are you supposed to do with all the love you have for them? It also makes me crazy thinking he'll be seeing other people. Thanks for whatever advice you have. — Billy

Billy, you are supposed to move on. You cannot force someone to love you. They have a right to lead their life their way and if they don't want to include you in it any more, that is their right also. It is your right to be angry, upset, confused and reluctant to stop loving them. At some time, though, you're going to have to get over your hurt feelings and pain and move on.

There's a chance that sometime in the future when you're less angry, less hurt, and more in control you'll be able to be friends. I don't see that happening until you become an independent person and stop trying to make him responsible for your happiness. — Queenie

♥

Hi Queenie, my best friend and I were in love with each other until 2 years ago. Although we're still best friends, we're not lovers anymore. She is no longer in love with me, but I am still in love with her. She has recently fallen in love with another guy and I'm trying to get use to it. She knows clearly how I feel, for I have told her.

Over the last month, things have been a little shaky with her new relationship and she doesn't know if she should continue it. She has told the guy how she feels, but he hasn't stated that he feels the same way although his actions

appear to indicate that he does. He has refused to verbalize it. She's had sex with him now and feels like "a fool" for giving herself to him when he didn't state clearly his feelings.

I'm angry with her for giving herself so soon to anyone. I wouldn't feel so strongly about it if I wasn't in love with her. Of course, she lied to me when she told me that she didn't have sex with him. I know that she did, because I walked up on her saying to her sister that she wants to ask him "was sex the only between us for you?" I pretended not to hear. I want to confront about this. Should I?

I'm still in love with her and still believe she's a wonderful person. She made a huge mistake by sleeping with him. But, should I just keep the friendship and move on or confront her about this? I really want her in love with me again. She said the door is not closed to having a relationship with her. — Adam

Adam, she doesn't owe you an explanation about her current relationship. She is a single adult who may do as she wishes. Your feelings toward her do not obligate her to be faithful to you, nor does it mean she must tell you the truth about whether or not she is having sex with her current boyfriend.

I, personally, think you need to walk away from this situation for your own best interests. She is living her life as she wishes, and because you are still in love with her it is causing you more pain than you need.

You need to get past this relationship and stop hoping that she'll come back to you. Maybe she will. But she'll see you in a much better light if she sees you dating others and if she thinks that someone else might take her place in your heart. Right now she has no competition so she has no reason to be more than just a friend. — Queenie

♥

Dear Queen of Hearts, how do you get on with your life after 10 years of still wanting someone that that was never worth wanting from? I hope you know what I mean. — Barry

Barry, it sounds like 10 years of wasted time. Too bad. So why would you want to keep wasting more time? Just move on. — Queenie

♥

Queenie, this is pretty pathetic, so prepare yourself. I knew this girl in high school...met her freshman year. I always had a sort of crush on her, but I really wasn't experienced enough in boy/girl matters at that point, so I didn't really try to "woo" her or anything. I'm 21 now, by the way.

Ever since then, I've become increasingly obsessed with her. This got even worse when I found out through a few friends of mine that she "liked" me way back when. It all made sense, too. I remembered certain things she did: called me a few times to invite me places, slipped hints as to her affection into conversation...but I was too stupid at the time to realize what any of this meant. I think about this girl at least once every single day, usually more. I've almost sort *of set her up in my mind as the perfect woman. I'm *sure* there's some sort of specific psychological term for this.*

How can I get her out of my head? I've recently been swept up in a new attitude on life and my former problems (mostly shyness, unrequited love, etc.) with girls have pretty much vanished...except for Her. HELP! — Virgil

Virgil, in other words, you're obsessed with the idea of this girl you knew in high school who probably had the hots for you but you were uncool back then and couldn't see the forest for the trees?

Are you sure you aren't just hanging on to the embarrassing aspects of this non-relationship and making a bigger deal out of it than it actually was?

Believe it or not, lots of us have that one person (maybe that first one person) who for some reason just seemed perfect but we couldn't get the right words to say how we felt and they are lost to us forever. Lost, that is, until we attend our 20th or 30th or maybe even 40th high school reunion and there he or she is, and suddenly we know (and are thankful) why it never came to be.

You're wasting a lot of useful dating time dreaming about this girl. As I see it you can either forget her or try to locate her and see if there is anything between the two of you that might develop into something worthwhile. Put a current face on this fantasy and it might answer all your questions. — Queenie

♥

Dear Queenie, I lost the girl of my dreams last year. She was killed in an auto accident. I am having trouble letting myself get close to any one at this time. I have met many wonderful women but just can't seem to allow myself to fall in LOVE again. Any suggestions would be greatly appreciated. — David

David, there is a period of mourning that you will go through when a relationship ends. Death is the worst kind of relationship end because it leaves so many things undone and unsaid. Everyone has different ways to grieve but one year is not too long to still be feeling the pain.

Don't force yourself to fall in love. That will come with time. In the meantime, let yourself work through the grieving process so that you keep her memory but move it to another spot in your heart so that you'll be receptive to finding new love. Incidentally, most experts say you shouldn't consider any serious relationships for at least one full year after the death of, or divorce from, a loved one. Good luck. — Queenie

♥

Dear Queenie, at the beginning of this year my boyfriend (ex) and I split up after 2 years of on and off being together. We've lived together and apart, and were very intense. We had the usual problems of money, insecurities ect. Both are in our early 20's.

The final breakup occurred after he ran into my ex-best friend of 10 years (who married my first love), she told him many of my secrets and even made up some too. These secrets included a lover I had during a long period of separation between my ex-boyfriend and myself. I never told him when we got back together because I didn't want to hurt him. He also believes I still carry a torch for my first love which isn't really true, it's more like a sentimental memory.... anyway he broke up with me over the phone, calling me every name in the book.

Now six months later I still want to work this out even just to be friends. He doesn't. I keep telling myself to move on and have made lots of effort to do so: dated other guys, made new friends thrown myself into work, but I still long to have some kind of relationship with him. Help! — Tamara

Tamara, keep telling yourself to move on. There appears to be too much bad history for him to overlook. Or, perhaps he was just looking for an excuse. Whatever the reason, consider him history and concentrate on your future not your past. — Queenie

♥

Dear Queenie, up until last week I was good friends with a girl that I had dated on and off for the last 3 years. I have to admit that she was not the perfect woman. She was very possessive, had a baby at 18, and really didn't have much of an education. I still loved her though.

I had been hearing from people that she was going out with other guys behind my back, and I started to investigate it. I believe she is going back into her old lifestyle of being promiscuous and such.

My question is if I still love this girl, how do I get her out of my system so I can have meaningful relationships with other women that suit me and respect me? She is a very loving girl, and I think it may be hard to get over this... What do you think? — Malcolm

Malcolm, it's always difficult to leave someone we love. Memories of the good times and "how it was supposed to be" can get in the way of moving on. You already know her faults, remember them when the good memories come flooding back. — Queenie

♥

Dear Queen of Hearts, I met this girl my age, who I immediately connected with, in a mental/spiritual fashion. She and I became best friends, and after a few months of friendship, we began dating. Our love for each other was magical—she and I both felt we had found our soul mate; it was indeed true love.

Everything between us from the day we first met was magical, a sort of storybook romance. We always talked everything out, usually starting out as a mild fight, but after an hour or so, we would once again see eye to eye.

We shared so many experiences together and made so many memories, those that last a lifetime. I was even her first sexually—she truly felt that I was "the one" that she wanted to spend the rest of her life with.

As our relationship progressed, I started to take her for granted, the things she did for me, and all. Occasionally, I would even take out my anger on her, not physically by any means, but verbally, telling her that she wouldn't understand — we would go out to eat, and sometimes there was just silence.

But through and through, we always worked out the problems facing us short-term, at least up until we had a big fight, and she broke up with me the next day, basically saying that she couldn't take it anymore and that I needed to regroup; she still loved me and wanted to be with me, but my attitude needed to change.

Shortly before she broke up with me she met this guy who is exactly opposite of me — a lying, selfish, cheating, deceitful player who has never dated a girl he hasn't cheated on. Full of BS and a real smooth talker, once he found out she was MY girlfriend, he started coming on to her. Aware of his track record and his personality, she swore to me that she brushed him off. Liking a challenge, he continued to call her for a week or so — she says she got rid of him by asking him if he wanted only to be friends with her, to which he replied something along the lines of he had never had a female friend who he didn't "hook up" with.

After a week of spending all her free time with him, it was obvious that she started falling for him, even though she would call me and my friends, who know him whining about how she liked him, but she just couldn't trust him. When this became obvious to him, he convinced her to give him a chance, which he blew by cheating on her at a party. He admitted to her that he had cheated on her, but whined to her that he loved her and how he had made such a mistake. Right after it happened, she came to me for comfort; we spent the night talking about them and us — she made it clear that she wanted him back, simply because she was having fun (and not sex, as she swears).

I'm so confused (she says she is too), and I have no idea what to do now. I mean we really, truly loved each other. She knows I will always be there for her, as I have been in the past — it really hurts me to think of her with him and not me, and to see her setting herself up like this. Everyone who knows me and her well feels like this is just a phase she's going through and that she'll come back to me.

Lately, I've been having my doubts, not because of other girls, but rather the fact she's in so deep, and doesn't seem to know which way's up. She doesn't seem to think he's the one, and before when they were together, they weren't all that serious. Your thoughts and ideas on how I could "reel her back in" are immensely appreciated. — Allan

Allan, your relationship with her is very typical of what can and does happen with "first" love. It takes "having more than one" to know who is best for us. Neither of you had a prior experience history and while that is good in theory, in practice it leaves a lot of unanswered questions before making a lifetime commitment to one person. She isn't ready for you to "reel her back in" and it's possible that you and she may never be any more than the best of friends for the rest of your lives.

I won't even try to tackle the "why would she stay with him when he's a rat?" situation since she didn't ask for my advice and I doubt that she would even care if she won't listen to her friends. All I can say is that this is not an uncommon situation, and while you're right about tigers and their spots, that doesn't mean there won't always be people who believe their love is all someone needs in order to change bad habits. There's an element of excitement and danger that some people need in their lives, no matter how much they may whine and cry otherwise. (That is not your clue to change your basic personality to mean and nasty to try to win her back!)

It hurts you as you watch her with him. I certainly understand why it would; you love her and want her back. Unfortunately, that's not going to happen right now. She has no motivation to change anything she's doing since she has him (when he wants to be with her) and she has you for your support when she needs a strong shoulder to cry upon. Not a good situation for you, but it's a perfect setup for her needs at this time. Sadly, though, even if she were to leave him, she would probably not return to you other than as a crying post when her next relationship had problems.

Have you watched "When Harry Met Sally" or "Four Weddings and a Funeral"? Don't you wonder where the plots for movies come from? Try real life. Let her go and take a look around you at all the other wonderful women nearby, one or more of whom could be your next soul mate. Very rarely is "the first" the "only." If the two of you are meant to be together, you will be. Good luck. — Queenie

♥

Dear Queenie, I broke up with my boyfriend whom I have been seeing for over a year. Perhaps I was wrapped up in the romance of things but I have fallen out of love. It hurts so much knowing that he hurts too. I asked if we could remain friends and his reply was that it would hurt too much to ever see me again and that he was going to try to forget he ever met me. I understand that he needs to go through what ever it takes to move on. But it hurts.

It is like I miss the little gestures he'd do for me to show that he loves me. I miss his love, but I know deep down in my own heart that I am unable to reciprocate the love back to him that he deserves and it is tearing me up inside. What should I do? The pain is so heavy upon my heart and I am feeling so scared...but I am not quite sure of what. Please help me. — Angela

Angela, you dumped him and now you want to be friends so that you don't hurt so much because of how much he's hurting? Uh, have I missed something here? This is what happens when couples split up. He's trying to move on. Let him. He'll get over you. Now it's time for you to get over him. — Queenie

♥

Dear Queenie, I dated this girl for about 3 months. It started Valentine's Day of last year. She said she liked me and that I'm an ideal husband. I was smitten. I decided that I will love her no matter what. After the 3rd month she told me that I was too nice and that she prefers "chicer" guys. She dropped me like a hot potato.

More than a year has passed. I have failed to get over her. I still love her. The pain is still with me. I asked her several times to lunch but she said she has a boy friend. They met right after me. I need your advice. Should I pursue or give it a rest. If you advice on the latter, tell me how to get over her and get on with my life. — Robbie

Robbie, if you want to keep getting hurt, keep going after her. She can't make it much clearer that she's not interested. Being dumped is painful but only you can put a stop to the pain — if you want it to stop. You can do it. While you're chasing her there's someone else who would be much better for you who can't catch your eye. Look around. — Queenie

❤

Dear Queen of Hearts, last week I broke up with a guy I had been seeing for over 3yrs, because I wanted more than just seeing him on weekends. He said he didn't want more but if he did I would have been perfect. Well, I found out, from him, that he is already seeing someone else. I am so incredibly hurt and angry I can't see straight! My question is: how can I get through moving on. What are some tools I can use to bounce back without resenting all men in general? I don't want to attract any more men that cannot give me the type of relationship I truly want in my heart. Thank you. — Flossie

Flossie, falling in love is a gamble. That means you take a chance on someone else caring as much for you as you do for them. Sometimes you win, sometimes you lose. To hold all men responsible for what one has done is doing all men a great disservice. Somewhere there's a guy who is your soul mate. The only way you'll appreciate how wonderful he really is, is by meeting a lot of losers as you search for him. Good luck. — Queenie

❤

Dear Queenie, I was going out with a guy for a year and a half and I cheated on him with one of his best friends. So my boyfriend and I ended up breaking up because he couldn't decide whether or not he could forgive me. We didn't have a really perfect relationship in the first place but I loved him and was happy with him for most of the time. During the last month or so of our relationship we started to have some problems and had some pretty bad fights but we had had worse. Anyway we have been broken up for almost 2 months. I am now going out with the guy that I cheated on my ex with but I can't stop thinking about my ex. I really like this new guy but I don't know if it's just because he has always been a great friend or if I really like him.

I also have feelings for my ex and I am so confused. I fooled myself for a while thinking that I was over him but I don't think I am. I don't know what to do. Please help me. I need some outside advice. — Christy

Christy, if you were ready to settle down to one guy you wouldn't have so many guys on your mind. What's the rush? Enjoy yourself. Some day one guy will come along and you'll know he's the one and you'll forget about everyone else. Good luck. — Queenie

♥

Queenie, if I have managed to keep a friendly relationship with my ex after the breakup, but he doesn't even bother to call me during holidays or my birthday, does it mean that he isn't even worth my friendship after all? (I happened to have remembered to call him on his birthday and even took him to lunch). I didn't call him either during the holidays because my mother was in the hospital, so I had many other things on my mind. But he was fine, so he should have at least given me a call to see how I was doing during that time even as a basic sign of continued friendship. (By the way, he was the one who dumped me).

He did call me a day after my birthday to ask me how my mother was (he had heard about her sickness from a friend, and not me), without even mentioning my birthday the day before. Is he playing games, or has he simply stopped caring about me in every way? I'm confused and let down. — Nora

Nora, there comes a time when a relationship must end. That means that each person goes their separate way and maybe, if each is comfortable doing so, they will have casual contact in the future. It does not mean that they must call regularly, remember birthdays and holidays or check on family members. These things are actions of the past and dredge up emotions that are best put to rest.

Perhaps, since you place so much importance on what he has not done, you have been displaying much more of an emotional involvement than he was comfortable with and this is his way of letting you know that the relationship is truly over. Stop being confused and stop feeling let down. Meet some new guys and socialize. He's not playing games; he's getting on with his life. — Queenie

♥

Dear Queenie, I know it's over and I don't want her back. But is it impossible to stay, just friends, with your old girlfriend when you have met a new one? Or is it a fantasy that you hold on to when you can't bare the thought of never again seeing your ex, with whom you have shared so many feelings. Should I just try to forget my old girlfriend and go along with my life? — Jonathan

Jonathan, there's a fine line between "just friends" and "old lovers." Of course you've shared some important times with this ex-girlfriend, but that's the past and if you want to be able to have a good, true relationship with a new girlfriend, the past needs to be closed.

Ask yourself this: Does my new girlfriend feel threatened by my friendship and feelings for my ex-girlfriend? Am I sure I don't wish that things were different and we were back together? If I had the chance, would I make love to my ex-girlfriend? If she had the chance, would she make love with me?

There is no reason that ex-lovers cannot be friends as long as the friendship does not cause stress in current relationships. Sometimes, too, old girlfriends (and boyfriends) like to make the new girlfriend (or boyfriend) uneasy — perhaps unintentionally and sometimes fully planning to break up the new relationship just to prove they can do it. Weigh what you want and who you want in your life then make your decision. Good luck. — Queenie

♥

Dear Queenie, several months ago I met this girl through some friends who I fell completely in love with. I never really believed in love at first site till I met her. Anyway, due to many uncontrollable circumstances she never gave me a chance, so unfortunately nothing ever happened between us. I know we could have been great together. I was quite distressed over this for some time. I hadn't seen her in a while and I thought I was over her, but I saw her recently and now I find myself thinking about her all over again.

How does one attempt to forget about someone whom they cared for so much especially when you'll see that someone often? I find myself at quite a loss as I've never felt this way before. — John

John, there never was a relationship between the two of you except for the fantasy one that you alone have had. It's time that you stop thinking about what might have been but never was. — Queenie

♥

Dear Queenie, a guy I like and I have gone out now and then two years ago. This year we did again. We have liked each other for 5 years and now that we broke up he won't tell me why. I love him and if he asked I'd go back out with him but what is his problem, and/or mine? — Tammi

Tammi, it's your problem. Just because you think you love him, he is not obligated to return that love. You need to stop trying to get him to love you and find yourself a boyfriend who will care for you. — Queenie

♥

Dear Queen of Hearts, I have recently gotten out of a four year relationship. Sometimes I don't know how to deal with this, and I'm hoping that you can shed some light on the subject. I am twenty-one years old and the relationship started out when I was seventeen and he was twenty-seven. (I realize now that this was a mistake.)

He was married at the time. His wife found out and they separated. A few months later, I was living with him. Earlier this year I packed my bags and moved back in with my parents. I left the diamond engagement ring he had given me on the kitchen table.

A little voice inside of me had put doubts inside my head, so I got out. Somewhere deep inside I knew he wasn't ready and our marriage would end in

divorce. Our problems weren't out of the ordinary, but I was young and had never been in love. I guess you could say that I had been burned by love's flame. He was a womanizing jerk that would build up my self-esteem only to break it back down. He was very controlling on some issues and at other times, he was very loving and gave me a lot of attention.

My father hated him and we didn't speak to each other for a year. Now, since I've moved back home, everything is fine. Here's the worst part: My ex started dating someone else three weeks after we split and she moved in with him last month. I live in a very small town, and I can't get away from him or her. I hear and see everything. It's pretty obvious that he's gone on with his life, and I'm stuck being afraid to open up my heart to someone else. I feel that the only reason that he did get into a relationship so soon with someone else is because he can't stand to be alone. She just happened to be the first girl to pay attention to him, so he reeled her in. He was my world, but I don't regret leaving him. I still think about him and I love him.

I feel like he has replaced me and she is living my life. I feel sorry for her because she doesn't know what she has gotten herself in to. I'm sure he treats her like a queen just like he did me at first, but it doesn't last for long. I'm so afraid to let myself go with another person. What do you think? — Lisa

Lisa, this man was the most important person in your life for four years. He was your first major love. It doesn't matter that he didn't deserve that honor, he held the post anyway. It takes time to get past the hurt and the bitterness.

Some days the need for him will be stronger than others but at some point he will not hold such an important role in your life. You saved yourself a lot worse heartache by dumping him now than by living more of your life with him. You know that already.

Most probably history will repeat itself with his current girlfriend but guys like him can always find some woman who believes "all he needs is the right woman" to straighten him out. No one intentionally wants to get hurt in a relationship. Denying yourself a chance at a new relationship to spare yourself pain from its failure is to deny yourself the possibility of the ecstasy of success. — Queenie

♥

Queenie, thanks for your recent advice to my situation. I'm not pining away for him. I've known since the day he left that he was never coming back. I wish that I could control what goes on in my mind, but I can't. I keep hoping that his memory will die, but so far, it hasn't.

I do have a life. I go out and I have a genuinely good time. The only problem I have is feeling that I'm doomed to let a memory control my life forever. If I could go in my brain and turn off the switch, believe me I would.

No one has ever had this much power over me before, and it has nothing to do with the fact that he treated me good or that he liked to do lots of things (because he didn't), it's because I felt like I was floating when I was with him.

I know it's stupid, but when you're with someone and you don't care what they wear or what they say and you can't wait to be with them again, you can't help but wonder will I ever feel that way again.

I've been seeing a great guy for the past two months, but something's missing. Thanks again for all your advice now and in the past. — Marie

Marie, a friend of mine, a usually cool, organized, level-headed business woman, still gets weak in the knees, five years after she and her boyfriend broke up. Never mind that their differences far outweighed their similarities. Never mind that theirs was a relationship of only a few months' duration. Never mind that she wasn't the only one in love with him at the time.

She, too, has a wonderful man in her life but that little "spark" just isn't there. She, too, would like to not feel this way. If humans were computers we could easily replace the defective "relationship chip" with a new one. But we're not. Thank goodness! — Queenie

♥

Queenie, well, here I go again. It's been almost a year now since my boyfriend dumped me and I still can't stop thinking of him. To make matters worse, last Friday was my birthday and guess who I just happen to run in to. His mother. We hugged and started talking, naturally I had to ask how the family is. She told me that he was still with the same girl that he started dating less than two months after we broke up.

I work a full-time and a part-time job on the weekends and I also go to school, so I'm plenty busy. However, I still think about him and after I talked to his mother I went home and cried. Why do I want to be with someone so bad and how can someone want to marry you one minute, then tell you that you don't belong together the next?

The worse part is that right after he broke it off with me, he started dating someone else and I can't bury his memory deep enough to allow someone else to come in to my life. I compare everyone to him, and believe me he had no personality, he hated being around people and he drinks.

I'm tired of this nightmare. I'm tired of a ghost having control over me. I keep asking myself what I did wrong. If he didn't want to be with me, then how could he turn to someone else so quickly? -- Marie

Marie, what advice would you give to a friend who came to you and told you they were still in love with an old flame, someone who had no interest in them any more, someone who had no intention of coming back into their life? Would you tell them they should continue to pine away and think about that person every waking moment?

Would you agree with them that there had to be something wrong with them for their lover to leave them and take up with someone else a short time later? Would you encourage them to continue to learn everything they could about the ex and his current activities?

Relationships can be downright mean sometimes. One partner wears their heart on their sleeve and the other partner gets on a ladder to step on it to break it.

Things happen for reasons we don't understand sometimes until years later. That's when we look back and say "now! I know why we broke up! it makes perfect sense! why didn't I see it before?!" But we didn't see it before because we were too busy punishing ourselves, taking responsibility for the failure of the entire relationship, when it had run its course and it was time for us to move on to something better.

You're right. You won't meet the right man until you get the wrong man off your mind. You can do it! One day at a time! — Queenie

♥

Dear Queenie, I have been out of a serious relationship for about 4 1/2 months. The relationship lasted a little over a year and was the most perfect thing that could happen to me. But it all came to an end. She realized that she had "loved" her best guy friend. Ever since the day we "broke up" I have still been in love with her. I still care for her and would love to have her back. I find myself crying night after night about her.

I can't get her out of my mind and I try so damn hard. She has now since broken up with her friend and I asked her if it was possible to get back together again. She said not now. I don't know why I asked because she doesn't love me anymore. I just want to get her out of my mind. She just gave me so much but to let me go. So do you have any advise on how to get over such a great love? — Andrew

Andrew, it isn't easy getting over a great love, but you really don't have any choice. Just as she found another love, so can you. Stop going to the places special to the both of you, stop listening to the sad songs, stop driving past where she lives, stop thinking about her every second.

Reshape your life with activities so there's not any time left for thoughts of her. When you find yourself thinking of her, remember that she left you for another guy. Get angry so you can move on.

Love relationships, unfortunately, don't usually end at convenient times for both people involved. That means one of them is going to get hurt. This time it was you.

Please remember the pain you are feeling so you will have some empathy in the future when you decide to end a relationship with someone who thinks you're her perfect match. It will happen. — Queenie

♥

Queenie, this probably sounds stupid, but is it possible that a person will never get over a lost love? Sometimes I feel like my heart will just explode from all the hurt I've experienced in the last eight months since me and my husband-to-be split. Even though I never see him, I still think of him almost every day. It's enough to make a sane person go crazy. I know that if someone else came into my

257

life, then hopefully this pain would go away. However, I'm beginning to feel like that NO ONE is going to take this guys place. I keep asking myself is this ever going to end or am I doomed to forever think about this guy. — *Myra*

Myra, the way you feel doesn't sound stupid. But it's sad when you love someone so much more than they love you, and that's apparently what happened between you and your husband-to- be.

Mourning a lost love is acceptable behavior and everyone has a different time frame for the grieving that takes place when we lose someone we love. It's no less a loss than when a spouse, close family member, or dear friend dies.

Your boyfriend did choose to leave so you're also probably trying to figure out what you could have done differently to make him stay. Possibly nothing. Some relationships, no matter how good they appear to be, aren't going to last forever. We assume that if your boyfriend wanted to return to you, he would be welcome — but he chooses to be elsewhere.

Getting over him will take work. You'll need to have a goal of erasing him from your thoughts. Get involved in volunteer activities or a social club, or intensify your career path. Keep your free hours busy. Spend time with friends. Learn a craft or take up a hobby. Get out and get active! With him crowding your thoughts and emotions, there isn't room for someone else to come in to take his place. Push him out, make some room. He's not the only man in the world for you. — Queenie

Cyberspace Romance

Cyberspace Romance

"I've been talking to a very special woman through e-mail for a few days now, and I know this sounds pretty stupid, but I feel that I love her."

Cyberspace is a fantasy singles bar filled with all manner of potentially good, bad and downright ugly dating experiences. Through the miracle of technology it is possible to meet someone thousands of miles away, carry on a romance, and get dumped, all without leaving the comfort of your home or office. I don't want to put a big "X" on online dating because true love can flourish in cyberspace but so can major heartache.

The anonymity of the Web gives courage to otherwise shy men and women. Unlike singles bars and real time events where what you see is pretty close to what you get, cyber lovers can be anything they wish to be, young, single, handsome, voluptuous, talented, beautiful, tall, slim, or wealthy. The perfectly charming gentleman with all the qualities of the ideal mate could in reality be a prison inmate who is working that online charm on several women at the same time. The wonderfully witty woman of any man's dreams may be the collective creation of college kids with too much free time and very active imaginations.

There is a false sense of security when "chatting" on the Web, the feeling that people are "real" and honest. Unfortunately, virtual reality leans more toward dishonesty and misrepresentation whether it's a married man claiming to be single or a young teen claiming to be of legal age.

Romance on the Web isn't all gloom and doom and finding your soul mate online could happen to you as it has happened to thousands before you.

Be cyber smart and avoid the pitfalls of Web relationships. Don't believe everything you're told. Don't give out personal information without being absolutely sure of the identity of the person you're giving it to.

If you're meeting a cyber friend face-to-face for the first time, tell family and friends where you're going, who you're meeting, and bring a friend along at least for the first half hour or so until you feel comfortable being alone with the person you're meeting.

If you don't feel comfortable once you've met, have a pre-arranged signal with your friend for "get me out of here!" and use it.

Trust your gut feelings and don't put yourself in the position of being a statistic if your new cyber friend turns out to be a cyber psycho.

♥

Dear Queenie, my boyfriend is overseas for three months. The other day I found a disk with a picture of a 16 year old and several files I could not open tiled — —picture file, and —chat. About a month ago the day he left I found a picture on the computer of a girl approximately 18 no more, starting to pull her sports bra down, he said that he has no idea where it came from, but the time stamp is marked a few minutes before I got home from an appointment. He of course was on the computer. When he is home he is always on the computer saying he dislikes the shows I watch, but when I offer to change them he stays on the computer. He had to begin working out for his job; I kept noticing that he was gone 5 hours at a time, never responded to my pages. I drove to the base one day and found him on the computers at the library.

I know he is doing something, at least talking to someone else. But he seems to think I am stupid. Why won't he admit it? He wants me out of our apartment after a year of living together...He is usually so nice and sweet the other night he was so callous, is telling me w/out saying the words? He professed to love all the time before I confronted him, even crying how much he missed. Is this relationship hopeless? — Dev

Dev, based on what you have written I'd say you need to walk away from this guy. Quickly.— Queenie

♥

Queenie, I caught my boyfriend cruising' chat rooms to meet women. He actually met 3 of them (via a date) during a 10-month period. Since he's been "discovered" he swears he hasn't had the urge to "chat". He claims it stems from his childhood (being smart and a geek) and also because he hates being alone. He is seeking outside counseling. He is 29 years old. Should I believe that his urge for "chatting" has dissolved? Should I stay with him? Any advice would be appreciated. Thank you. — Shelley

Shelley, I can't tell you what to do; only you know how much you're willing to risk being with this man. Hopefully counseling will help him overcome his emotional needs but only time will tell. In the meantime, may I suggest that you practice safe sex whenever you and he "chat"? His "chatting" puts you at great risk.—Queenie

♥

Queenie, I have been talking to this guy on the web for about a week and he is already acting as if he is in love with me. But I have never met him. We seem to have a lot in common but he is already buying me Christmas presents and wanting to meet my parents.

This is too much too fast. I just gave him my telephone number. And he is wondering where I'm going and who I'm with. And if there are any men around me is this a psycho or what? I told him that I was overweight and have a deformity but he said he didn't care. What do I do? — Liza

Liza, tell your parents about this and tell them your concerns. A week is too short a time for anyone to be in love over the Internet. Just because you've been talking, it doesn't mean he has any ownership, nor do you owe him any explanations.

He could be someone with a hidden agenda that could be harmful to you should you meet.

Next time, Don't give out your phone number or any personal information for a long, long, long, long, time. — Queenie

♥

Dear Queenie, I have been corresponding with a man on-line for almost 2 yrs. We have a lot in common, have exchanged pics and talk on the phone regularly. We both have very demanding careers and travel frequently for work. We have had some cybersex together but it's infrequent. We've become quite close in terms of friendship and perhaps more.

We are going to meet for the first time this week. I have read lots of advice on the do's and don'ts. But I am freaked out. This is like a blind date with my best friend!! We are having a casual lunch first to test the waters. Help! What do I wear, what do I say, how do I react if/when he doesn't match my expectations/ fantasies? Any advice appreciated. — Tamara

Tamara, go slowly and try to keep it as casual and as upbeat as possible. No doubt he's as scared about this encounter as you are. Wear something that shows you're a lady. You may have had cybersex but it's not the same as an actual physical encounter. Until you actually meet there is not enough to base a love relationship on.

No matter how much you think you may know him, try not to get intimate too soon or you may just ruin what could be the beginning of a really great romance. — Queenie

♥

Dear Queenie, I met a man over the internet. We've spent several weekends hanging out together. Other than one mild encounter, there has been no intimacy. This is my choice. He lives 2 1/2 hours from me. He is a nice guy, a little obsessed with sex. We've talked. He just wrote me an e-mail stating that he would like to take our relationship to the next level. However lonely for a lover I am, I do not feel this way for him. Please, I do not want to hurt our friendship. I've been down this road before and I need to know if I should do what I've done in the past. Help me!!! — Chandra

Chandra, do not let you him force you into something you don't want to do! Tell him that you think of him as a very good friend but that you don't think of him as a lover. If he gets angry, back away.

I don't know what you've done in the past but if you've given in, then I think this time you should stand firm and see just how good a friend he really is. If he stops making contact, you'll have your answer. — Queenie

♥

Dear Queenie, I have known someone in the web. The feeling is mutual that we love each other. I have been calling him for several times and he told me that he doesn't want me to spend so much for calling him. He asked for my telephone number but I refuse to give it to him cause of the news that there are many murder cases that first come through e-mails. Knowing one another through e-mails and meeting one another and rape, murdered etc. Should I trust that guy? Should I give my number to him? — Angela

Angela, perhaps I have missed something here. You say you are in love with him and he feels the same about you and yet you don't trust him enough to give him your telephone number? First of all, you cannot be in love with someone you have never met. You can be in fantasy but that's not the same thing as love.

Second of all, if you don't trust him with your telephone number you better make sure you're calling from a pay phone because if he has caller ID on his telephone he already knows your number. — Queenie

♥

Queenie, I met this lady on the internet. She is 21 and I am 36....We finally met and it went okay...We made love and all. We met again about three more times since then, and again have made love every day we where together. She tells that she loves me as a friend and now says she has a boyfriend she is really happy with. If this is the case with her then please tell me why she would still call me 5 or more times a week to say much about nothing. Oh she also lives over 1000 miles away. I am confused as to what her intensions are.

Please could you help me try to understand her motives a little more clearly? Do we ever have a chance to be with each other as a couple or what? It still hurts me to just chat with her as friends because I feel I do really love her and make her very happy. But I don't feel I can go on communicating with her just being friends. What should I do? — Raymond

Raymond, this relationship has a couple strikes against it: the physical distance of more than 1000 miles between you and the distance between your ages.

Don't get me wrong, older man/younger woman relationships can work. But both people have to really be in love with each other and this doesn't appear to be the case between the two of you if she has a boyfriend that she says she's happy to be with.

Does she know how much it hurts you for her to tell you about what's going on when you'd like to be her boyfriend and not just her friend? If she does, then she isn't being too considerate of your feelings. If she doesn't, then you need to tell her.

Some internet relationships turn into major love relationships, some only turn into sexual contacts that lead nowhere. It would seem that your relationship might be the second type. — Queenie

♥

Queenie, I am 32, self employed, work in the outdoors all day long, and live a normal life. I met this girl, who is only 16, over the Internet basically by an accident as I was not looking to meet anyone over the Internet. We exchanged e-

mails and have been doing so every day since leading to some great conservation. We truly have become good friends at this point in time. We have also talked about more personal things, including sexual experiences, fantasies, and eventually meeting someday.

We have exchanged pictures, (her idea), talk about meeting sometime in the future, possibly next summer or definitely after she is finished with high school and in college. We have talked about taking romantic trips together, having hot steamy relationship at the times I visited her, but both agreed not to get serious with it. She has no problem with the age difference, but has made it clear with me that her parents would not approve with it at all. She has had just a few sexual encounters in her lifetime, and never has been in love.

My question, is this a healthy friendship/relationship to be having over the Internet? The age difference is rather significant being that she is 16 and I am 32 and it is a great deal of concern to me with possible unrealistic expectations. This girl is a lot more mature than anyone would expect from a 16 year old, and really do not think about her age at all during our great conservations that we have.

I feel this relationship getting stronger every day, but am somewhat reluctant to go anywhere else with it other than just friends as I do not want to take advantage of the situation, since she sounds like she is already crazy for me even though we have never met in person. On the other hand I think about her often and wished I could meet her in person sooner in spending some time together even if it was just friends. I think she feels the same way. Any advice on the whole situation would be greatly appreciated. Thank you. — Danny

Danny, you're playing with fire! You know it isn't a good relationship, so why ask me to validate it for you? For that matter, how do you know you're dealing with a 16-year old girl? Exchanging photos isn't proof. It is very easy to email photos of someone else; they're available all over the Web.

This "girl" could be a police detective looking for guys who chase underage girls. This could be a bored housewife who enjoys playing guys like you. This could be a guy who gets his kicks this way. It doesn't have to be just one person, it could be a bunch of college kids seeing how far they can string you along.

Personally, I would drop this one very quickly before it turns into more trouble than you could possibly handle. — Queenie

♥

Dear Queen of Hearts, I need someone to advise me. ..I have met a most wonderful man on the net. We started in e-mail, and now go to a private chat room every day. We have each others pictures and know each others real names. There is one big problem now....we are 3000 miles apart.

We are in our 50's, both very lonely people. We have become so very close. We also seem to have a mind bonding which you can feel in your heart. I don't know if you can understand unless you have experienced it. We want to

meet, but the distance is so great. I am afraid it will not work out. What I want an opinion on is: Should we meet and should he be the one to travel the 3000 miles? If everything works out, I plan to move there in near future.

I know it probably doesn't seem like a big problem to you... but believe me.... it is to me. What should I do? If you could e-mail me back.... I would gratefully appreciate it. — Norma

Norma, there are many emotions that can be developed through words and pictures that are not accurate when people meet in person. That might happen between the two of you. It also might happen that the two of you will have an instant 'in person' bonding.

Whatever might happen, the best course at this point is caution. You only have to read the newspapers to see how some online romances have turned disastrous.

Having said that, I have to ask if there is a reason that the two of you can't each travel to a half-way point for this first meeting. This does not mean that you share the same hotel room nor that you choose a remote setting. It means that if there is a location mid way that might appeal to the both of you as a good mini-vacation spot, why not both share the travel burden?

If the first meeting works out, I would think that before you make a permanent move to his location that you take a short trip to see how and where he lives and whether or not you feel comfortable and compatible to the surroundings. Good luck. I hope he's all you think he is, and more. — Queenie

♥

Hi Queenie, I'm 22 yrs old and I met this girl 2 weeks ago online from my town also, and we've been talking on the phone now for almost two weeks. Lately we've been talking for at least 5 hours a day.

We've connected on a level that I never would be possible over the phone. I care deeply for her and so does she. We keep talking about when we're going to meet and how great it's going to be. We've both been hurt before, and she has had terrible experience with men, and even though she knows she's finally found a great man in me, she still really doesn't trust men all that much.

Personally as scary as this may seem, I seriously think I'm slowly falling in love with her, but she keeps telling that she doesn't want to fall in love any time soon cause of all the pain she previously went through before, but I know that even if she's saying that, that she's also falling in love.

She knows how I feel to a certain extent but not the full extent and I really want to tell her how I feel, but I'm afraid that I'll scare her away if I do so. I'm kind of confused on how I should approach this cause I really feel an intense connection with her and really don't want to lose that. — Benjamin

Benjamin, you two haven't actually met. Talking on the phone is not the same as being in the same room and seeing if there is actual physical attraction and getting to know each other on that level. It's way too early to be thinking about love.

Relationships die because both people jump too soon into believing what they feel is love when actually they have a fantasy idea about who the person is that is nothing like the real person they finally meet and get to know. Everyone is on their best behavior for a time, but when the 'new' wears off, that's a whole different thing.

Take it slow. Don't talk about forever. Keep love out of it and get to know each other as friends. If you find that you have similar interests and really, really like being together, if you laugh a lot, if you just can't find enough hours in the day to be together, and if this feeling lasts for months and months (not a few days or weeks) then maybe you've found true love. — Queenie

♥

Dear Queenie, I met a guy on the internet but I do not know what to do. He acts like he likes me, but I think he wants miss skinny Minnie. I am a little heavy but not fat. Should I tell him I am not fat but not skinny or just let him assume? Thanks for your advice. — Danielle

Danielle, honesty is the best way in all relationships. Why get your heart broken by a guy who is disappointed when he finds out you're not the person he thought you were. You're already mad at him for wanting someone skinnier than you. Why aggravate yourself even more by pretending you're someone you're not? — Queenie

♥

Queenie, can you really fall in love with someone online? When I first got online, and started chatting in the chat rooms I had no idea I could actually develop feelings of love for someone you haven't really met in real life. I have heard of such things, but passed them off as being absurd. And then I met a lady that has totally taken over my thoughts.

We have been chatting with one another for about six months now. We have become very good friends. We have found out that we have a lot in common in interest, likes and dislikes. Even the way we run our lives are almost the same. It is really a little spooky.

Our online chats have now become long phone calls to one another. We get on the phone with one another, and talk for hours. We really enjoy each others company. Needless to say my phone bill and hers too, are a little high. She lives about 3,000 miles away.

I have not wanted to admit to myself, but I believe I am really falling in love with the lady. She will not come out and tell me how she if she feels the same or not, and I'm a little afraid to ask her how she feels toward me. I have hinted to her how I felt and she has not really tried to discourage me. She just hasn't really responded like I hope she would. She did say she would like to meet me someday, but we both know that is a little unrealistic with the distance between us.

I guess my question, or questions are this; is love really possible online, or is it just an 'idea'? A fantasy? I pride myself in being realistic, and don't want to make a fool out of myself. So is it really possible? — Mitch

Mitch, anything is possible. And there have been some love matches that have started online. Those are the rare exceptions. I think you're probably in fantasy. — Queenie

♥

Dear Queenie, I've been talking to a very special woman through e-mail for a few days now, and I know this sounds pretty stupid, but I feel that I love her. I can't stop thinking about her. She's smart, kind, caring, she loves children, I could go on forever. I wanted to know, when is the right time to introduce the idea of romance to our e-mails?

I want to let her know I love her with all my heart, my soul, and everything that I am. Do I just tell her? I don't want to scare her off. Can you help me, please?

I know after a few days sounds ludicrous, but this could possible be the woman for me. How do I let her know how truly special she is to me and when should I tell her? — Roger

Roger, you have fallen madly and passionately in love with someone you have been emailing for the past few days? Okay... Have you talked to her by telephone? Have you seen a picture of her? Have you met her in person? Have you shared a sunset, a walk through the forest, a cup of coffee, a tender moment after a movie, some tears, some heartache, a morning after, a night before?

You cannot possibly "love her with all my heart, my soul, and everything that I am". You don't even know this person! Words are only that. "She" could be anyone, but not necessarily someone you'd ever want to meet.

Scare her off? Until you have met and spent some quality time together, you should slow down and forget instant love. Perhaps a very cold shower would also help. — Queenie

♥

Dear Queen of Hearts, exhaustive searches have turned up nothing re info on fantasy online romances and profiles of men who seek out women for email sexual gratification. I think I have recently been a victim of a consummate con man who is in a few singles ads with his pictures, didn't hesitate to give his address and phone which checked out, and after a 5-week hot exchange of email including much substantive nonsexual content, 3 phone calls, and explicit pictures, and plans to meet this month despite the long distance, has not contacted me in 9 days nor answered my email of 2 days ago.

I am engaging a private detective to do some checking to see if he is married, if he is who he says he is, and if he has been incapacitated. The detective told me that these con men are legion and that they seem perfect, but if a meeting

is discussed that as that time nears, they disappear. He in fact proposed flying up to meet me—I had never brought the subject up—or he said I could visit him. The revelation of phone and address info baffles me. I'd think anonymity would be part of the scam and this man has a rather high profile as owner of a part-time business and the singles classified ads with photos of him, his house, grandchildren.

This raises a lot of questions. He has three email addresses for one thing. Does this constitute harassment which would cause him to be dropped, or is it considered consensual. Are there listings of individuals online about whom such complaints have been voiced? Any help would be appreciated. — Kayla

Kayla, I have a couple reactions. First, it is possible that he is completely legitimate, but either sick or having major computer problems so that he cannot contact you via email. Of course, that still leaves the telephone. He could still be sick or incapacitated to such a degree that he cannot easily contact you.

However, the anonymous nature of email and other computer contacts such as chat allow for such cons as you outline. It is easy to make a quick evaluation (although perhaps not a completely accurate one) when someone is standing in front of us, but completely impossible when all we have are a few typed emails and some chat room contacts. Photos are easy to come by, as are fantasy families.

It would be a simple matter for a computer smart 'kid' to create any persona he or she would deem appropriate and useful and obtain the photos from online and clipart sources to further the image. Same with unsavory characters wishing only to 'get off' and move on if you get too close. Internet contacts are strangers. They're the unknown. The nice guy or the pervert. The kid or the con. The single guy who really has looked in all the wrong places or the wrong guy who turns the personals into his personal pleasure zone. The single woman who seeks true love or the married woman who wants a little fun. The stalker. The cyber nut. Welcome to the dating zoo.

Anyone can be anyone else on the Internet. Proceed with extreme caution. Don't believe everything you're told, see, or hear. Don't arrange a meeting without letting friends know the details and take a friend with you. Don't meet in a private place where it's just the two of you (your home, his home, a hotel, dark alley, an office at night — you get the idea).

Arrange to meet in a very populated, public place where you can even 'look' before you meet so you can leave if you don't like what (who) you see.

Don't give out your home phone number. Don't tell your home address. Get a P O Box and an anonymous email through hotmail or similar services. Don't provide job contact information.

Engaging in cybersex can be as dangerous as engaging in real sex with a stranger. You may find yourself stalked or otherwise victimized. At the very least, you'll have developed an emotional dependency that cannot be fulfilled. Think of it as cyber AIDS. Protect yourself. — Queenie

♥

Dear Queenie, I am doing a research and speech about online relationship advice websites. I need help on how you define relationships and making it work...I hope that you could help me! Thank you very much. — Kathie

Kathie, I define relationships as interaction between two or more people. As far as making relationships work? There are as many answers as there are relationships. — Queenie

♥

Dear Queen of Hearts, I met a terrific woman on line two months ago, and for most of the last month we've talked almost every night on the phone. We both found ourselves very attracted to each other and made absolutely no secret of our desire to meet, which we did last weekend, we live fairly close to each other. I feel very close emotionally to her, I'm feeling a lot of love right now and I strongly feel she does also; we've made arrangements to see each other again this week and weekend after next.

My problem is this-something seems different now. I hear a change in her voice when we talk on the phone, when I left a message that I needed to just hear her voice because I was having a terrible day at work I ended up calling her because she didn't call.

Normally she would have been right on that. Yet when I ask her out she doesn't hesitate in her answer and when I ask if I can see her over dinner one night this week, again no hesitation. I am very sensitive and very attune to things though and I feel something different from her. I just can't put my finger on it. HELP! — John

John, have you tried asking her if she feels something different? Communicate, communicate, communicate! The three most important words in a relationship. If she is 'backing off' somewhat it may be that she isn't ready for a full-time commitment and she may feel that is the direction you are heading.

It's a valid feeling considering the short time you two have known each other, so don't take it personally if that's the case. But you won't know if you don't communicate! Good luck. — Queenie

♥

Dear Queenie, I've been talking a guy on the phone for about four months now. Our discussions have recently grown rather intimate. We have never met, and yet I seem to have feelings for him. I think maybe I must be extremely lonely or I'm losing my mind. How can you "love" someone you've never met and only speak to over the phone?

The hard part was that the other night on the phone I almost let it slip that I was having these feelings. I am good friends with this person and don't want to scare him off. I'm just not sure how to deal with this sort of thing. Can you help me understand it? — Peg

Peg, you are not in love, you are in fantasy. You're certainly not alone as too many people believe they are in love with a voice, or even someone who they meet and 'type chat' with in chat rooms. It is easy for some people to know what another needs to hear and then expand upon those needs.

You have exchanged enough information with him, and he with you, that you have created a fantasy person to meet your needs. You could be very surprised how little the person behind the voice might match what you believe him to be.

I'd suggest that if you have a need to engage in phone sex, keep going with your intimate conversations. Otherwise, bring this phone friendship back to safe topics and keep it light. And find a picture of a goofy looking guy, paste it to the wall in back of the phone, and look at it when you're talking with him. Create a silly character for him in place of the 'dream lover' you have currently created. Good luck. — Queenie

♥

Dear Queenie, I met a guy online about 4 months ago...we live in the same city and have become very close...but our relationship is mostly based on telephone conversations...we know everything there is to know about each other, or so we have told each other...he is everything in a man that I want...we have only been out in public together 3 times. We talk on the phone almost every night, and when we miss a night for one reason or another I can't sleep that night, and he says he feels the same way...recently he told me that he loved me at the end of one of our phone conversations. I was so tired, that I didn't remember answering him, but recalled the conversation the next day, I asked him about it and I was right he did tell me that he loved me, and that I didn't dream it. He also told me that I told him I loved him also!

I live in the city that I attend school and this is the city he has lived in all his life, so since we met he has repeatedly asked me to go out places, because I go home to my parents home every weekend I declined his invitation every time.

This past Thursday a friend of mine and I finally decided to go out to the bar with him, I had a great night! He introduced me to all his friends, but he also ignored me for most of the night while we were at the bar, he was hanging off of a whole bunch of his female friends. He doesn't know how I feel about him and I'm very afraid to ask... He and I danced at the end of the night and I thought I was in heaven, I had never been more happy. He was so drunk that I had to hold him up on our way home.

My friend and I ended up staying the night at his house, I hadn't planned on anything happening but it did. If it wasn't for my friend sleeping on the chair, which was right beside the bed we would have had sex. I'm kind of glad that I didn't let it happen, the next day he slept until 4:30pm and my friend and I were long gone from his home. I called him to say hi but he was very cold with me, as he usually is every time I call him. It seems he only wants to have intimate or any type of conversations when he calls me at the wee hours of the morning. This is very upsetting to me and he thinks I'm reading too much into it...and he says that if he didn't care so much about me then he wouldn't call and speak to me as much as he does. I don't' understand why it's ok for him to call me at any time of the day or night. He even calls me at 2am and I still am willing to talk to him, but when I call him he doesn't have the time to talk to me and makes it seem like I'm nobody special.

After our encounter this past weekend, I thought things would be different or that our relationship would develop into something more, but as it stands now, nothing has happened and I haven't spoken to him. I'm leaving town and won't be back until the new year and he knows I'm leaving and hasn't called to say good-bye...this makes me feel like he doesn't care, or is it just that he is afraid to let me know how he feels about what happened between us?

Should I approach the subject with him and find out how he feels for me once and for all? I'm afraid to ask how he feels just in case it isn't what I want to hear...and if it's not what I want to hear will asking something like that ruin our friendship? I think I love him...by the way...what have I gotten myself into!? Please help me! — Sondra

Sondra, hiding from the truth doesn't make it any less the truth. If you want to know how he feels about you, you must ask him. I don't know him and certainly can't second guess his feelings.

In all relationships there is give and take. The 50/50 type of relationship that people would like to believe exists, does so very rarely. The relationship you wish you had with him seems to be very far away from the relationship that you actually do have. It is a relationship based on words exchanged on the phone and via the Internet. Words are easy. Actions are more truthful. His actions when you call speak volumes about his true feelings for you and this relationship (or lack thereof).

So far, everything seems to be on his terms or no terms. Not good. And this is the early stage of the relationship, when each person makes their best effort to please the other person. If this is his best, what can you expect in the future? And is that the future you wish for yourself?

I also sense that alcohol could possibly be an influence in his feelings for you. Specifically, perhaps he needs a few drinks to get that lovin' feeling, which could explain those late night or early morning phone calls. If this is the case, you might want to save yourself a lifetime of pain by saying goodbye now. Having a man who loves you only when he's had a few drinks is no slice of heaven. Good luck. — Queenie

♥

Dear Queenie, not a terrible problem just a bit if confusion that I know a different point of view could help with. This girl and I, whom I had known earlier, began writing email to each other, and it was going really well. We talk on the phone a few times, and there was a lot of interest expressed, on both parts.

She did tell me that she had just gone through three bad relationships, the most recent ending a month before our little beginning, so this would be a slow process, which I did not have a problem with.

We kept writing, and I went to see her (She lives in another state) and the first time I went to see her it was good. Nothing physical happened, just nice get to know each other stuff. So after that we kept writing (every day) and then after a real good phone conversation I asked to visit her again. Well this second visit was not too good. She pretty much ignored me, acted as if I was her lowest priority, even though she had to be with me as I had driven 8 hours to see her.

So after that it has gone down. And the thing is that were pretty in depth in our letters. About life, our personalities, God, family, and each other. In fact just before it went down, it was actually the best. So who knows? It is a little strange. But I really like this girl. I don't know if the distance got to her, if I pushed too much, she felt scared as we got closer, or she just simply met another.
— Brad

Brad, I don't know what happened either, but I think the relationship probably moved faster than she wanted it to move. Some relationships aren't meant to go any farther than just casual and this may be the case with you and she.

It sounds as though you two are pretty good friends, considering all the things you've been able to discuss. Why not keep it at that and let her know you think she's great but that you really don't want a serious "relationship" at this time. Perhaps if she realizes the pressure of a relationship is off, she'll enjoy being with you much more.

In the meantime, meet others and don't limit your opportunities. Good luck. — Queenie

♥

Dear Queen of Hearts, I've a bit of an unusual problem. I met this guy online about two years back and we hit it off right away as friends, since we had so much in common. At the time, I had neither the desire nor the opportunity to pursue anything past friendship, since he was still getting over a bad relationship. Conversely, I helped him get over the girl who had dumped him.

Well, needless to say, things got more intense, and we found ourselves calling each other girlfriend and boyfriend after several months. He came up to visit me, and things seemed okay for the first few days; barring the initial discomfort one would expect when meeting someone for the first time. However, he told me he just wasn't sure of the relationship, and wanted to back off a little. I went along with it. But a couple weeks after he returned home, he wanted to get back together with me. I went along with it.

Recently (two months ago), he came up to visit me again, and I felt like he was taking things too fast. Same thing happened again, and a few days into it, he told me he wanted to back off and be friends. Thing is, our relationship was much more comfortable and enjoyable as 'friends'.. the thing that confused me is that he still wanted to hold hands, hug, make out, etc.

When he returned home, he called me up and said he still loved me and wanted to try this again. I care about him very, very much, but I'm not sure if taking him back would be making a huge mistake. Help? — Carla

Carla, apparently he can't live with you and can't live without you. My guess is that he's afraid of commitment so soon after having a relationship fail, and he's probably right.

You certainly have a vote in this relationship. What do you want to do? If you want to date him but not commit for the current time, tell him this. A slow and easy friendship building into something more might be the proper course. Certainly don't do anything you're not comfortable with. — Queenie

♥

Dear Queenie, I've been on the internet for a short time and I have been conversing with this man from the United States. I am beginning to have really strong feelings towards him and him towards me. I feel comfortable in writing to him but I'm not sure if these feelings are possible without knowing the person for a length of time and not seeing him face to face. We have been talking about meeting in real live. What do you think I should do? — Tammie

Tammie, you have strong feelings based upon what you think this man is like. He is an unknown fantasy for now. What he really is like could be entirely different than what you believe him to be. While there are many fine people making contact through the Internet, there are also many others who use it for evil purposes. I strongly believe you should do whatever it takes to make sure that your actions don't put you in danger should he not be the man he says he is.

Have you told your family and friends about this person? If not, we think you should. Have you exchanged photos? Does he have your address and you his? (It is not a good idea to give anyone a street address, but rather rent a P O Box.)

Have you talked to him on the phone? If not, have him give you his phone number, do not give him yours, and call him or call him through a phone chat program over the Internet.

Have you and he conversed in "real time" through a chat program such as ICQ? It is easy to take lots of time writing the perfect email response, but quite a different matter making intelligent "chat" in real time. Does he act the gentlemen in his correspondence or is he getting sexual? How much do you really know about him?

Please be careful and good luck. If you do plan a meeting, take someone with you! No one who has your best interests at heart would object to this arrangement, as a matter of fact, they would provide you with as much personal information as it would require to assure you they were as they represent themselves. — Queenie

♥

Dear Queenie, I'm in a relationship with someone who spends most of his time on computer chats, even when I am there he stays on the computer, he has been chatting with someone for a long time, he tells her his thoughts but will not talk with me about his feelings I can't believe I'm jealous of a computer. — Tori

Tori, it's fairly safe to tell your deepest thoughts to someone in a chat room because most times you do not know the person and whatever it is that you need to say will not go any farther or be held against you. He obviously has a need to talk to someone without feeling vulnerable. Do you have a computer? Can you go online? If so, try to talk with him this way. — Queenie

♥

Dear Queen of Hearts, I have begun an e-mail relationship with someone really special. My problem is that we live across the country from each other. We've grown attached and I don't know what to do. We keep saying that we know we'll never meet, but, we care a lot about each other. I'm in an emotional pickle. I really want to continue the relationship. But it hurts that we can never be together. Do you have any advice on how to deal with this? — Liz

Liz, have you exchanged pictures, have you talked on the phone, how much do you actually know about each other or is everything based upon email correspondence? Do you have absolute assurance that the person you believe you care so much about is real?

Unless you have travel restrictions, there should be nothing to stop you from visiting each other. If he has the same feelings, he will meet you half way. — Queenie

♥

Hi Queenie, I'm 17 years old and have a problem; I have totally fallen in love with a girl I met on the internet. She lives a few hours from me and is in high school as well. I know whether she loves me or not, she really thinks I'm a great guy. So should I tell her?

I don't want to scare her if she doesn't feel that strongly and if she does what then? I mean at least for a year, neither one of us will be on our own, and be able to visit each other. I might be going to college near her, but not till next year. I don't care if she stays my friend or becomes my lover, I'd be happy with either, but I do want to tell her how I feel. Thank you. — Mark

Mark, it's a little too early to start thinking about her being a lover. Right now, you need to concentrate on school and she does too. Don't get too involved in this "internet love" since real life is waiting for you away from your computer. Nothing wrong with maintaining a friendship as long as it doesn't get in the way with schoolwork, going out with friends, and planning for college. — Queenie

♥

Dear Queenie, I met a man online about seven months ago and we wrote back and forth for a little while. One day he wrote me a long letter confessing to me that he had fallen in love with me. I was floored and a little scared, but I finally responded with a letter saying that I'd give him a chance. Well, I fell head over heels for him after a while and our relationship bloomed and we began talking of marriage.

Here's the problem: he's been on parole for a couple of years (we'd gotten past that) and he just recently violated it before meeting me by moving without permission. No serious crime. But his parole officer filed to revoke. I was really upset, naturally. To make an even longer story shorter, the last I heard from him was the morning of the hearing and he promised to write me. It's been a month and a half with no word. I have no idea who to contact to learn of his whereabouts'.

I don't want to abandon him if there's a problem and he needs me, but should I just wait around or try to find him? Or should I try to forget about the special relationship we have? I love him so much! If I were to give up on him I'd be breaking my own heart. What do you think I should do? — Lilac

Lilac, if your friend wanted to contact you, he could. Even if he has been returned to prison, he could write or telephone. He has chosen to discontinue contact. Violation of parole is a big deal. He knew the consequences yet chose to take the risk. Too bad you've already made an emotional investment in this man.

Don't wait around hoping he'll get in touch. The special relationship is now a sweet memory. It's time to move on. Broken hearts heal. Good luck. — Queenie

♥

Queenie, I recently had my first date with someone I met online. I was just in short wondering about any detailed advice on how to check the pulse of this situation to see what kind of impression I've made. I'm worried that even though she suggested we meet next time in my neck of the woods, how serious she actually is. Any way to check this? She even got directions to my place before we left the restaurant so I'm figuring that's a pretty good sign.

I don't want to appear desperate or pushy in any of this. I even left her a nice message on her machine the day after thanking her for having lunch with me. I'm bothered I didn't get a return message. We visited Sunday. It's Wednesday and I left her an E-mail at her work. If I don't get a response by Friday I'm going to be nuts. I also told her in the E-mail I'd be calling her later in the week. Any advice? — Tom

Tom, you sound as though you might be more serious right now than she is, or at least than she is giving the impression of being. Slow down. You've had one date. That does not mean anything is happening within this relationship. Yes, it is a "relationship" just as any interaction between people is a relationship. Right now it just isn't a serious relationship. It may never be, but you won't know without following it through. Slowly. Cautiously. Without words of commitment. Without demands.

Love means taking chances. If you don't take a chance you won't get hurt. You also won't find love. Good luck! — Queenie

♥

Hi Queenie, I thought I would update you about my first online date. I met her one Sunday for lunch and afterwards she asked for directions to my place saying she might like to visit next Sunday. Called her Friday to possibly confirm plans and she said she'd try and call me Saturday. Saturday went by and no call. Sunday I left a message at her home telling her I expected to hear from her sooner and hoped everything was O.K. No show Sunday. Finally I E-mailed her a nice note. She E-mailed me back saying it got hectic on the home front and she was ignoring everyone, trying to deal with her own problems but that she did want to get together again, she just wasn't sure when.

I gave her an opportunity to accompany me to a movie on a week night since she told me that would work out better for her. I E-mailed again my ideas for dinner and a movie. No return message.

How do you get someone to own up to what they're really feeling and how can you tell if this is truly her good intentions without the intestinal fortitude to carry them through? What can I do about a possible noncommittal situation? — Tom

Tom, a lot of people are so stretched out with career and other commitments that, even though they really would like to have a special person in their lives, it's difficult to find the way to work them in. So, perhaps her response was perfectly legitimate.

On the other hand, perhaps she is telling you in the most gentle way possible that she isn't ready or interested in any more than casual contact at this time.

There is also the possibility that she is very interested but she is scared that you're moving too fast too soon. I hope you will make contact with others and develop many friendships so one such as this does not have paramount importance should it not play out the way you wish it would. — Queenie

♥

Dear Queenie, my girlfriend saw my phone bill and noticed I had several long calls to 900 numbers. Now she wants to know what kind of chat lines I was calling and why. I am very embarrassed and don't want to talk about it. How do I convince her to forget about it? — Harvey

Harvey, if she is demanding to know about these calls, then she is out of line. You're an adult, aren't you? So, why do you have to be embarrassed or explain yourself to your girlfriend? You're not a kid and she's not your mother.

Of course, if she pays the phone bills, then she probably deserves an explanation as to why they're so high.

As an adult, it's your personal right to call whomever, whenever you choose, as long as you're paying the bills. — Queenie

♥

Queenie, I am going crazy because my lover with whom I live has been having a very romantic secret relationship with a girl he met in a chat room. They use terms of endearment such as "darling, my love, etc.," they also write to each other about sex. My problem is I am very jealous, I told him about my feelings; he said he would stop, but instead he just tries to hide it now. Please help. — Pearl

Pearl, there's something exciting about fantasy and interactive fantasy is even more exciting. Your lover has a fantasy love relationship with someone who doesn't really exist. Okay, this person does exist, but they may not even remotely resemble the person he believes her (or him) to be. The Internet gives people the ability to assume any role, to be anyone or anything they want to be. His girlfriend may be a group of teenage boys or a prison inmate or.... oh, how it boggles the mind as to the possibilities. (At some point you should begin to see the potential humor here.)

Before you become consumed with your jealousy, you need to cool down and consider the worst that could happen. Even if they enter into phone chat, most of today's software programs offer voice enhancement to change gender, etc. In other words, you can't believe what you read, and you certainly can't believe what you hear. If they're trading photos, you can't believe what you see, either.

The Internet fantasy lover can hide flaws extremely well — no warts, no wrinkles, no potbellies or sagging breasts. Try to visualize someone other than last month's Playmate sending love notes to your lover (that may be who he's visualizing, but those babes don't need to grab guys off the Internet).

It's time to do something to bring his attention back to you and turn his fantasies into some exciting realities for the both of you! Why don't the two of you read "her" responses, particularly the ones that are most blatantly sexual, and then, when you're both turned on .... Well, it would get his mind away from "her" and enhance your personal life! In other words, make this a game, an interactive game with this cyber fantasy providing the stimulus to add some zip into your relationship so even if he does go elsewhere for his "warm-up," he directs his passion to you.

A certain amount of jealousy is fine — you wouldn't be jealous if you didn't love him. Which makes me wonder what his reaction would be if he happened to find a steamy email from some fantasy lover of yours. – Queenie

Lust or Love?

Lust or Love?

"I am 25 years old and thought I was in a great relationship until I met a co-worker. I fell totally head-over-heels for her in just two days."

I don't believe in love at first sight lust at first sight is another matter. Lust isn't a bad thing because sometimes it will last long enough for love to develop. The down side of lust is that it can be so powerful that otherwise sensible people will throw good lives away in pursuit of relationships based on lust. Lust doesn't last; it can't, because it burns too strongly to have lasting power.

In lust people do some very stupid things. They leave long term relationships mistaking the blaze of lust for the kiss of a soul mate. They rush into commitment, even marriage, before the sizzle loses its glow and when the fire dies, so does the relationship with disastrous consequences for everyone involved.

Love builds slowly and once it has developed it will withstand much. Lust is a rush of emotion that masquerades as love but doesn't have the staying power. Love can survive the ups and downs of day to day contact, lust cannot.

People in lust don't think with their heads or their hearts which is why lust may be the most dangerous emotion shared by two people who don't know enough other well enough to also be in love.

Lust is the perfect accent to a relationship; it should not comprise the entire meal.

❤

Dear Queen of Hearts, do you think it is possible to start falling in love with someone after a couple of weeks? I don't know if it is possible, but it seems to be happening to me and it feels right. — Darryl

Darryl, love takes months, sometimes years to develop. Lust happens quickly and when lust happens, it feels right. At least for the moment. — Queenie

❤

Dear Queenie, what if you are in a relationship and the guy starts out wanting to see you every night and then all of a sudden he wants to slow down. What does this mean? — Pam

Pam, it means the lust is wearing off. If the two of you have common interests you'll still have things to talk about other than how much you like each other. If not, then your relationship won't last too long. — Queenie

❤

Dear Queenie, just wanted to take a moment to thank you for all the wonderful insight and advice you have given to me. I do appreciate your honesty and candor in helping with my past dilemmas. As of now, my dilemma isn't much of a dilemma... I'm able to think more rationally and objectively now, after a few months of self-examination, where I'm going, where I'll be, what I'll be doing, and so on. I do, however, want to fill you in on what has happened lately.

The attraction I had felt for the "just-friends" man-in-a-million has grown on both our parts. We are now settling into some sort of exclusive relationship. Neither of us has the desire to date anybody else, but we also recognize that we both have our own lives to live and we care deeply about each other. It has worked out wonderfully for me by just being patient and expecting from him only what he could give me.

Somehow what I needed wasn't all that important in the long run: my basic needs for understanding, caring, and acceptance were already being met by him. We see each other when we can and settle for phone conversations at least once a week when we can't. He is opening up to me in ways I'd never imagined he could. The last time we were together, he pampered me like a princess and showed me how affectionate and loving he can be. Everything is going wonderfully, except for the distance. Right now I'm an hour away from him, and I can't see him often.

It will be worse in graduate school, when I am several hundred miles away. But he is perfectly happy seeing me once a month while I'm completing school, as long as we stay in touch (email, phone, etc.). He is being very patient, and I admire his efforts.

I would, however, like to have some freedom to date other people, if the opportunity arises, while I am in school. I would also want him to do the same, if he found someone that he could have fun with while I'm away. I would hate for us to miss even better partners for the sake of sustaining our semi-Utopia. I don't know if this feeling is because I'm taken aback from all this newfound love, if I'm apprehensive about commitment, or if I'm just afraid of the unknown.

Maybe it's because I haven't yet been attracted to him on a physical level. There is abundant mental, emotional, and spiritual chemistry, but only a little physical chemistry. I can't explain it. We have agreed to save a sexual relationship for marriage only, out of our own choosing, if that sheds some light on the situation. I've always been more physically attracted to my former boyfriends. I know that many people never reach the deeper levels of attraction he and I feel for each other, and so I shouldn't complain, but this deeper level of attraction is very new to me. I realize all four levels are needed eventually for lasting love. Is this relationship healthy without the physical attraction?

Thank you for being so patient with this long letter. Again, thank you for being so helpful in the past. Without your advice, I would not have found so much joy in life. — Lorna

Lorna, this was a long letter but you have provided some important comments and insight that others who are experiencing some of the same problems will find helpful. As you have found out, time has a way of bringing things together if you're willing to be patient.

You're asking what is normal in a relationship. There is no "normal" when you're talking about people's needs. In some relationships it is the sexual attraction that provides the fireworks and the joy. Such a relationship without portions of mental, emotional and spiritual harmony may eventually burn itself out. Is this what has happened with those other boyfriends to whom you were attracted?

Who can say whether physical attraction will become stronger in this relationship. Being in physical harmony is very important for the long term success of a marital relationship. Lack of a physical attraction has been the cause of much grief for many of the people who write for advice.

That does not mean your relationship would be the same, but it does mean that if it is a cause for concern now, and if, as happy as you are, you still are open to dating and possibly finding someone more suitable, then it is a problem to your relationship. Of course, if the sexual harmony was as strong as the other components in your current relationship, you wouldn't be able to wait until marriage to have a physical relationship.

Sometimes, too, when life is too perfect we feel obligated to do something to screw it up. If your "comfort zone" is in relationships in turmoil, then it may be very difficult for you to be comfortable for a long period of time in a relationship such as the one that is developing with this man. Perhaps you don't believe you deserve to be as happy as you are in a relationship such as this. If that's the case, and you recognize that it is happening, you can learn to accept and be comfortable in this type of relationship.

Of course, perhaps you and he are meant to be best friends but not lovers. There would be nothing wrong with that and such a relationship might last a lifetime. Frankly, you may be in love with this man and scared that you're going to get hurt very badly because of the new feelings he has awakened in you. Of course it could happen. But love is a gamble and it is better to take the risk, no matter the outcome, than to turn it down.

This relationship is new and so far neither of you has asked the other for commitment so there is no reason that you or he should not date others as long as both of you agree to this arrangement. If the two of you are meant to be, you will return to each other. And, if either of you should find someone more suitable, there should be no reason that you can't remain best friends — as long as that friendship does not cause friction with his, or your, new love. — Queenie

♥

Dear Queen of Hearts, about three months ago I started dating this girl. We are in our 20s, and we are both graduate students. Anyway, the relationship started out real intense. We were seeing each other every weekend, going out of town together, staying the night at each other's apartment.

We thought that we were madly in love with each other. Within three weeks of the relationship I started talking about moving in together next year as a step toward something bigger (i.e., marriage). She liked the idea. Then suddenly

about four weeks ago, she started to pull away from me. She told me that she needed some space. Two weeks ago, she tells me that she is not in love with me, which is fine because I realized that I was not in love with her either. We agreed to continue dating, however, things have been noticeably tense between us.

I blame myself for a lot of this because I am the one who started talking about marriage (she went along with it though) so early in the relationship. She told me that the more she thought about this, the more scared she got, so she backed out. I also agreed with her that we really only had a fantasy that was not based on true friendship. Nonetheless, we still like each other and still want to see each other, but I'm not sure I like the idea of being just friends.

Is there any hope for this relationship? Is there any chance it will go back to the way it was before? I know we screwed up by getting caught up in the novelty and fantasy of being in a relationship, but we both still want to see each other. But I need more than a "friend." What should I do? — Steve

Steve, it's a shame that lust got the upper hand in this relationship because you never had a chance to take it slowly enough to learn about each other, to develop a deep liking for each other, to start as friends and then progress to lovers if that was to be the plan. You became intimate before you knew if you really liked each other. When the passion started cooling down and the two of you took a good look at each other, you weren't sure that you were ready to settle down for a lifetime together.

It's difficult to break up. You tried to do it slowly and that didn't work. So you tried to call it "being friends" and that isn't working. It's difficult to forget about intimacy when you've been there, done that. It is time to sit down for a little talk and decide that you need to go your separate ways for now, continuing on your search for that special someone who will be a friend and a lover. Hopefully, you and she can keep in touch as caring friends would do.

Now that doesn't mean that you two won't ever get back together again in a relationship. But if you do, learn about each other's hopes and dreams, see if you have some common ground and interests upon which to build a solid relationship foundation before you hit the sheets. — Queenie

♥

Dear Queenie, I am 25 years old and thought I was in a great relationship until I met a co-worker. I fell totally head-over-heels for her in just two days. The problem is I don't know if the signals I was getting were friends or more than friends. She did say once that if I were not in a relationship she would think that it was fate us meeting.

The signals I have confused are — she leaned back on me and I put my hands on her hips and she did not move or brush me away. We ended up holding hands for about 45 seconds. We have stared into each others eyes for minutes at a time. We have had lunch and talked about intimate times with other people.

When I left (I was a temp for two weeks), she gave me a long hug. I think I felt passion in it. She said to stay in touch and we do but I seem to do the most of *the calling. She seems happy when I call and we talk into the night, she even told me one night what she was and was not wearing. Now she's out of the area and I am going crazy.*

I really love this woman. I have my breath taken away sometimes when I look at her or think about her. I wrote her a letter about my feelings and she called me and wanted to have dinner.

I messed that up and she seems to have gone cold on me since then. Now it is up to her. She has my number and I am waiting by the phone for her return. Do you think she was a friend or a possible lover in the future? Help, Please! — Mark

Mark, you are in lust with this woman. You haven't known her long enough or been involved deeply enough to know if you love her. You haven't lived with her and seen her at her worst. The two of you have not shared the good times and worked through the bad times. She is who you imagine and want her to be. That is not reality and it's not love.

What happened to the "great relationship" you were in when this hot lady came into your life? It would seem you weren't as committed to it as you believed.

You don't say how you messed up or why she has gone cold. Is it that you are still involved in your other relationship? Based on what you've said I am assuming that the other relationship is over considering the amount of time you are spending obsessing over this woman. If it isn't over, and if you are afraid of ending it in case the other doesn't work out, you're not being fair to anyone.

What do you want from her? Do you want a friend? Do you want a lover? Do you want a lifetime of commitment and caring? Decide what you want and back away from your emotions far enough to decide if this woman is the one who can provide these things. If so, then IF she contacts you again, slowly build the relationship into a strong one. – Queenie

Dateless and Clueless

Dateless and Clueless

"I am shy, but not incapable of initiating conversations with friendly people, and suggesting number exchanges and activities when there seems to be interest. But after that I'm clueless!"

Why do intelligent men and women turn clueless when it comes to dating? And why must a date be any more than *just* a date? Regardless of today's fast paced world, it takes more than one date to make a "couple" and more than a couple dates to make a relationship.

Men and women go into dating with great expectations. They expect to find the one person in the entire world who will complete them, which, of course, is an impossible task for anyone.

Instead of searching for Mr. or Ms "Right" it makes more sense and is less intimidating to look for Mr. or Ms "Right Now". With the pressure off for turning a new relationship into a lifetime commitment, each person can fully explore the similarities they share and decide whether or not their differences are deal-breakers or worth compromise.

Meeting someone who is date worthy shouldn't be intimidating, either. Even if you have been in a committed relationship for the past few years and are newly single, the world is not comprised of happy couples and you. The world is full of singles and the best way to meet them is to get out and mingle since it's unlikely that the perfect date is going to magically drop into your living room.

Dating takes courage. Dating is a gamble. You lock eyes with someone and then must have the courage to say hello and take a gamble that their interest in you matches your interest in them. It also means you begin early in the "getting to know all about you" phase of dating to find out if they are already involved with someone else since not everyone who appears available is.

Dating isn't commitment until both partners are in agreement that they are in an exclusive relationship. Asking someone for a date and having them say "no" isn't rejection. Liking someone doesn't obligate them to date you.

Going out once doesn't guarantee a second date but any date deserves to be ended with promises that will be kept which means if you say you'll call later, call later. If you're dating after a recent breakup keep your baggage light, don't unload all the ugly details of your past relationship(s).

❤

Dear Queenie, at college over the past few years I keep on running into the same guy. This past year we finally met. When we see each other we smile and say hi. And sometimes in the distance or in a crowded room for example we always seem to catch a glimpse of each other. We have talked a little. A little here and there like hi and how are you doing? I am a graduate student and he is a junior. Too different schedules you could say.

We have very similar interests. I doubt he has a girl friend. But I am not sure what I am looking for, maybe just a good friend. I have never had this sort feeling of being drawn or compelling feeling to look at anyone but him. The feeling you could say is magical and each time I see him. I wish to say more then just hi. Maybe it's my nerves, or we catch each other when both are on our way someplace else. We both have one yr. left at school, which will start up again in the fall. This summer he is overseas and I am here in states working. So we will not see each other until the fall.

First I would like to get to know him better as friends. I know some of his friends and we both share similar interests. At school we have each other at some of these gatherings, which have many other people there too. I guess I am just wondering what this could be, maybe or may not be. I am not looking to get married. Hey if it ends up to be nothing, cool then I just have another great friend too. Either way it's cool. Please just help - I hope I am not going. Anyway thank you for your time and have a nice day. — Myra

Myra, there's a saying "nothing ventured, nothing gained" that comes to mind when reading your words. You are interested in him and he might be interested in you but you don't know for sure and you're afraid of letting him go when there might be something, etc., etc.

Okay, here's what you do: Go up to him and say "I heard you're spending the summer in South America. I've always been interested in learning more about other countries. Would you be willing to correspond with me while you're gone and give me some firsthand details while you're there?"

If this guy has even the slightest interest in you he should jump at the chance to keep in touch. If he can send email and has access to IM, ICQ or a chat program all the better. If he says he doesn't want to take the time, well, there's your answer also.— Queenie

♥

Hi Queenie, my question is: I have a very good friend who has always been there for me and who is always looking after me. My friends tell me that his behavior towards me is not of just friends but that he may like me but because his religion and family prohibits him from dating outside his culture that he may never say anything to me.

I don't know what to believe I like him and I would like to be more than just friends but I can't sit around and wait for him to tell me how he feels about me. Should I date other guys and maybe lose him or should I wait for him? — Buffy

Buffy, why are you listening to your friends? Friends are always trying to put people together, sometimes when they're better off as good friends and nothing more. Perhaps the religion and family (culture?) are obstacles that would be too difficult to overcome. Why would you even consider waiting for him and not dating others in the meantime? Do you think that if he did ask you out that would signal instant commitment?

If you're trying to find out if he feels the same way you do about taking this friendship to the next level why don't you jokingly suggest that the two of you go on a "real" date sometime. If he doesn't leap at the chance you're probably not thinking the same thoughts about each other. — Queenie

♥

Dear Queenie, I have been through some tough relationships where I have always been the one who got hurt. And more often than not, it was pretty bad. All but two of the women I have dated have cheated on me (of the 7 or 8), and all of them lied to me and not about little things. And because of this I tend not to trust people. Even my best friends, I have found that I don't tell them when things are bothering me or pretty much any information that might make me vulnerable.

I want to know if there is something I can do. Is there something I can do to help me to trust people again? And is there something I can do so I stop getting hurt so much? I don't want to be the person getting hurt anymore, but I don't want to become the one who does the hurting. And I know that getting hurt happens in relationships, but I feel that I have had some extreme cases. Please give me some advice; I don't want to spend the rest of my life alone because I didn't take a chance worth taking. — Michael

Michael, you're learning that love sometimes hurts. Sad to say, that's a lesson everyone will probably learn at least once in their life. Keep taking those chances and don't hold the mistakes of others against the new people you meet.

There's someone special looking for you but you won't meet up with her if you don't work your way through the people that are blocking the way between the two of you. — Queenie

♥

Dear Queen of Hearts, I just met a guy at a pool he was the lifeguard as I was leaving the pool he made a pass at me; unfortunately I never got to talk to him. I didn't live in that town, but I would really like to call him up and talk to him. But I have no idea what to say. Please help. — Joyelle

Joyelle, I suspect he may make passes at a lot of the girls at the pool. If you don't think this is the case, I'd suggest that you go swimming again and see if he remembers you. Calling him is really chasing a bit too hard for a simple pass, don't you think? — Queenie

♥

Dear Queenie, I met this guy at a bar, and we had fun talking a lot of the night. We exchanged phone numbers, and we talked a few days afterwards. I went with him and a friend to have a beer or two, and we had fun.

Thing is, is that I know he likes me more than I like him. He asked me out on a date; and I feel like I would be leading him on if I went out with him and let him spend money on me, knowing I don't want anything more than friendship. And, so I feel like a total idiot for ever giving him my number. I'm just not ready for a relationship or dating or anything like that.....please help me out......thanks.
— *Gretchen*

Gretchen, why in the world does a simple date have to lead to more than friendship? If a guy spends money on you do you feel obligated to put out or get serious? Wrong, wrong, wrong, wrong!

If you want to get rid of this guy quickly, tell him you only date guys who you plan on marrying and you're not ready to get married right now. Otherwise, mellow out and enjoy his company. You might find he's a nice guy. And he might just end up being a really great friend. — Queenie

♥

Dear Queenie, I have recently asked a woman whether she was interested in going dating. She thanked me for the question but said no. My question to you is whether I should pursue the reasons for not going dating for example, to ask whether she is in an existing relationship just for clarification. — *Chris*

Chris, is there something about 'no' you don't understand? She owes you no explanations. — Queenie

♥

Hi Queenie, I'm 20 years old and had been in a relationship for over 2 years. It has been almost 6 months since we broke up. I have been trying to look for another girl for the past 6 months with no luck I feel like I'm never going to find someone again and I'm scared of growing old being single.

Where can I go to meet women? I don't have a lot of time because I work the night shift and I go to school. Can you help? — *John*

John, if you were 60 and desperately dateless, I'd try to give you a few pointers but you're only 20, and it's time to get your priorities in line. First, get through your schooling. Get yourself started in a good job or career path. Then you'll be able to handle the responsibilities that go along with serious relationships.

Finding someone is never a guarantee that you won't grow old being single. As a matter of fact, that's one of the worst reasons I know to search for someone to love. You can always get a nice dog to come home to, or a friendly cat or two.

Sometimes, the best way to find love is to relax, quit trying, and let it find you. At 20, you've got a lot of time to let the right one find you. Besides, if you find someone now, before you're situated with school, etc., they may not be the right one for later. — Queenie

♥

Dear Queenie, I have a crush on a girl that I don't even know her name. I don't know any of her friends and none of my friends know anything about her. How do I go about getting to know her? By the way, I am 18 and have never had a girlfriend, and it's been awhile since I even noticed a girl. — Robert

Robert, if you don't know her name or anything about her then you have a "crush" on the fantasy person you think she is. If you get to know her in real life you may find that she isn't anything like the person you have a crush on.

I suggest that you find out what her interests are, and if any of her interests are the same as yours, then try to be in the same place at the same time as she is, and strike up a casual conversation with her. But, if you do get a chance to date her, move very slowly or you'll definitely scare her away. — Queenie

♥

Hi Queenie, I am looking for general advice for starting and maintaining relationships, friendships as well as romances. I am an attractive and intelligent young woman, yet for some unknown reason (to me, at least) I have very few friends and date only once in a blue moon. I have always suffered from mild depression, nevertheless, I am certain my personality can't be particularly abhorrent, and no one has ever pointed out any significant flaws.

I am shy, but not incapable of initiating conversations with friendly people, and suggesting number exchanges and activities when there seems to be interest. But after that I'm clueless! For the last 5 years (at least) all promising looking leads have gone nowhere fast. Prospective friends and dates stop calling or responding to my calls and invitations, without any obvious reason. I am getting tired of being alone. Please help me or direct me to where I can find information on relationships and social skills. Thanks. — Lenore

Lenore, sometimes 'shy' is mistaken for 'aloof' and while it's difficult for the shy person to understand how anyone could consider them to be aloof, it does happen.

Perhaps, too, you are trying to develop these friendships and relationships at too rapid a pace and 'scare off' potential friends and 'lovers.' Do you repeatedly contact a new friend or do you make a call and suggest a meeting and then wait until they make the next move to see if they're as interested in developing the friendship as you are? Do you get people to talk about themselves? Are you interested in learning about them?

I really don't have a clue as to what the problem is, since you may just be trying to develop friendships and relationships with the wrong people — wrong for you since perhaps there are not enough shared interests.

Have you tried joining groups or clubs in which you have a strong interest? If you're around people who have your same interest levels, you'll have an easier time starting and maintaining conversations and friendships.

Get into your comfort zone and you'll find others in there also. Good luck.
— Queenie

♥

Dear Queenie, when someone is tired of the bar scenes, where do they go to meet down-to-earth people? — Jean

Jean, they join special interest groups, hobby clubs, volunteer organizations, religious organizations, and business clubs. They get involved in activities they enjoy, which is where they will meet people with whom they are compatible. They go out with friends and meet their friends. They visit, and perhaps join, local singles groups.

Perhaps they take dance lessons, or go to college for a refresher course, or get season tickets to some local event they enjoy. They learn to enjoy their own company so that no matter where they are, they are not desperately seeking the attention or approval of others. — Queenie

♥

Queenie, I have been having many problems with women lately. I am pretty good at meeting women, but usually only stay friends with them for a couple of months. Some of them (women) call me a superficial person, and all that I am interested in a girl is looks. However, this is not true. I have no idea why people feel this way, but they do.

I have not been in many relationships. I would like to go on many dates, but I feel that women no longer like me. I might meet the most beautiful women, become great intimate friends with her, but it all falls apart within a few months. I do not understand it. These have really lowered my self esteem. I am not as outgoing as I used to be, because I think that the women aren't noticing me anymore.

My question(s) is: How do I stay friends with women that I meet? How do I become friends with women that I used to be friends with? How do I raise my self esteem towards women? I would really like it if you could answer my questions. Thank you a lot. — Steve

Steve, perhaps the key is that you "become great intimate friends with her" too quickly. Good relationships are built on friendship and mutual interests (without sex) first, and then progress to more, if both people want it to go in that direction. In other words, if your relationships are based only on sex, when the sex ends, so does the entire relationship.

Maybe all you are interested in is looks. Maybe you are superficial. Why don't you take a good look at a couple that has been together for many years and study each of them to discover what it is about them that keeps the other with them? — Queenie

♥

Dear Queenie, I have a girl that I know was interested in me. At the time I was interested but wasn't sure if things were right. We had previously been

writing for three years as I had been moving around. Now I ended up in the same city as her. How do I get her attention? Every time I make an offering she says ok but ends up canceling. Am I waiting for something that will never happen? — John

John, how about the direct approach? Ask her: "I think you're really great, and I'd like to get to know you better. So far, our dates haven't worked out. Am I wasting my time?" It's the first step in communication. And, you should get the answer you need, even if it may not be the answer you want. Good luck. — Queenie

♥

Dear Queenie, I have a lot of women friends and it is very difficult to sustain a friendship since most of the time, they are unavailable because of their tight and long working hours. Notwithstanding the fact that friendship takes time, a friendship like a relationship needs effort from both sides for development otherwise it is just another acquaintanceship. I am not saying that all career women share the same priorities. Nowadays, women are more aware of what materialism can do for your future and spending. Is it simpler and sensible to have friends who have lesser ambitions and love homes and families more? — Charles

Charles, you should choose for friends those people with whom you have the most compatible interests. If your interests are more oriented toward home and family, then you would probably be happier with friends who place home and family ahead of intense career development.

Nowadays, women are more aware than ever that they could find themselves supporting themselves, and possibly their children, without assistance from a spouse. Many women choose to become involved in the types of careers that will provide the level of income they need for the lifestyle they wish to have, without being dependent on finding a man to provide it for them. — Queenie

♥

Dear Queenie, I am a 24 years old male. I'm not at all bad looking, very smart, and a very nice guy. So how come I always end up being "just friends," no matter what I do to try and change that. I have never had a girlfriend, and it is going on 5 years since the last time I had sex. I am very worried about my future in this department. What can I do to change this? — Michael

Michael, if you are just looking for someone for sex, you can pick up someone, lie to them, and dump them when you're tired of them. Hopefully, you're nicer than that.

Some people mature later than others when it comes to making lasting romantic relationships. If you can enjoy yourself and others, if you like being who you are and aren't desperate to find someone, anyone, for romance, someone will find you.

Perhaps, though, you are looking for the perfect woman, and overlooking all the nice ones. Redefine the type of person you'd like to meet and then hand out those requirements to your "just friends" and ask for their help in finding you someone to date. They'd probably love to fix you up and maybe one of them would like to be more than "just friends" herself. Good luck. — Queenie

♥

Queenie, I am a 36 year old SWM who is thoroughly perplexed with the concept of relationships. I feel as if I am missing something by not having a significant other. It has been nearly four years since my last relationship, and the loneliness is tearing me up inside. I have tried personal ads and dating services w/ o any (good) luck. Most of the time I get stood up and other times, I wish I had. Blind dates really don't work. I'm not very attractive, nor do I have a lot of money. And, as a recovering alcoholic, the last place I want to go to is a singles bar. Not that I could talk to anyone there.

I'm terribly shy and have no self esteem. I know I don't sound like much of a prize, but I'm being honest. I always thought there was someone out there for me, but lately I've begun to lose hope.

I'm a kind and gentle man with a heart full of love, going nowhere. Is there anything I haven't thought of, or, in your opinion, something I must do, to get peace of mind? — Darryl

Darryl, as long as you don't like yourself, why should anyone else like you? I think your first step is going to have to be to make peace with the person you are and learn to like and love yourself. When you can stop finding fault and develop some self esteem, you'll be on the road to attracting others who will appreciate the kind and gentle man inside. — Queenie

♥

Dear Queenie, I'm 61 yrs. old a good figure and sexually active. I can't find a guy my age that doesn't want a much younger woman. Doesn't experience count? Where do I go from here? — Bebe

Bebe, experience isn't the first thing a man sees when he looks at a woman. It's an unfair world for older women and it gets more unfair as the emphasis continues to be on young physical perfection instead of content. Physical perfection is much easier to achieve than it ever has been and more young women are submitting themselves to plastic surgery than ever before in order to achieve that perfection.

Guys your age are fighting the aging process as hard as they can. They're scared. They need reinforcement that they are still attractive. It doesn't matter that they're attractive to you, they need to prove to themselves that they can still attract younger women. It's a badge of honor and vigor to parade a much younger woman in front of their friends.

Not all guys your age are this desperate for their lost youth. Some are more than willing to date within their age range. I'm willing to bet you think those guys are too boring and settled and not exciting enough for you. I suggest that you stop trying to attract the guys who want younger women and start dating the guys who are hitting on you. Good luck. — Queenie

♥

Dear Queenie, I want to know how to get together with someone if she won't talk to me or even listen? — Sam

Sam, it is the right of every person to have relationships with only those persons they wish to have relationships with; no one can or should be forced to have a relationship with someone they're not interested in. Find someone who wants to be with you and build from there. Good luck. — Queenie

♥

Dear Queenie, I have an interest in this girl (I think she maybe interested too) from class, but I never had enough nerve to really talk to her (just an attempt, but nothing substantial came out). Semester is over and I thought that was it and I have to move on since I'm transferring out to another collage (I happened to know she's not going to the same collage I will be going to).

Recently I had to go back to my college to request a transcript transferred and there she is working in the records office! She looked at me which seems longer then normal. Now I'm thinking about this all over again. On one hand, I keep telling myself to concentrate in school and get it over with and who knows there are others. On the other, It would have been interesting to get to know her.

What should I do? And if you suggest get to know her, then how do I do it? Make up an excuse to go to the records office again? I can't do that without looking silly. Maybe stick a note on her car? Or forget it and concentrate on school! — Tom

Tom, all of us look silly some time over love, why should you be any different? If you think she'd be nice to date, go into the records office; slip her a note that says "You have the most incredible blue (or green or brown) eyes! Would you think it too forward of me to ask you for a date? I have two tickets to _____ (think of something) and I'd love to take you with me."

She'll either think it's the most romantic thing she's ever read or she won't. What, really, have you got to lose? Good luck! — Queenie

♥

Queenie, I am very happy with my life in everyway except one. I don't know how to find someone to be my friend and companion. I really am on the shy side and don't know how to go about meeting people. Any suggestions? — Mavis

Mavis, shyness is difficult to overcome, both by you, and by someone who might want to meet you but who thinks your shyness is actually you being "stuck up." Get involved in activities that interest you. That will give you something to talk about with people who have the same interests. Good luck. — Queenie

♥

Dear Queen of Hearts, this will probably be a pretty standard question, but... I believe that I have met the girl of my dreams. Unfortunately I don't know much about her. What can I do, without scaring her off to get her to like me, or to have her even drop hints if she does. We've flirted before and exchanged e-mail and phone numbers. Help me. — Jack

Jack, it may be a novel approach, but have you asked her for a date? That is usually the way things begin. A simple, non-threatening movie (no XXX, extreme violence, etc) and maybe a stop for coffee afterward. Keep the conversation light and find out about each others likes and dislikes. Let her do a lot of talking. Of course, if she understands the art of listening, then share in the talking and the listening. Good luck! — Queenie

♥

Dear Queenie, there's this guy I really like a lot. But it seems as though girls are not of interest to him. But he's not a gay, o.k. He's probably just not interested at the moment. I really want to get this guy. I'll do anything to have him. I know I have a chance I can feel it. But I don't know anymore what to do 'coz I'm not really very good at this. So I need your help. I need you to make a big difference in my life. Thank you. — Susan

Susan, don't put the pressure on me to make a life for you! If he's not interested but you just have to "get" him, perhaps you thrive on the challenge of the conquest and not the quality of a relationship. Be his friend, if he's willing. If he doesn't even care to have a friendship, then look elsewhere. — Queenie

♥

Dear Queenie, there is this female I like. I asked her for her number several months ago and she told me to just get it off of the phone number sheet at work, we work at the same place but not together. Well I wasn't sure if she was serious so I didn't call. Several months later I seen her at another party and we made some serious eye contact.

I really like her but don't know what to do, she is about 5 years older too. I have been told she wants a relationship but nobody will ask her out. Thanks. — Sid

Sid, get her phone number, as she has already told you to do, and call her. — Queenie

♥

Queenie, it happens all the time. When I go up to talk to a girl I like, after a while, I get a bit jittery inside and run out of things to say. Then, there is a very tense silence for a while. Any suggestions on what I can do? — Mark

Mark, it happens to all of us. You're probably trying to make the very best impression you can and are too afraid to relax. So, relax. Don't look for things to "say" look for things to ask about her. Get her talking about things she likes, her hobbies, current events, the weather, favorite movies, etc, etc. People love to talk about things in which they're interested, get her talking and see if you and she have any common interests and work from there. — Queenie

♥

Dear Queen of Hearts, I have a comment to make then the question. I am going to take out a girl that I have liked for a long time now. The question is, what do women like to do?? I have been on dates and stuff before, but I want to make this one very special and romantic.

What is romantic for a woman? What do they want to do? I really want to sweep her off her feet. Any advice? — Todd

Todd, to try to answer a question that applies to all women would be like trying to answer a question that would apply to all men. One woman may be moved to tears by a guy who brings her a handful of wildflowers; while another woman may rant that he's cheap. One woman may consider picnics romantic, while another may be romanced only by expensive wine at a four-star restaurant. See?

Your date will be special and romantic if you treat her like a lady. Bring her a flower if you wish, open doors for her if you're so inclined.

Don't try overly hard to impress her on your date, your effort will keep her ill at ease and won't let the real you shine through. Keep the conversation light and discuss interests the both of you share. Don't put major moves on her.

Sweep her off her feet with courtesy, respect, and interesting, (sometimes humorous), comfortable conversation. Most of all, be yourself. — Queenie

♥

Dear Queenie, at the college I go to, I have a clique of about 5 people I hang around with all the time. I have totally fallen for one of the girls in the group and now I don't know what to do. Her body language is very confusing to me, sometimes she seems interested and other times she seems like she just wants to be my friend.

Everyone else in the group knows I like her but no one is quite sure about her. What should I do? Risk screwing up our friendship and tell her how I feel, or should I look for some signs that she likes me? I'm very confused. — Ozzy

Ozzy, have you considered asking her for a date? It's a unique approach, but in olden times people used to go out to the movies and concerts and other non-committal things such as that and if they found that they really liked each other's company, they'd pair up some more and sometimes even go steady before they got down to telling each other they were in love.

Considering that we have even longer life spans these days, what's the rush to talk about "true feelings" before getting to know someone by casual dating? Perhaps once you got to know her better, you might only want to be friends with her ... or the two of you could end up being another great love story. — Queenie

♥

Dear Queenie, I need to learn to lighten up and let my softer side shine through! How do I go about doing just that? It's a very hard thing for me to do! Trust is the most difficult thing of all! Can you help me? I want a boy friend but it would not happen unless I receive some help from you! — Danielle

Danielle, you are the only one who can help you! You know the problem which means you know the solution. Lighten up! Relax! You don't have to always try to make the best impression. You don't have to impress everyone you meet.

If someone doesn't like you for who you are, why do you need them? That isn't to say you shouldn't cultivate some social graces, but don't try to be someone you're not.

As far as wanting a boyfriend, if it was so easy to get a boyfriend, I wouldn't have any questions to answer. There are probably some perfectly fine guys who think you're swell, but you don't care for them. And there are probably a couple guys you'd like to get to know better who have their eye on someone else instead. — Queenie

♥

Dear Queenie, recently, after having been through a rough time as "the other man" (and thank you for your advice at that time) I decided to get out more and try and meet other people. I went with a female friend to a night spot, a place I almost never go and I had to be coerced at that. Anyway, while there a very nice, attractive woman asked me to dance. Although I don't dance, even though I like to, I accepted, and it was great. It turned my outlook around.

I liked this woman immediately, but I don't like this getting the phone number thing and don't do it well. Still, I was encouraged and the following week she was there again and we spent more time together talking and dancing. Again, however, I blew it, and did not follow through.

She has not been there anytime since (three weeks) but I can't stop thinking about her. Now, the problem is, I don't know if I'm making too much of this, a rebound kind of thing. We really did hit it off. I called information and her phone number is unlisted. I know where she works, should I contact her that way? Should just write it off or continue to hope she goes out again? Any suggestions? — Jason

Jason, there is certainly nothing wrong with contacting her at work to see if she is planning on going dancing soon. Just tell her what you told me, you're not too great about making first moves but she's such a great person you just couldn't let the chance for another dance go by.

She'll either be flattered and this will be the start of something wonderful, or she'll be otherwise involved and you can stop daydreaming about her. Either way, it's worth a call. Good luck! — Queenie

♥

Queenie, I'm usually a shy person but open up once I get to know someone really well. The fact that I'm shy and also picky when it comes to having a relationship with the opposite sex has left me with few dates. I am currently interested in one of my male friend's friend and am wondering how to go about letting this guy know I'm interested in him without being too forward. My friend doesn't want to have anything to do with this. — Heather

Heather, your male friend may be afraid that your picky nature will make for a short relationship with his friend and he doesn't want to be caught in the middle. This one you're going to have to do on your own. Whenever you see this man you'd like to date, you're going to have to go out of your way to talk to him.

Shyness is not an option this time. Simply smile at him and talk about the weather (yes, it's still a safe opener for conversations), current news (something happening in your hometown in which the two of you might share an interest) or whatever pops into your mind ("you've got wonderful blue eyes").

Of course you take a risk being this bold since he may run screaming from the room (how many times has this happened to you?) or he may continue the conversation and it could lead to something more. The first time is always the hardest. Practice, practice, practice and soon you'll have no need of friends to make introductions for you. Good luck. — Queenie

♥

Dear Queenie, I'm a single man, 27 years old, I just have one "serious" girlfriend but I broke with her a month after we began dating. I didn't like her. In a long time I just had the girls as friend's and I have a lot of beautiful women as friends that I never try nothing, not even a kiss. And it's happening again and again and I need a lover!

I see her and I want to try dating her but she is afraid to go and she only go out with me with other friend's, I know that I should talk to her but I don't want to lose the friendship. I know I'm wrong, but now I have a lot of women's friend's but no lover. I just want to know if I'm normal, and what have I to do to

change it? I think if they like as a best friend, why not as a lover? What to do? —
Jackson

Jackson, this is a question you should ask one of the ladies that you trust the most. Pick your best lady friend and ask for her honest opinion about what you need to do to attract a girlfriend for more than friendship. You may not be doing anything wrong, perhaps you just need to ask for a date. — Queenie

♥

Hi Queenie, last semester (collage) this girl and I kept exchanging glances at each other, but I never got the nerve to say "hi" because I don't really know if she is interested in me. This semester she is now sitting right in front of me and I finally got enough nerve to ask her how the weather is. All she did was smile. I didn't ask or saying anything else.

Two questions: I'm 24 and she is about 18? What is the normal age limit? Should I slip her an anonymous Valentine card or a note saying "hi", or should I attempt small talk again? to see if she has interest? Thanks, — Ted

Ted, what is the worst thing she might do if you were to make small talk with her? Do you think she might slap you? Laugh at you? Shoot you? Run away in fright? Call the police? Run over you with her car? See? What possibly could happen that would be so bad that it's not worth taking the chance of making light conversation to open the way just in case she's as interested in you as you are in her?

While you certainly can't disrupt class talking to her, you can wait until the time is right and ask her questions about the class material to draw her into a discussion about the subject matter.

Don't try to show her how much you know so that it comes out like bragging but rather discuss the topics with an even exchange of ideas. If she is interested in continuing the conversation with you, she will. If she isn't, she won't. But at least you will have made an effort to converse with her. Nothing can be accomplished if you don't even begin a conversation.

Assuming you haven't already been married or have some other maturing factors in your history that would make you considerably emotionally older than 24 and assuming that she is at least 18, there shouldn't be any age difference difficulties. That takes care of question number 1.

I wouldn't suggest any anonymous valentine cards or notes, etc. Why continue the suspense as to whether or not she would welcome some interest from you?

Please remember, she might already have someone special in her life so she may not be interested in anything other than a casual friendship. Don't take any rejection, should it occur, as a personal putdown. Good luck. — Queenie

♥

Dear Queenie, everywhere I go, guys are always flirting with me and they invite me for a date. I don't have problems meeting guys. People always tell me that I am beautiful, etc. The problem is that some of these guys are not available (they are married or have girlfriends). They are very insensitive. Also it is very difficult for me to have male friends because they want more than a friendship.

I have had bad experience with female friends too. I did not know my best friend was a lesbian until she became jealous because I told her I was dating someone. Then she told me she was in love with me. Other female friends I had put me down every time they had the opportunity.

I don't have these people in my life anymore. I am trying to live a healthy life. The problem is that I don't know how to find healthy people. — Nathalia

Nathalia, pretty women don't have difficulty meeting men of all types — available and unavailable — particularly if they flirt well (which I suspect you do). Some men interpret flirting as an open invitation to much more than a friendly conversation.

Some women don't know when or how to stop flirting, or even that they are flirting, and this can get them in trouble in other relationships such as female friends who mistake it for something more or other females who look upon the flirtatious female as a predator after their men (particularly if their men are interested).

When you're standing alone, you must first take a look at yourself to see if there is something you are doing that is causing certain reactions in others. If you find that there is, and you do not enjoy the reactions, then you can modify your behavior to produce reactions from others that are more to your liking. Healthy people are all around you. Look and you will see. — Queenie

♥

Dear Queenie, I'm an 18 year old guy, a university student and I've met this girl that I really like. It's not like the "love at first sight" scenario, I've spent some time with her including this last weekend. I "think" she likes me, but then again she may just be being polite. Anyways, I really want to get to know her and was thinking of asking her to dinner and a movie.

I don't know how to ask her, as for the first time in a long while I'm feeling shy! And if I do ask her, and she says no then what to do? Or if she says yes, what to do? Do I make the night special, and something to remember, or do I just take it slow? You see, I really like her and want her to be around me everyday, not just for the one night! Please help me out, I'm feeling really confused at the moment. Thanking you in advance. — Mel

Mel, "shy" is a nice attribute, girls can respect that. There's a difference between shy and wimpy so don't cross the line. You probably don't know how to be wimpy so you're safe.

Dinner and a movie is a nice idea. Walk up to her at a convenient time (when the two of you can talk privately just in case she has to turn you down) or call her on the phone or send her email (if her email is private) and suggest a movie, something funny or light adventure or classical. If she says yes, suggest that the two of you add a light meal to the date. I suggest a light meal as opposed to one of those formal candlelight things because this isn't the time.

If she doesn't already have plans (she might and they could be perfectly valid that she can't cancel even if she really, really, really wanted to), keep the date casual, fun, and end it at a reasonable time, at her doorstep, with an appropriate casual ending. Then, if you say you're going to call her again, call her!

Oh, a single rose or daisy or something whimsical like a little stuffed bear might just set the right mood when you show up to pick her up. Nothing expensive, just cute! — Queenie

♥

Dear Queenie, I am interested in this guy, but he doesn't know it, and I don't know how to tell him. All of my friends think that he likes me, but I'm afraid of the rejection. — May

May, whenever you see him, smile and say hi. If he's interested he will probably do the same. Hopefully, once you've gotten that far, one of you can think of something casual to start a conversation, like "what classes are you taking this year?" or "did you see Independence Day?" you know, that kind of thing. — Queenie

♥

Queenie, I really like this guy who I don't think he even knows that I exist. He is a construction worker. He works a lot at night. He has gotten my phone number four times but still hasn't called am I wasting my time. Just as I get over him he seems to stop in at my work and ask why my friend and I don't go and see him at the work site.

I thought he liked my friend but she says no. She tells me he acts interested in me. But why won't he stop in when I'm there. He would have us pull over and he would talk to us for awhile but when I went to see him on another site he just waves and smiles.

My friend's boyfriend works on the site driving so he really doesn't talk to him. Also he is the son of the owner of the company. And he started flirting first. So I just pursued it and nothing has happened yet.

Everyone tells me that they just like the attention of people driving by and beeping. Should I give up? — Lana

Lana, you could tell him that you'll call him the next time he asks for your phone number. Then call him. Invite him to a movie or bowling or the races. Something fun, informal and inexpensive. If he says no without having a good excuse, consider that he's just a flirt. — Queenie

♥

Queenie, I don't know why boys do not ask me out, some of them look at me but that is all. why they never ask my telephone number? Sometimes I think I am not too pretty but I have heard some boys like me but they just comment this to his friends and I definitely believe they only want to have sex with me.

This confuse me because I am not an easy girl, I haven't gone out or dated or kissed any man in a long time so I really don't get it! They just want sex but they not even approach to me to talk, to get to know me better, they just look and I am dying to have a relationship. — Nicky

Nicky, you do not tell me enough about yourself (age, etc) for me to know how to respond. Perhaps you act too desperate, or perhaps too shy. Sometimes a very shy person is thought of as stuck-up because they don't smile or speak to people easily. If you are still in school, even though you don't believe it now, there is plenty of time to meet a nice guy. All things take time.

You must be happy within yourself in order for others to seek your company. In the same way, you should value yourself highly and not feel that becoming sexually involved with someone is the way to make them like you.

It may seem so for a while but a relationship of this type does not last. You must value yourself before others will have a reason to value you. — Queenie

♥

Dear Queenie, how do men respond to a woman's initiative to inviting them? — Sylvia

Sylvia, it depends up the man, the woman, and the culture. Some men are very flattered when a woman takes the initiative because perhaps they were interested but were afraid she wasn't interested and would say no. In some cultures, though, the men and women are not enlightened and the old ways of men making the first approach still hold true. In that case, a man might be embarrassed or even shocked to have a woman approach him.

If there is no social or cultural problem with making the first move and you have someone you'd like to get to know better, by all means, invite him out. Invite him to a concert or a picnic or a movie — some place that is "safe" and non-threatening.

For example, inviting him home for a candlelight dinner would be a little too serious for a first date while inviting him to a concert or a similar event in which you both have an interest would not. — Queenie

♥

Dear Queen of Hearts, my question is this: Where are all the nice girls? I'm a 25 year old man and for quite some months now I've been back in the dating game after yet another failed relationship. (This time I was dumped because I

refused for the nth time to get drunk and party all night with her and her wild friends). I don't seem to have too much difficulty approaching, attracting and dating women. My problem lies in finding a nice girl.

I've never had a "casual relationship", I don't drink or smoke, I train at Gym five days a week, let's just say I'm the sensitive type. Where are the girls who still believe in love? I mean real love, complete with trust, understanding, passion, togetherness, equality and commitment? Obviously I'm looking in the wrong places. Where are the right places? I know nice girls exist. I've got some good friends (already taken) who are wonderful people.

I've tried everything I can think of to find someone like myself. I mean I'm not lacking, I've got the looks, the good job, education, even a house. I'm Mr. Stable and Reliable. Surely this should attract a nice girl. I've tried asking the aforementioned friends for a set up, but they can't think of anyone. I've tried asking out the girls at Gym, but they've all been taken already. I've even gone as far as dating people I've met in town while shopping, but they've all been shallow too.

I'll ask again, just in case I haven't repeated myself enough: Where are all the nice girls? Please respond with some practical advice, other than "just do the things you enjoy and you'll meet someone with similar interests". This advice, while good, hasn't helped me. Oh, and I'm not the religious type either, so while there might be some nice girls at a church group somewhere, I'd feel a little guilty going along to such a thing just to meet some who was worth while.

If there is some secret hiding place where all the genuine people go, I would like to know about it. I'm at the end of my tether. I'm starting to think that I've missed the boat. All the happy couples I know met years ago, back in high school or Uni. Help! Thanks in advance. — Mason

Mason, I'm having trouble coming up with an answer for you. I still don't have one. Frankly, the world is full of nice, suitable women. They probably work beside you, live in the same town, go to the same places you go, participate in the same activities as you.

For some reason, you overlook them, choosing instead the party girls then expressing surprise when "what you see is what you get." Or, as a lady recently related to me, her alcoholic husband responded to her criticism of his drinking: "What did you expect? You met me in a bar, didn't that give you a clue?"

From your description of yourself, it sounds like you're too good to be true, over qualified as it were, for almost any ordinary female. I don't know where someone who has it all would find someone like himself. I don't know of any secret places to find the home loving, sensitive, caring types. Generally, those types hide out in the bright sunlight with everyone else. They sometimes just don't stand out because they're not quite as flashy, and their demeanor is non-aggressive. They're the ones that are strong on "content" but sometimes lacking in "packaging." (You know: "Have I got a girl for you!" "Is she pretty?" "She's got a great personality!" "Oh, a real dog, huh? No thanks!")

Past suggestions still apply: get involved in activities of interest to you and you will meet others that share your interests. You don't have to be the "religious type" in order to attend church, so get over the guilt and check it out. If all of the women in your gym are married, you need to change gyms, find one with a larger single membership.

Have you tried classified ads, dating services, matchmaker services, singles clubs? If you're really serious about meeting someone, no effort is too great. I suspect, however, that you will be critical of anyone you meet, no matter how qualified they might be. — Queenie

♥

Dear Queenie, I recently met a man that I find very attractive and would like to get to know better. I met him through a friend who is encouraging me to make a move. She says he is a little shy and usually waits for the girl. I'm not accustomed to making the first move and also my ego has been a bit deflated since my fiancé broke up with me over a month ago.

I'm not looking to jump into another relationship, I would just like to start a friendship and go from there. How should I go about this? — Sara

Sara, one of my male friends, a gentleman well experienced in these matters, offers the following advice: "Tell her to find out what he does, think up a question related to his work in which she might have an interest and suggest she call him to meet for coffee to discuss her question. And if that doesn't work, have her call me." I'm relaying his message but not his phone number.

It is difficult taking the first step after a relationship fails but the steps become easier the more you take. There certainly is nothing wrong with making the first move to meet a man, particularly if he's shy. Dating times have changed completely and smart women know how to chase until they're caught. – Queenie

Three is a Crowd

Three is a Crowd

"I really like this guy and he seems really sincere when he tells me he likes me. I know he's never with his girlfriend because he's usually with me. Should I give him a chance?"

Perhaps the pages that follow should have been included in the chapter on cheaters and cheating but that was getting a little massive. So here's more people who haven't been able to disengage themselves from relationships in which there are three (or more) people involved.

Personally, until someone has actually slipped a wedding ring onto their significant other's finger, my feeling is they are "fair game" in the game of love. Of course, the fact that they are involved in a committed relationship but still shopping around doesn't speak too well for their personal dating habits.

Getting involved with someone who is already involved with someone can be risky at best and disastrous at worst. The trust issue would definitely be a problem.

♥

Hi Queenie, I've been friends with this guy for several years we recently got intimate but he still has a girlfriend. I know this wasn't the best time for this to happen but what might come of this? This isn't the first time we've been close either. — Karin

Karin, this guy cheats on his girlfriend. Frankly, he doesn't sound like a prize. I'd throw him back and look for someone who doesn't already have a girlfriend. — Queenie

♥

Queenie, I'm sort of dating this guy that has a reputation for being "around" and using girls. He has a girlfriend, and he said the only reason why he isn't breaking up with her is because she is suicidal.

I really like this guy and he seems really sincere when he tells me he likes me. I know he's never with his girlfriend because he's usually with me. Should I give him a chance? — Mona

Mona, if his reputation is correct, look at his current girlfriend and you'll see your future. It's up to you. If you just have to go for it, try not to get hurt too badly. — Queenie

♥

Hi Queenie, my boyfriend has this one particular female friend that I feel is coming between our relationship. She constantly calls, and comes over to his house. He says because they are friends and nothing is going on, that I should not be worried about anything. I told him I do not like her coming over and calling so much and he allows it even though I have a problem with it. To me, she and him have no respect for our relationship nor my feelings. Many arguments have come from this subject and nothing has changes. I told him that I can no longer deal with it and am thinking about ending this 2 year relationship. — San

San, is this female friend friendly to you or does she avoid you? Are you welcome to join in when she visits him or do the two of them get together when it's inconvenient for you to be there? I suppose it's just my suspicious mind but I've never much liked guys to entertain female friends when their girlfriend is clearly feeling threatened by the other female.

If you're ready to give him an ultimatum and can handle the outcome no matter what it may be, go ahead and do it. Or, you could make an effort to turn her into a friend of yours also. Of course, if she doesn't want to be your friend that might be a big clue as to how she really feels about him. — Queenie

♥

Dear Queenie, I've been at my current job for about a month now, and I've seem to become very good friends with one of my bosses. He's handsome, charming, and great to be around. I'm 18 and he's 25, and engaged. We talk all the time about sex, and relationships. We talk about the relationship we both want to have with each other. He asks me if I think about him, how much I think about him, and why I haven't made a move yet.

I know he really like me but I'm unsure why he hasn't made a move, but what can I say I haven't either. I think I'm falling in love with him. I work everyday and spend the whole time either in his office talking or in mine. I know he likes me, he tells me he knows what I'm thinking all the time, and he seems to know. I really like him and would like to see what's there, what do I do. Please help!!! — Melissa

Melissa, this falls into sexual harassment, whether you feel that way now or not. He is your boss and he is putting sexual pressure on you. Add to that the fact that he's engaged and you've got a really fine guy there.

If the two of you are spending so much time together, both of you are wasting the company's time and money and when his escapades come to light, guess who is the most likely to lose their job. One clue: It won't be him. What do you do? Start looking for another job, now, and this time forget about flirting with the boss. — Queenie

♥

Queenie, I'm fairly new in the navy, and when we got a new female on my ship, right away we hit it off (as friends), but for me it was love at first sight. We were always around each other drinking, going out to restaurants, or just watching television at her house. 2 months into our friend ship (I still haven't confessed my feelings for her) she starts dating a guy off of the ship.

Me feeling the way I did I never said anything. They dated for a couple of months, then there relationship slowly got old and they became just friends, so we started going out again (as friends). One particular night we were drunk, and we

kissed, and I finally admitted the way I had felt for so long, and luckily she felt the same. But now we have a secret relationship behind this guy's back because she doesn't want to hurt his feelings. "He's a good guy" she says and I understand, but when it comes down to the way I feel I don't give a DAMN about the way he feels.

I know that might sound selfish but this girl and I are talking about marriage and kids in the near future and keeping this guy hanging on it putting a strain on my progress and I'm ready to tell him, but she's not.

I know that their not intimate anymore but I just don't want him to think that he has a chance to get back with her. I'm stuck and confused please help.
— Navy

Navy, I agree with you. As long as she continues to lead him on, and that's what she's doing, he has every right to think that there might be some chance for them getting back together. Perhaps she's also thinking along those lines.

When you love someone, you put them first. You don't treat a "friend" who means "nothing" better than the person you're considering spending your life with even if they are a "good man". Would you treat her this way? Sneaking around, not wanting people to know the two of you are in love?

Unstick yourself and tell her you aren't interested in being her secret lover while he enjoys her company the rest of the time. Bring her commitment to you to the same level as yours is to her or, if she isn't ready to take it to that level, slow down and stop talking marriage and kids. — Queenie

♥

Hi Queenie, there's this guy from my college. he is an employee, not a teacher, I feel as if I fell in love with him the 1st day I met him, but he has no idea I like him, in fact he doesn't even know I exist....and I think he has a girlfriend, I don't know what to do, I'm really inexperienced in this thing...can u help me? — Margaret

Margaret, forget him. Concentrate on your studies and the guys in your classes. No doubt there's more than one who would like to go out with you. — Queenie

♥

Dear Queen of Hearts, she and I first met about six weeks ago. we meet each other at least once a week. her best friend told me she likes me. I like her alot too. however, the setback is that she have a boyfriend, that's her biggest hurdle. her relationship with her boyfriend is NOT at a healthy state.

Her best friend told me that she wish to leave her boyfriend for sometime but doesn't know how to. Her boyfriend will be out of town for two months, which will give me some room to make my move. Should I??

I am willing to wait for her. I'll wait forever if she says she will be there for me too! Should I tell her I'm in love with her? She's always on my mind, 24 hrs a day; should I move like a marine or just be cool? Please advise. — Louis

Louis, how shall I say this? She has a boyfriend who just might think she's waiting for him also. Would you wish someday to have another guy asking our advice as to how she should handle the fact she has feelings for someone other than you?

If you're willing to wait for her, be cool and wait until she has broken up with the other guy. It's the right way to do these things.

If she doesn't know her feelings well enough to tell her boyfriend she no longer wishes to be committed to him, or if she doesn't have the strength of character to tell him, why would you want to be in love with her? She wouldn't have the ability to be honest with you, either.

Slow down. You met her six weeks ago. If you've been meeting her once a week, that's six times you've seen her. Way too soon to think you love anyone. Be cool! — Queenie

♥

Dear Queenie, I am in a confused state right now and I need some advice. There is this girl and she is going out with a guy and says she loves him. Well when I talk to her she also claims that she loves me. I know about her boyfriend, yet he doesn't know about me.

I am a Christian man so don't think anything of sex is going on. I have more pride than that. What I want to know is it right for me to go after her because of my feelings for her or would it be in the best interests to let her be. I feel as though I love her to.

It is kind of that feeling where when I see her I get all balled up inside. Well anyway... could you give me some advice on what to do about her? Thanks a lot. — Bo

Bo, I think you'd be better off letting her go until she is not involved with someone else. Right now, she seems to not care that she's hurting you or that she's cheating on him (and hurting him). There are plenty of unattached and nice girls around. Find one. Forget this one until her boyfriend is no longer in the picture. — Queenie

♥

Dear Queenie, I have fallen in love with a friend. I first met her years ago, and we were separated, but I recently met her again at a party, and we hit it off great. We now are good friends. The only problem is she has a boyfriend. I don't know how serious, weather just really good friends, or deeply in love. I don't think it is incredibly serious, but she speaks of him often, and seems to have a genuine like for him.

This is where my problem comes into play. I love this woman, but she doesn't know it. I am uneasy about telling her because of her boyfriend, and the

fact that I don't want to break up our friendship. I know she likes me, and trusts me, but I can't tell if she considers me anything more than a good friend.

I've sent her flowers, for which I received a hug, and a thank you, but there again, It is deceiving. Was the hug and thank you I sign of love, or just close friendship. I wouldn't push the issue, but I can't explain the feelings I have for this person. I almost cry at night sometimes because I know I don't have her. I'm not just out for cheap experiences, I want to hold this person, and be with this person. The most incredible person I have ever met comes along and she has a boyfriend.

I need to do something, but I'm afraid if I tell her my true feelings I may scare her or, I don't know, maybe I'm just afraid she won't fell the same way (which she may not), for she's so flirtatious, I can't if her hanging all over me and calling me means love, or is it just the way she treats friends in general. — Joe

Joe, I am always amazed how someone can be desperately in love with someone they don't know well enough to tell whether a hug is more than a hug. She has a boyfriend. Since she's a friend, ask her how serious they are and whether you can throw your hat into the boyfriend ring to try for her heart.

Pretty mushy stuff, huh? Well, since you say you love her, and she hangs all over you, it's time to be mushy and find out just how deep her feelings go. If she says there's hope for you, then go for it. Otherwise, just consider her a flirt and look for someone else to give your heart to. — Queenie

♥

Dear Queenie, I really like this girl I meet, but we are just friends and she really likes my best friend and it is ripping me apart. I told her how much I really care for her and I think that she is afraid of me because we have not spent time alone with each other for a while.

I don't understand some time I really thinks she likes me or sometimes I think that she is using me to get to my friend and some times I just don't know. Could you help me with some advice? — David

David, it sounds as though you need to look for a girlfriend who isn't already taken. I suggest staying away from your friends' girlfriends, if you want to keep your friends, that is. — Queenie

♥

Hi Queenie, I'm a 20 year old woman in a boring small town. I usually go to one particular store to buy items that I need like milk. That's when I noticed a cute guy working there. Since I was too shy to ask him if he was single one of my friends asked him for me. She ended up slipping him my phone number. He then said that he just might call. Later on I found out that he has a girlfriend. He won't cheat on her so I do respect him for that. Still even when I know he has a girlfriend I find myself wanting to see and talk to him all the time.

Lately I have been going into the store just to see him. There is a drink I buy when I go there and he always shakes it up for me. He looks so cute I don't even have to tell him what I want he just goes over gets me my drink and shakes it up. Even if he doesn't get to take my order he tells the person who does to shake my drink up for me. When he is busy he still makes time for me. I really like him alot and I'm confused about him b/c he always smiles at me and gets close to me.

So what should I do? Should I keep going there to see him or should I leave him alone? Why does he flirt with me when he already has a girlfriend? —
Faith

Faith, let me suggest that 'boring' explains a lot about the way you feel about this guy and the attention he's paying to you. He likes to flirt because he lives in this 'boring' small town, too, and it gives him something to do. Forget falling in love. This is lust a competition to see if you can "win" him from his girlfriend.

He has a girlfriend, he won't cheat on her but he flirts with you. Let's just suppose he dumps her for you. How long before he starts flirting with someone else? Then what do you do? You need a life. A real one without this guy in it. — Queenie

♥

Dear Queenie, I was set up with a friend of a friend and fell for him instantly, It turns out he has a beautiful daughter and an x-girlfriend living separately with him. She was to move out at the end of the month, and things have been postponed. I'm unsure whether it is worth pursuing this or not, I really care for him and I know that he feels the same way but we can't spend the time we wish together and when we do we have to sneak about in order not to upset the x-girlfriend due to the fact that she might flee with their daughter to another town and cause a large hassle with custody etc.

As my best friend is the friend that has set us up, she offers little assistance in this matter because we both now that this guy is right for me. I just wish I knew how to proceed with this. I would appreciate any assistance you could offer! —
Jessica

Jessica, from what I see, I see a guy who is cheating on his live-in girlfriend, the mother of his child (?), and a guy who doesn't mind sneaking around if you don't. Don't you think this is a little degrading?

If I was in this situation, I would leave him alone until he was free and clear. Otherwise you may be 'stuck in the middle' for a long, long time. — Queenie

♥

Dear Queenie, I've been involved with this man for several months now. He said he loved me and I in turn told him I loved him. I really only get a chance to see him on the week-ends. He rarely calls during the week, because a lot of times he's out of town and claims he doesn't want to run up phone bills.

When I first met him he was in a bad relationship and was in the process of breaking up. Once he broke up with her, he started seeing me and as the story goes on - we became intimately involved. I have found myself falling in love with this man. Well within the past few weeks, we haven't seen very much of each other, he says it's because of his job.

Last week I paged him because I hadn't seen him in about two weeks, talked to him on the phone probably two or three times. Instead of him paging me - it was another woman. She wanted to know why I paged him and how I knew him. I told her the complete story - I had nothing to hide. She told me she was his girlfriend and had been dating him for about two years and that they lived together and wanted to try and make things work.

I told her if that was the case I would interfere. The next day I receive a phone call from him and he said everything she told me was just lies and that he wanted to be with me. He came over the next night and apologized and said he didn't want her. We had a nice time together and he said he would see me the next night. Now the problem is I have not heard anything from him since.

I have paged him on several occasions, but he has not returned my phone calls. I do not know how to take this. I do care for this man a lot and think about him constantly. What should I do? — Carolyn

Carolyn, it sounds as though he has either made his decision and you are not a part of the picture or he is at least trying to make a go of it with her again.

You probably would prefer to hear something else, but, if it were me, I would forget him until he is completely and totally split up with and over this current girlfriend. In other words, stop thinking about him and stop paging him. If he really loved you, he'd be with you, not her. Words of love are cheap to come by; actions are what count. No matter what he may tell you, he's still with her. — Queenie

♥

Dear Queenie, I have a person that I have fallen madly in love with who is in a relationship with someone else but that person lives in another state. She is not in a committed relationship with this person mostly due to the fact that he has been afraid of committing to her.

We started out by saying we would just be friends but this quickly escalated into much more. I invited her on a fun trip for a week and she accepted. This was about two months before we were actually leaving for this trip.

During this time she went to visit the other man to determine if they were going to move forward or if she was going to concentrate on building a relationship with me.

I accepted that she was going because these plans were made well in advance of us even meeting for the first time, although I wasn't thrilled about it and she knew this.

When she returned she said they had come to an agreement that it was not going to work between the two of them and we were going to move forward

with our relationship. Our feelings started to grow even more for one another and I started to spend even more time with her and her nine year old child.

We had a fantastic time when we were away together for a week but spending that much time together was stressful and we learned more about each other that week than we had known. She told me that I was a very controlling person and always seemed to want to have the last word in what we do. I look at the situation at this point and can certainly understand where she is coming from.

We did have one fight the last day that we were there and it was due to me being jealous of her actions at a party we were at the last night because she was being very flirtatious with the waiter where we dined. We stayed mad through the next day and we had a heated argument the next night but we talked it through and everything seemed to be ok.

When she arrived at her home she had a call from this other person. Now he was telling her how much he missed her and that he wanted to come visit her to sort his feelings out and see if what he is feeling is simply because he is lonely and feels rejected or if it is truly that he is so much in love with her that he can not live without her. She agreed to this.

It finally hit me that if I did not cool it and start thinking logically about this and set my emotions aside for a minute that I was going to loose her because I was starting to scare her and she told me this. I thought the situation through and determined that I was the one that walked into their relationship knowing full well that they had been going out for the past year and a half even though he has been moved away for over six months. I also realized that she had not stopped loving him when she fell in love with me and she always told me this.

I am completely confused at this point what to do. Am I doing the right thing and would it be right to continue to pursue her when both of us love one another so much. She tells me she loves me. My solution was for her to continue until she either knows who she wants to be with or until one of us men gets tired of the situation and bows out on our own.

She told me once that she would not be with me if she did not want to be and I certainly would not want her to because that would not be a healthy relationship. But at the same time she is still in love with this other person. Why does love have to be so difficult? Please give me any advice that you can in this situation. Thank you! — Martin

Martin, you've come up with a good plan - continue with the relationship until she either knows who she wants to be with or until one of gets tired of the situation and bows out on your own.

There is some problem with this, however. The two of you "men" could turn this into a real test of your "manhood," pitting yourselves against each other to see who "wins" her love. This is fine if you like contests and the 50/50 odds. Actually, the odds are a little more in his favor since he has known her longer and she appears to still be in love with him.

May I suggest that there is another approach? You can remain in the running, but you can change your status. Instead of being the third person in this relationship play, why not add to the cast of characters? Change your status from "waiting patiently" to "single and looking." In other words, until she's ready to commit completely to you, you have no reason to commit completely to her.

When she realizes that someone else could come along and steal your heart, she may speed up her selection process. If she doesn't, you're that much closer to finding someone who will love only you. — Queenie

♥

Queenie, I like this girl but she has a boyfriend who doesn't treat her right and I like her a lot!! What should I do? — Bobby

Bobby, be a friend and if she gets tired of being treated badly perhaps she'll notice you and give you a chance. Don't hold your breath, though, she obviously likes something about this guy. — Queenie

♥

Dear Queen of Hearts, I have a problem, and I need fast response. My long distance boyfriend just notified me that one of the ladies he's been dating is asking for commitment or else!! Now he wants me to help him to get out of this or he is going to marry her on a certain date and he wants me to save him!!

I love this man very much, I have been so patient with him through 3 yrs of relationship, should I let it go, or try to save him for myself. Help. Thanks. — Mona

Mona, or else what? She's going to leave him? What? Exactly what does he want you to do? Marry him? Lie for him? Personally, I think you deserve better and would suggest that you let him get himself out of this situation. If this is his subtle way of asking you to marry him, and you love him despite his other girlfriend, then do what your heart tells you to do. If he hasn't come right out and told you what he wants you to do to save him, ask him. Then respond appropriately, depending upon your feelings at the time.

Frankly, it sounds as though he needs to have a little more time to "mature." Maybe, in three or four years, if he still appeals to you and he isn't married, or otherwise involved with someone else, you might want to give him another look. Hopefully, by that time, you'll care less. — Queenie

♥

Hi Queenie, I have been going out with A for about 6 months, even though she has been seeing someone else. I knew that it was risky; she wanted to break off with the current boyfriend and go with me.

He's the homely type and he is always at her house. He even eats dinner with her parents and family members. She said her parents told her to break off with me if she wants to go on with him and vice verse. Now she says she still loves him because he has "changed".

I did propose to her and she told me that she was not ready for marriage yet. She keeps telling me to slow down and reduce the pressure of getting her commitment to drop him.

I hope to make her either try to convince me that she's my best choice for a girlfriend or allows her to date others without worry from me. She says she does not want to use the break up word on us. I have told her that if we were to breakup, I don't think that I could ever speak or talk to her ever again since I love her very much. I may have to burn bridges. I don't want to lose her but I feel I may have to.

I feel stronger now and physically healthier and believe that the decision to break up should not be taken by me but by her. I will leave it to her decision. I have also reinforced my feelings to her and told her that I have not changed by mind of loving her and spending my life with her.

I don't think that I should pressure her to make a decision but continue to see her (to confirm my staying power), be my jovial self, see other women (there are other women!) and see how things go. What you think/suggest? Am I making the right decision? — Jon

Jon, if she has a boyfriend, and she chooses him instead of you, then I would think she has made her decision. If you two aren't good enough friends to be friends instead of something more, then perhaps it is time that you stop trying to convince her that she needs to love you more than him. — Queenie

♥

Dear Queenie, what do I do? I have fallen in love with my best friend! (A guy!) So I finally tell him that I like him but he is already seeing my cousin. (I never knew about this!) But I know that he doesn't really feel the same kind of closeness with her because he just met her and she lives thousands of miles away! How can he love someone without really knowing her?

I was the one he came to when he lost his friend! I was the one that took care of him when he needed me to. What did it mean when he held my hand, and held me in his arm the whole night as I slept? How can he, after admitting to me that he did have feelings for me, choose not to be with me? And I know that he cares about me a lot because of the way he looks at me. Why is he choosing to ignore his true feelings?

I know that I have gone away to college and it's easier to just stay friends, but I truly believe that true love will prevail! I suppose I have to get over him, but I can't shake this feeling that he still loves me! And I can't move on! Help! I need to know what to do! How do I begin to mend this broken heart! — Hope

Hope, if you believe that true love will prevail, then you know that if he truly does still love you, he will return. But do you love him so much or do you just want him back now that he has fallen for someone else?

Just because someone, in a moment of need or weakness, says they have feelings for us, it does not bind them to us forever. At some point, some time in his life, he told someone else he had feelings for them and yet, after that, he told you the same thing. It does not mean he didn't have feelings at the time, just that at that time and place he felt one way, and now, he feels another.

You have a choice. You're in college, you have lots of people you can hang out with, and you've got an education to take care of. All of this should keep you very busy and not give you too much time to worry about what he is doing. Or you can waste your college years by worrying about something over which you have no control. I'd like to think you're smarter than that. Good luck. — Queenie

♥

Queenie, became friends with a woman, which became a relationship after about 5 months. We are very compatible and get along great. Truly best friends. However, as the relationship became more involved, I realized that religious differences would not permit me to marry her. I didn't discuss it with her much, and didn't encourage her conversion. After about a year, I began pulling away a little at a time. I didn't know what to do.

Finally, we split for a few weeks after it came to a head and we talked about it. Again, I discouraged her from exploring religious conversion. However, we got back together, though it was never the same. At that point I was miserable and wanted it to end. I put on weight, and we rarely had sex.

Finally, she met someone and dated them. When she told me, I immediately left. However, she continued to call and we started getting together as friends. It was much more comfortable. However, after I discovered their relationship had quickly escalated and our time together was becoming sparse, I was angry. I asked her not to call. For 6 weeks she didn't. Then she called pleading for my friendship.

I know they are sleeping at each other's apartments almost every night and are constantly together. She's immersed herself in all his hobbies. Changing for him. It's been 4 months and they are together constantly. We've met once or twice in the last month.

She still wants me in her life, but I tell her I must move on with mine. I've asked if she still sees us getting together and she says yes. But how can she think this with a BF in her life! She's told me he's mad about us talking or meeting, even though its only been a few times. We're both in our late 30s, so we're not children.

I've decided I would encourage her to adopt my religion (which she says she would consider) if we got back together, but I hesitate to suggest anything of the sort. And I'm not sure I could ever overlook her current relationship. I'm torn between just letting it go and trying again. She lives nearby and is in a group I'm involved with, so she won't disappear from my life. So...friends, lovers, or let go?
— Enrique

Enrique, love shouldn't be a team event. She isn't being fair to you nor to her current boyfriend. She knows her friendship with him is hurting you and she knows that her friendship with you is hurting him. You don't have to ignore her when you run into her but I think you'd be better off getting involved with someone else. Good luck. — Queenie

♥

Dear Queenie, I've been dating my girl friend for two months now and I'm ready for a relationship of more than just friendship. One night on a romantic date, I asked her how she feels about me. She said that I am a nice guy and likes being with me... but she is in love with somebody else.

She is in love with this guy in the military and that they are away from each other at the moment and they are not getting along. Of course, I was hurt when I heard this. I haven't returned her phone calls nor seen her since then. I care for her very much and letting her go would deeply hurt both of us. How do I handle this situation? Thanks for your advice. — Mark

Mark, I would suggest you be cordial to her when she calls and don't be cold when you see her but let her know that you need to be more than a friend and you don't plan to be "on reserve" while she waits for her boyfriend to come home.

If she didn't tell you in the beginning that she was in love with someone else, I think she has a little cheating blood in her veins. You don't need to be second to anyone. Find someone who will put you first. Good luck. — Queenie

♥

Hi Queenie, I met this really great guy who I like very much. He asked me out and now he says he might get back with his old girlfriend. Her father is very prejudiced against any other nationalities and this has caused problems between him and his girlfriend.

Supposedly her father has changed now and she wants my friend back. He sounds so unhappy in this relationship. He told me he wants to keep in touch with me and if we are meant to be, we will be. I want a chance with this man.

Do I fight for him? Do you think her father will change?

Do you think I should make sure he sees me every once in a while? After all he did want to go out with me. He does like me. What do I do? Thanks! — Laura

Laura, he may have wanted to go out with you but that was before his girlfriend wanted him back. He may like you, but he still has feelings for her. Perhaps her father has mellowed and he will be more welcome now. If he feels a need to give it a try, then it is in his best interest to do so.

How do you plan to "fight" for him? Are you going to call him, send him letters, go to the same places he goes? This is a person, a free human being, not a prize to be won by whomever wins the game. If he chooses to get back with her, he is making that choice of his own free will.

Why don't you learn to be a caring friend of his, not a girlfriend waiting for him to return. If he makes contact, keep it casual as long as he is in any type of committed relationship with this girlfriend. Committed means he and she have agreed that neither of them is going to date others.

If he wants to turn your casual relationship into anything more, tell him that you won't be a "stand-by lover" and that you'll be glad to date him if and when he and his other girlfriend are no longer together.

Being always available is not an attractive trait. Nor is trying to seduce him if he really cares about this girl; it will backfire and could turn him against you. He's keeping his options open and so should you. You'll do what you want to do, but you asked and that's my opinion. Good luck. — Queenie

♥

Dear Queenie, this seems really complicated to me, but maybe you can help me figure it out. There is this woman that I really like. She's my age, and we have so much in common, it's almost unreal. We have so much fun together. But I am not sure if she likes me too. When we are together, we forget about everything else. Then, it seems like she realizes that she is having more fun than she should, so she makes up an excuse and leaves. We are hardly ever alone, just the two of us. She is part of the group of friends that I usually do things with. If I were to ask her how she feels, she'd tell everyone and I'd be humiliated.

She also has a boyfriend, who is also a friend of mine. She is very unhappy with him, but has been with him for almost a year. I know that if she would realize that I would be better for her, she would leave him. But I really don't want to hurt him either.

When she and I are together, there is this magic in the air that I want to feel forever. I can't just let it go—I have to do something. What can I do without getting embarrassed, hurt, or people mad at me? Thanks for your help. — Carl

Carl, this situation is ripe for getting embarrassed, hurt and having people mad at you. Let's get to the bottom line on this one. She has a boyfriend. She's an adult (you both are over 18 aren't you?). She can make her own decisions. She chooses to stay with him right now despite her apparent unhappiness in the relationship. No doubt she knows how you feel which is why she makes excuses and leaves when the two of you start having so much fun together.

Look for a girlfriend who doesn't already have a boyfriend. If you keep pursuing this one, you could lose her, him, and become less welcome in your group of friends. — Queenie

♥

Dear Queenie, there's a girl at work I'd been working with, the past 3 months. I'd known that she been giving me signals that she to do something with me, but I'd know that she has a boyfriend and I just think she want to play games. She is beautiful don't get me wrong, but she acts like little kid. What should I do about this matter? I'm 24 yrs old and I'd already went through this and I don't want to go through it again. Thank you. — James

James, ignore her signals. She's already involved with someone and you don't need to become a third party in a game that's meant for two. — Queenie

♥

Dear Queenie, sometimes life can be very confusing. Well, my life is confusing, right now. My friend told me tonight that she foresees her life with her current boyfriend in his hometown in view of what career plans that she intend to start there and to use the networks that her boyfriend's family has there.

I have never felt so low and have never met someone anyone who is so career/money driven who is willing to sacrifice her ability to explore her feelings to the fullest but instead is money driven. On the other hand, she tells me that she feels for me but do not want to lead me on if somewhere down the line, we would not talk to one another.

This stirred my emotions in the past when I felt dumped from a relationship and it made me never to speak to the person again. I do not know why I did that but it made me regret what I did. Maybe, I was rushing things too fast. Well at the end of out discussion, we agreed that we should give one another a chance. She tells me that she will take it as a challenge.

My question is in the long run, am I barking up the wrong tree? My happiness means the most to me. Should I place hope on this relationship and initiate some interest? No doubt in the relationship, I understand that there are ups and downs. I feel sometimes my feelings goes up and drops like a pile of bricks. I basically fear of getting hurt again.

I was thinking of going out with another friend who is slightly older than me and go slowly on this relationship with my other friend. I feel that the issue of money and career will crop up again in the future and I doubt that I can run away from this if I pursue the relationship.

I am generally very personal with my feelings and I feel that if we were not in a relationship, we would still remain as friends and I do not think that I will be able to talk to her on that personal level again and we would just remain as acquaintances. Please advise me. — Frank

Frank, as long as you fall in love with women who are in love with someone else, you will get hurt. She has different goals than you do, choosing money over relationships for her happiness. Some people do believe money will make them happier than having a good relationship, and for them, it probably does. A sad life to the rest of us, but not to them.

If you continue to pursue this woman with the thought of a personal relationship as the outcome, you are going to have pain. That will be your choice because you already understand her needs and motivations. Not only that, you understand your needs. Try to clear your thinking so that you see this logically and you will know what you should do. Good luck. — Queenie

♥

Dear Queen of Hearts, sometimes at the time when you least expect it, you find someone find someone who you can trust/build a relationship/friendship with. I have just tendered my resignation recently and found someone who I normally work with but never had the chance to talk to, as a special friend.

She is dating someone now, whom she had known since university. She told me that her boyfriend is rather quiet, and not career minded. It seems that her parents want her to take over their business and the family assets when they pass away.

She told me that her parents are very materialistic. In her own words, she finds me to be "dangerous" and she says that she has never spoken to anyone like me before. She has indicated to me that she wishes that she had known me earlier and if she dumped her boyfriend now, she would not have any regrets.

I respect her relationship with her boyfriend and suggested that we take our friendship slowly in order to see where the friendship may lead and cultivate our feelings which she agreed.

We are seeing more of each other every day mainly because we work in the same company. I will be effectively leaving the company soon and she has been transferred to a subsidiary company near to my company. I feel that I can relate my feelings to her without being trampled and I think we are getting closer each day.

My problem lies with parental pressure. I understand that her mother has suggested that she marry a rich person in order to go back to the rich life that her family had several years ago. Well, she tells that she does not mind marrying someone who is not rich but have ambition and must be able to win her heart. Please advise me. — Marc

Marc, the best way for a relationship to have a chance is for both people to be free to develop their feelings without hurting others in the process. If she chooses to dump her boyfriend and take a chance that your relationship with her will lead to a lifetime commitment, then you may have a something worthwhile.

She is an adult who should be able to make her own decisions. Of course, in some cultures this may not be an option. If she lets her family influence her choice of mate, you will just let yourself in for heartbreak if you try to win her heart. Continue slowly, particularly as long as she has a boyfriend. You have a good grasp on the situation and I hope she will be able to see what a worthy boyfriend you would be. Good luck. — Queenie

♥

Dear Queenie, this girl and I have been friends for 3 years now. 2 years ago, I really started liking her (in that way), but she had a boyfriend. However, one day she broke up with him so I thought about asking her out on a date, but I figured that her breakup was kind of hard on her so I asked my friend what I should do. He said I should wait a couple of weeks.

Meanwhile, he was dating this other girl but as it turns out, he got in a car wreck and was put up in the hospital for about a week. That week is also when

I went on a cruise, and when I returned, I find out that he asked my friend out because he dumped the other girl.

I'm the kind of guy that doesn't get angry out in the open, but this is the most supreme form of backstabbing I've ever experienced. They have been going out for almost 2 years, and I know, because I still hang out with him, that he doesn't really love her. He admits it whenever he's drunk. And all she does is bitch about him whenever he's not around. She flat out says he embarrasses her.

I'm still in love with her I'm just waiting for her to break up, but I know that's probably not the best thing to do. However, when they do break up, how do I go about telling her that I love her and telling him that I love his ex-girlfriend?

Also, how can I egg them both on to break up with each other? Their relationship is driving not only me, but many other people crazy. Thanks. — Brian

Brian, first of all, you certainly have more consideration for his feelings than he did for yours. As far as how you should tell him that you love his ex-girlfriend — just do it if you get the chance. He knew you wanted to date her two years ago but he waited until he had the advantage and asked her out himself.

Getting involved with a goal to break them up is not a good idea. Even though they act as if they dislike each other, they're still together. That means there is something keeping them together, and love takes many forms.

Your best bet is to distance yourself from both of them. It has been two years and you've wasted time wishing for a girl who could dump him for you if she wanted to — just like she dumped her other boyfriend. It sounds as though you need to meet someone as nice as you are and get away from this battling pair. — Queenie

♥

Dear Queenie, a relationship with a former lover has been rekindled. How long should I wait for him to give up his current flame before I consider breaking off the relationship?? I was the one who broke it off before. We have discovered we both love each other very much and it is much more than a casual relationship. — Marian

Marian, do you believe you love him because he's involved with someone else? Are the problems that caused you to break up with him before resolved or has distance from him and seeing him only at his best made you forget the bad parts of your former relationship with him?

If he feels the same about you as you believe you do about him, he should do the honorable thing and disengage from his current relationship. His girlfriend is going to be hurt no matter how long he waits — and there never is a right time for dumping someone.

I think you should get on with your life (oh, how I hate using that line but what else can I say?) and let him see that his inaction may lose him your love this second time around. After all, he has no reason to cut loose of his current girlfriend if he has no competition for your affection. — Queenie

♥

Dear Queenie, my problem is: Number one falling for a girl who I never really told that I liked her and that eventually turned into love. Number two she's messed up, I don't mean drugs or sex. She is very committed to herself and what's going on in her life. The thing is she's not too selfish, (we all are) but she doesn't seem to do anything with anyone. All except for her boyfriend.

I wish it didn't happen like this, she doesn't like to talk about it, and she doesn't want to hurt me. But I have to tell you it's screwed up. When we do stuff, once a month, we have a great time. I guess it's really annoying because she felt this way at sometime, but she couldn't tell me, I just pushed too hard at the wrong times. Now I've kind of moved on. I have a glimmer of hope that she might correct herself while I'm still single and go through college. I know we can make a good couple, and if she changes when I'm still around, that's great. Now my biggest problem is trying to be friends with her. I just want to preserve any chance I have in the future. It would be great if we hooked up but this friends thing is screwing me up. She's so impossible to reach or do things with that I convince myself that she hates me. I know she cares for me, she's told me after another story, but she never shows it.

I would like to know what I should do. Should I test her out somehow? I really don't want to screw this friendship or possible relationship up so any advice you could give me would be much appreciated. I'm happy I did this and maybe this will be a good way to deal with it. Please write me back, I need help. Thank you. — Tim

Tim, I am a little confused here. You think this girl is "messed up" because she spends so much time with her boyfriend and not enough time with you? That's the way "couple" relationships are — and you bet that should she become your girlfriend you would want her spending all of her time with you, not with some other guy. Right?

If the two of you are getting together once a month as "friends" there isn't much doubt in my mind that you're being very aggressive trying to turn the friendship into a romantic relationship. This probably has her uncomfortable.

You'd be better off leaving her alone and finding yourself a girlfriend who doesn't already have a boyfriend. If, in the future, she becomes available, perhaps the two of you will be able to develop something more romantic in nature. Right now, it's not a satisfactory relationship for you, for her, or for her current boyfriend. — Queenie

♥

Hello Queenie, I am writing you this letter to tell you a story of something I did yesterday. It was for a very good friend of mine who I work with. She is just

a friend. Yesterday I had a crazy idea of sending her a rose knowing she is seeing someone. When she got it she was happy but didn't know who it was from. I later confessed and she thanked me for it. My question is Do you think I did a dumb thing by sending her a flower? Also do you think she was only being nice in thanking me when deep down she may have been mad? — Stan

Stan, in answer to your first question: what do you think? In answer to your second: it may have embarrassed her and it could have caused trouble in her current relationship, both of which could be grounds for a bit of anger. But I am not a mind reader and what's done is done. Don't make more of this incident than it is... a simple flower from a friend to a friend. — Queenie

♥

Dear Queenie, I am a 35 year old single male. I am very shy when it comes to dating and meeting women. When I see a beautiful woman I would like to get to know, I become very nervous, I babble quite a bit and I lose all train of thought.

Recently I decided that I needed to get more confidence talking to women and so I decided to ask several ladies at work out to lunch. I figured that this would be a safe environment with which to practice conversing with women. Little did I know that I would fall for one of the women. She is single, attractive, and smart and has a current boyfriend. I am not sure of the relationship between her and her boyfriend, only that they have been together for a little while.

My question is where should I proceed next? I want her to know that I like her, but at the same time, I do not want to scare her away. We work together and while we do not see each other constantly, there is interaction on a regular basis.

What should I do and how should I proceed? Any advice you could give me would be well appreciated. We have gone to lunch several times, mostly in groups, but we did go out alone a couple of times.

She has not yet said no to lunch. I think that is because she is a nice person and not because she may be interested. Bear in mind, this is just lunch at work and not a date so that might be all there is to that. How would I know? Are there any tips you can give me? — Arnie

Arnie, ask her for a real date. Maybe a concert or a movie (nothing too romantic or too gory) or something else that's fairly casual and not too intense or expensive. (I say not too expensive because many times a guy will spend far too much money on a first date in order to make a great impression when the first date is a time for getting to know a person enough to decide if a second date is a good idea.)

If she says she has a boyfriend and doesn't date, you've got your answer. If she says she has a boyfriend but will sneak a date with you, think about what you're getting into. If she doesn't mention the boyfriend at all and is willing to go on a "public" date, you've also got your answer.

Keep it light, don't rush, enjoy yourself, and laugh a lot. Good luck. — Queenie

♥

Hi Queenie, I would like to ask your advice on something that has been bothering me. I met this guy a few months back and we've been really good friends. We complement each other. He's the silent, brooding type while I can talk about anything. Although we've gotten really close, we've always known that our friendship could never turn into anything more.

You see, he's still in love with someone else while I'm recovering from a broken heart and not ready for a relationship just yet. But something happened 2 months ago that changed everything. We kissed and although we both didn't talk bout it afterwards, you can feel the tension whenever we're together. Then last week, we went out.

When he brought me home, we talked about his girl, his life our friendship...then we started kissing. It didn't stop there though. We made love that night. We didn't talk about it afterwards. Now, when we're with other friends, we act normal sometimes to a point of ignoring each other. When we're alone though, it's different. In fact, we pretty much act as if it never happened.

I'm really confused. I don't deny that I'm attracted to him and that I care for him. I just want to know the whys and what nows. One thing is for sure, our friendship means more to me than anything and I wouldn't want to lose that. What should I do? Thank you very much for your help. — Brittany

Brittany, does his girlfriend know about you? Have you met her? Does she believe that he and she are in a committed relationship? He may love her but it would seem that there is something lacking in their relationship that he may be finding in the relationship with you. Unless he is married or otherwise committed, there is no reason that your relationship with him can't develop further. Now let's look at the negatives.

This is a difficult situation because you don't want to make a mistake in choosing the wrong person as your new love. Being in "rebound" could cause that to happen. He offers a sympathetic shoulder and kind words as well as the warmth of companionship. These are dangerous combinations when we're in pain. Even more dangerous when the other person has no intentions of going further. At some point you may find your heart feeling like ground round.

Loving someone who is in love with someone else is asking for heartache. You're in deep enough now to understand what kind of pain there is... are you sure you want to get in deeper for the whole experience? Do you really want to be his standby love?

He is not treating you fairly if he is secretive about your relationship while still professing his love for her. No matter how much you enjoy this friendship, if you keep it going before he/she/you are resolved, you're in for pain. Explain it to him and let him know that you don't want to lose him as a friend but you're going to have to start a search for someone who will qualify as your new sweetheart. Then do it. If he has romantic feelings for you, let him disentangle himself from her first. — Queenie

♥

Dear Queenie, I like this girl she is one of my best friends. I have liked her since I met her 3 years ago. I can't tell her I can't even put how I feel about her in to words never mind say them to her. She has a boyfriend now they are getting serious and she is happy.

The guy is one of my less personal friends I have no wish to ruin my friendship with either of them or hurt there relationship even though he told me to tell her. The longer I wait the more I think about her and how I feel. And the more I want to have her for a girlfriend. Should I tell her or wait or what? Please help. — Walter

Walter, if her boyfriend says to tell her how you feel, then go ahead and say something to her like, "You know if you and — (her boyfriend's name) weren't going together, I'd ask you to be my girlfriend." This isn't the same as asking her out but it does let her know that you like her and if she has any interest in you, this gives her the chance to tell you. — Queenie

♥

Dear Queenie, I have recently met a woman that is the girl of my dreams. But the problem is she is in a relationship gone bad and can't seem to decide if she wants me or to stay in this unhappy relationship. — Jon

Jon, unless you're searching for a badly battered heart, you better get away from this situation as quickly as possible. You don't want to invest your tender feelings into someone who can't make up her mind. Wait until she's been out of this relationship for a few months and is sure she's over this guy before you make her your dream girl. — Queenie

♥

Hi Queenie, friend of mine has a boyfriend. However, we found that we also like each other. We would go to a dinner or movie. We would always have great time. But many times we would just passionately gaze at each other.

I do not want to make any move, because I would not like to hurt her, but it is becoming harder for me to control my feelings towards her.

What would you do? Should I talk to her about my feelings, or should I just find some reasons not to go out with her. Thank you in advance. — Eric

Eric, talk to her about your feelings. If hers are the same she needs to get out of the relationship she's in; if she doesn't you need to cool it and find someone else to go to dinner and the movies with. — Queenie

♥

Dear Queen of Hearts: Please, Please, Please HELP ME. This lady that works for me is just driving me crazy with temptation but tells me I can't have her. She says she loves the guy she has been living with for two years.

When this teasing started she said she was not in a very strong relationship and living alone. Now that I found out differently and confronted her with it (I checked up on her) She seems to do damn near everything to make me love her and I also do very nice things for her.

She asks me things like would I get a HIV test. I said I would and I did. She tells me how she likes to make love. Tells me how she does it with the guy she is with.

She says her home life has improved dramatically since working here as she does not go home all pissed off like she did at her other job. She now loves her boyfriend more than ever but just today she was talking about how she liked to make passionate sex that she likes lots of cuddling and hugs.

She is a great worker and I desperately need a person like her to work for me. I do not want to loose her as an employee but something has to change. I just love her so much I cant think straight when I am around her. There are some considerations about her boyfriend. She lives in his house. She drives a rusted out pick up truck 36 miles each way to work. She has no nice clothes, has not had her teeth cleaned for at least three years. She admits she is like his servant. She seems to have little money but he makes around $1,000 per week and lives in a $100,000 home with her.

I am starting to think this stuff is such a damn distraction that I just may have to consider ending her job. She is 21, her boyfriend is 37 and I am 36 years old. Just in looks she is a 7 to 7 1/2. I am a 8 1/2 or a 9 on a scale of 1 to 10. People say I could easily get a nicer looking girl. I love her so much that if I could I would fly her to Las Vegas and marry her ASAP. I am head over heals in love with her and I think she knows it. She would have a new car, house and a life. How can I tell if this is what she wants? I can't stand it any longer. — Walt

Walt, of course she's playing games with you! Love? Hardly. She knows how to keep you in heat — and you need to take some cold showers and then do whatever it takes to regain your life without her. She lies, she cheats, she wastes your valuable company time, and you think you love her enough to give her everything you own. You're in lust and it isn't pretty.

She might have the basis for sexual discrimination suit against you based on what has been happening during working hours. As clever as she is, perhaps that's the whole idea.

You're going to do what you want to do, but I think you should stop thinking below your belt and figure out how to get away from this bad situation before she takes everything you own and goes on her merry way. — Queenie

♥

Dear Queenie, I have a friend (female) that I dearly love. We went out a little while ago (said she just wanted to be friends) and talk to each other on the

phone almost every day. I compliment her whenever I can and buy her occasional gifts, just not too much to make it look like I'm coming on to her.

She says she doesn't believe in second relationships and that just put a big pit in the bottom of my stomach. I think about her every day and really want to go back out with her and have no earthly idea of what to do to get her to go out with me or just become better friends. What should I do??? — George

George, is the lady involved with someone else? Is that what you mean by "second relationships"? If so, you need to stop the pursuit and settle into being a good friend. Just because you have such strong feelings for her, she is not obligated to feel the same toward you, especially if she already has a love relationship with someone else.

Take the pressure off and find some uninvolved single women to date. — Queenie

♥

Dear Queenie, I started a new job and have been working closely with a woman that I have grown to care about very much. We have been having "relations" for the past 2 months and she has recently expressed the fact that she is falling in love with me. I too feel very strongly for her and I can see myself having a future with her.

The problem is she is engaged to a man that she has dated for almost 2 years, and they moved in together around when we initiated our physical relationship. She has told me that she is unhappy with her fiancé, and finds the relationship boring. The problem, as she describes it, is she is afraid to break up with him because she does love him and she does not want to make a mistake. I think she is afraid of the "fallout" that would come as a result of breaking up (the families have grown close). I truly want what is best for her, but I also believe that what is best for her is to be with me. What can/should I do???? Please help me as this is very important to me. — Chris

Chris, she wants it all — and right now she has it: excitement with you, and a safe, boring relationship with him. She's falling in love with you but she loves him and won't break up with him because she doesn't want to make a mistake? Shortly after the two of you meet, she starts a sexual relationship with you, at the same time taking a step toward further commitment with him (moving in together).

The lady is not too tightly wrapped! She can only cause you a lot of pain, the kind she's already causing him. It's time to think about what is best for you, since she's taking care of herself just fine. You need to get out of this mess now, while you still have your heart. Run, run, run, RUN!!! — Queenie

♥

Dear Queenie, I have been best friends with this girl for 13 years.(Since 5th grade) Over these years there were times when she didn't seem to be my type *to try and pursue anything further but for the past few years I have been more attracted to her then anything.*

I can honestly say I love her with all my heart and I would do anything to have her. Problem...... She currently has a boyfriend. I'm pretty sure she isn't very happy with the relationship. I know I see her probably more then him and would surely be better for her but I'm very nervous and scared about what and how to tell her my true feelings.

I know a situation like this is risky because of the friendship but I've got to have her. Please help!!!!!!! — Tim

Tim, if you and she are best friends then you are in the perfect spot to be there when her love relationship fails — if it should fail. You can offer the support she will need to get her emotions repaired and hopefully she will begin to regard you as more than a friend, and feel about you the same as you feel about her. This would be a safe, passive approach.

You could take the active approach and tell her now how you feel, and hope that she feels the same way even though she's involved with someone else. This would be very risky. It would make her uncomfortable, if she doesn't feel the same way. It would put pressure on your relationship with her, particularly if her boyfriend gets wind of your feelings.

Love doesn't happen between people at the exact same moment. It can, but usually it doesn't. That's why there are so many sad love songs. Do you really think "Unchained Melody" would be so popular worldwide or that so many country/western songs would be at the top of the charts if it weren't for the great numbers of people longing for someone they don't have?

I'd suggest you keep being her best friend and keep your true feelings as hidden as possible. I'd also suggest that you date others and meet a lot of different people with the thought that somewhere there is someone else just right for you. Your girlfriend might be very happy with her current boyfriend, despite your observations, and may be very happy with you in a best friend only role, now and in the future. – Queenie

www.ingramcontent.com/pod-product-compliance
Lightning Source LLC
Chambersburg PA
CBHW031145270326
41931CB00006B/153